D0476234

THE STRUGGLE FOR
DEMOCRACY

PARLIAMENTARY REFORM, FROM ROTTEN BOROUGHS TO TODAY

ROGER MASON

The
History
Press

Waltham Forest Libraries	
904 000 00427823	
Askews & Holts	15-May-2015
320.441 MAS	£17.99
4655634	

Cover illustrations
Front, top: How to Get Made an MP cartoon. (William Heath, 1830). *Front, bottom, and back:* The Houses of Parliament, London. (Wikimedia Commons)

First published 2015

The History Press
The Mill, Brimscombe Port
Stroud, Gloucestershire, GL5 2QG
www.thehistorypress.co.uk

© Roger Mason, 2015

The right of Roger Mason to be identified as the Author
of this work has been asserted in accordance with the
Copyright, Designs and Patents Act 1988.

All rights reserved. No part of this book may be reprinted
or reproduced or utilised in any form or by any electronic,
mechanical or other means, now known or hereafter invented,
including photocopying and recording, or in any information
storage or retrieval system, without the permission in writing
from the Publishers.

British Library Cataloguing in Publication Data.
A catalogue record for this book is available from the British Library.

ISBN 978 0 7509 5626 0

Typesetting and origination by The History Press
Printed and bound in Great Britain by TJ International Ltd

Contents

Preface

This is my nineteenth book. Most of the others have been on the subjects of finance and company law, and I have enjoyed writing them all, but this one is special. It has been a new challenge and writing it has given me the most pleasure. I hope that you enjoy reading it.

Many years ago I acquired a love of history whilst a pupil at Aylesbury Grammar School, and it has remained with me. My two history teachers were Mr Byford and Mr Dalby Ball, and I have much to thank them for. I recall Mr Byford teaching us about Parliamentary Reform, and in particular an inspired lesson on the 1867 Reform Act, which is covered in Chapter 10. It has remained in my mind and it is perhaps not fanciful to think that it provided the germ of the idea for this book.

I have attempted to tell the story faithfully, but at the same time to make the book interesting and enjoyable. It is something that Roy Jenkins and Antonia Fraser have managed so well, and I have tried to do the same. I hope that you will think that I have succeeded.

Finally I would like to express my thanks to Geoff Wright, my wife's cousin. He read through the manuscript and made a number of very helpful suggestions. He has a special insight because he is a former publisher, and twice stood as a candidate for Parliament.

Roger Mason

The Unreformed Parliament

In *The Sound of Music* Julie Andrews memorably sang, 'Let's start at the very beginning, a very good place to start'. It is sound advice for this book. The first two landmarks in the story of Parliamentary Reform are Catholic Emancipation, which was achieved in 1829 and is the subject of Chapter 2, and the Great Reform Act of 1832. This first chapter briefly describes the development of Parliament from the very beginning, and then moves on to the state of the unreformed Parliament prior to 1832.

The English Parliament is often, and with some justification, said to be the mother of parliaments, and it is certainly one of the oldest. It was not invented and did not have a clearly defined starting date, or even an unclearly defined starting date. It evolved, and of course continues to do so. At times the evolution was rapid, but for long periods there were very few changes.

The different parts of England and later England itself were originally governed by absolute rulers, the chief or monarch. He (with due respect to Boudica the personal pronoun is carefully chosen) was a virtual dictator, and if necessary got his way by the exercise of force. He could only be thwarted by greater force or by assassination.

The earliest assembly worth mentioning is the Saxon Witan, which was summoned at the discretion of the king. He called whom he liked and he did so when he liked. The Witan could inform the king and perhaps influence the king, but it could not overrule the king. After the Norman Conquest there was a small but permanent inner council of advisers and from time to time the king would also call additional earls, barons and churchmen. This council formed the basis of what in time would become the House of Lords. For many years county moots had included a representative element. After the Conquest these became known as county courts and incorporated the tentative concept of representative local government. Representatives of the county courts formed the early basis of what in time would become the House of Commons.

Of course, as all schoolchildren should know but perhaps don't, in 1215 King John sealed Magna Carta, which required him to listen to the barons and at least up to a point accept their advice. The use of the word 'parliament' commenced in England in 1236. It is significant that the word is derived from the French word 'parler', which means to talk or discuss. It is not derived from a word meaning to legislate or decide.

The forerunner of the modern Parliament was set up in 1265 by Simon de Montfort, the nobleman who was leading a rebellion against Henry III. As well as the barons this included representatives from each county, and also from the cities and towns. De Montfort was killed in battle soon afterwards, but Henry's son Edward I developed the institution when he became king in 1272. Edward summoned Parliament forty-six times during his thirty-five-year reign. As well as nobles and churchmen there were elections for two representatives from each county (the knights of the shires) and for two representatives from selected cities and towns (the burgesses).

An essential part of the Parliament's work was to agree taxes. After this had been accomplished the work of the knights of the shires, the burgesses and the clergy was usually done. The king would then discuss laws and other matters with the earls, barons, bishops and abbots.

The representatives of the counties were publicly elected at county court meetings. The process for electing burgesses, who represented the boroughs, varied from town to town. These arrangements did not substantially alter until the 1832 Reform Act. After the early seventeenth century there were very few changes in which cities and towns sent representatives to Parliament, and after the fifteenth century there were not many changes concerning who was allowed to vote.

The power of Parliament relative to that of the monarch progressively increased after the death of Edward I in 1307. Apart from anything else a civil war was won by Parliament, and Charles I was executed. Furthermore, in 1688 Parliament removed James II and invited the Protestant couple William and Mary to be joint sovereigns. In the following year passage of the Bill of Rights was secured. This laid down the limits on the power of the Crown and the rights of Parliament. Subsequently the power of the monarch relative to Parliament waxed and waned. In 1780 a disgruntled House of Commons passed the motion 'that the power of the Crown has increased, is increasing, and ought to be diminished'.

The English Parliament became the Parliament of Great Britain in 1707 upon the union of England and Wales with Scotland. This in turn became the Parliament of the United Kingdom upon the admission of Irish constituencies and members in 1801. Appendix A shows the full list of parliamentary constituencies at the time of the 1830 general election. The breakdown by type of seat and by country is as follows:

	Borough	County	University	Total
England	202	40	2	244
Wales	12	12	0	24
Scotland	15	30	0	45
Ireland	33	32	1	66
Total	262	114	3	379

This does not mean that there were 379 MPs and it does not mean that the distribution between the four countries was in these proportions. The total number of MPs was 658, the main reason for the discrepancy being that most constituencies returned two members. The distribution of the MPs was as follows:

	Borough	County	University	Total
England	402	82	4	488
Wales	12	12	0	24
Scotland	15	31	0	46
Ireland	34	64	2	100
Total	463	189	6	658

England appears to have been the winner at the expense of the other three countries, and some cynics will say that it was ever thus. Within England the south did better than the north and cynics will probably make the same comment. The county of Cornwall had no fewer than twenty-one boroughs, each returning two members. This meant that, with the two county members, Cornwall sent no fewer than forty-four MPs to Westminster. This was 6.7 per cent of the total for the UK. Lancashire, including Manchester, Liverpool and other large towns, sent fourteen MPs. Accurate population figures for the time are hard to obtain (especially for Ireland) but the following is typical of several estimates for 1831, the year of a primitive census in Great Britain.

	Population	Population Percentage	MPs Percentage
England and Wales	14.0m	57.9%	77.9%
Scotland	2.4m	9.9%	7.0%
Ireland	7.8m	32.2%	15.1%
Total	24.2m	100.0%	100.0%

The Irish figures are for the whole of Ireland and are at a time approximately fifteen years before the potato famine and emigration significantly reduced the island's population.

It is true that 658 MPs seems an awful lot. The United Kingdom, then as now, had one of the world's largest legislatures. The House of Commons currently has 650 MPs and many people think that the number should be reduced. For comparison purposes it should be remembered that the whole of Ireland was included in 1831, but that the Republic of Ireland is now an independent country. Only Northern Ireland is within the United Kingdom. The United States, with a population in excess of 320 million, manages with 100 senators and 435 members of the House of Representatives.

All but eight of the English boroughs returned two members, six returned one member and two boroughs returned four. All the Scottish boroughs (or burghs) returned one and so did all the Irish ones except Dublin.

All the Irish and English counties returned two members, with the exception of Yorkshire which after 1826 returned four. All the Welsh and Scottish counties returned just one. However, in an extraordinary exception, three pairs of Scottish counties voted at alternate elections and were disenfranchised at the other.

Apart from Yorkshire, after 1826 the counties were treated equally, regardless of their populations. In Wales, Anglesey had the same weighting as Glamorganshire. In England tiny Rutland had no more than 600 electors, whereas Yorkshire had more than 20,000. The average for English counties was around 4,000. Interestingly the United States Senate operates on the same principle. Alaska (population less than 750,000) and California (population more than 38 million) each send two senators to Washington. Districts represented in the House of Representatives are though of roughly equal size.

The voting qualifications differed between the counties and the boroughs, and they differed enormously from borough to borough. In the counties it was simple: all forty-shilling freeholders had the vote. A forty-shilling freeholder was a person who owned the freehold of land that was capable of bringing in rent of at least forty shillings per year. Since the fifteenth century the expanding population and inflation had meant that an increasing number of adult males had the vote. Exercising this right caused some of them considerable trouble and perhaps expense. There was usually only one voting point in each county, and the forty-shilling freeholders may have had to make a long and difficult journey over difficult terrain. It could take a couple of days or more to get from one part of a large county to another part.

The qualifications for voting in the boroughs were very different from the counties, and they varied from borough to borough. Looking back from the comfort of the twenty-first century one can only say that the variations were ludicrous. The voting arrangements were sometimes derived from a borough's charter and sometimes from custom lost in the mists of time. In a few cases they were fixed by the House of Commons following determination of a disputed election. In some boroughs the franchise was so extensive that the 1832 Reform Act reduced the electorate. In others the qualifications were very restrictive and there were many variations in between.

Preston, at least for a time, was the borough with the widest franchise. By a determination of the House of Commons in 1661 the right to vote was invested in the inhabitants, which had been interpreted as meaning the resident freemen. The poll in the 1768 election was conducted on this basis and the mayor declared that Sir Peter Leicester and Sir Frank Standish had been elected. The other two candidates, John Burgoyne and Sir Henry Hoghton, petitioned, basing their case on a literal interpretation of the 1661 determination. The petition succeeded and on a poll of all the inhabitants they were elected. This was universal male suffrage in the borough of Preston. What is more, 'inhabitant' was interpreted as anyone who had slept the previous night in the borough.

Apart from Preston, the widest franchise was in the so-called scot and lot boroughs and also in the so-called potwalloper boroughs. After 1768 Preston was restricted to being a scot and lot borough. In such boroughs the vote was given to everyone who had resided there for six months, was not a pauper and who had paid scot and lot. Definitions varied and pauper was sometimes taken to mean a person who had received parish relief in the qualifying period. The phrase 'scot and lot' refers to taxes paid to the borough for local or national purposes. 'Scot' was derived from the old French word *escot* meaning a payment, and 'lot' was derived from the old English word *sceot* meaning portion or share. So the phrase meant payment of a share. Those who avoided paying their taxes got off *scot free*. A potwalloper was a person who had control of a separate doorway to his dwelling, could provide his own sustenance and had a fireplace at which to cook his meals.[1] He had to be a resident and not a pauper.

Another class of borough was the so-called freedom borough, of which there were sixty-two.[2] The freedom of a borough could be acquired by right in certain ways. Examples were by inheritance, marriage to the daughter of a freeman and completion of an apprenticeship. It was also possible for the corporation to elect freemen, a practice which was open to abuse. If it seemed likely that an election would be decided against the wishes of the majority of the corporation, they could elect the required number of freemen known to be willing to vote in the required way.

That seems bad enough, but even worse were the so-called burbage-boroughs. In these the vote attached to a property rather than a person. In many cases it was not necessary for a voter to occupy the property, and in some cases it was not possible to do so. To take just one extreme example, at Droitwich some of the burbages were shares in a dried-up salt pit.[3] Burbages could be bought and sold, and could be conveyed for just the period of an election. This allowed a nominee to cast the vote. Non-residence was common in many areas and, for example, 44 per cent of the electors for Cambridge did not reside in the constituency.[4]

Another extremely unsatisfactory form of constituency was one where a close corporation elected the members. The freemen and other residents had no say at all. The three university seats complete the picture; the voters in these had the potential to cast two votes – once in the university election and once in their county or borough. Voting in more than one constituency was not confined to the university seats and some enterprising citizens arranged to be able to vote in several. This was possible because the polls were normally open for two weeks. It could be to their advantage to travel round and participate in the hospitality and inducements.

In many boroughs the electorate was low or very low. As well as making them unrepresentative this greatly increased the scope for corruption. Figures are unreliable but shortly before the 1832 Reform Act the adult male population of England and Wales was around 3½ million. At the same time the total electorate was around 365,000, or just over 10 per cent. However, the fifty-two counties provided 200,000 of these and the 212 boroughs provided just 165,000. There were of course very big differences between the boroughs, but some of them had tiny electorates. This and the fact that so many were under very close control justified the descriptions *'pocket boroughs'* and *'rotten boroughs'*. A pocket borough was under the control of one person, one family or a very small group of like-minded persons. The borough was said to be in their pocket.

The distribution of the boroughs and the size of their electorates never was logical, but the passage of time progressively worsened the anomalies. The boroughs did not reflect the consequences of the Industrial Revolution and the migration to the cities, particularly in the north of England. Mighty cities did not have separate representation while rotten boroughs had just a handful of voters.

Perhaps the greatest injustice was Manchester, which did not have separate representation. In the early eighteenth century its population was around 10,000, but according to local censuses it had grown to 182,016 in 1831. 'Cottonopolis', as the city was sometimes called, had good reason to feel aggrieved. Birmingham too did not have separate representation. Its population grew from around 74,000 in 1800 to around 150,000 in 1830. The citizens of the so-called 'workshop of the world' had good reason to feel under-represented. Representation of these two great cities was only via their contribution to the elections in the counties of Lancashire and Warwickshire respectively. Sheffield was another major city that did not have separate representation.

Many of the boroughs were under the control of families or individuals, and very often they were aristocratic families and individuals. Furthermore, some aristocratic grandees controlled not just one but several of the boroughs. This aristocratic influence is well illustrated by Lord Chesterfield's words to Philip Stanhope, 'You will be of the House of Commons as soon as you are of age, and you must first make a figure there if you would make a figure in your country.'[5]

It is tempting to say that the practice of bribing electors was universal. That would not be correct but it is not too far from the truth. A few high-minded candidates did not do it and some high-minded citizens voted according to their consciences, but the practice was widespread and varied from favours and inducements right up to the blatant purchase of seats. At the minimum many electors expected to enjoy hospitality, often involving copious amounts of alcohol. Elections were popular with tavern keepers; as an example the Duke of Wellington (then Arthur Wellesley) entertained the electors of Rye to a dinner prior to his election for the borough in 1806. Perhaps we should be charitable and assume that it was a reasonable and necessary expense to enable him to explain his policies.

Examples of blatant bribery are numerous but the following extract from the excellent book *The Genesis of Parliamentary Reform* by G.S. Veitch, first published in 1913 and reprinted in 1965, well illustrates some of the extreme practices:

A pretence of ignorance was, indeed, idle when seats were openly advertised for sale in the newspapers; when £5,000 had been left by will for the purchase of a seat in Parliament, when a seat had been reckoned amongst the saleable assets of a bankrupt, and when a defaulting debtor had paid the market price for a seat in order that, under the protection of parliamentary privilege, he might evade his creditors by escaping from England without arrest. The capital value of a seat can be estimated from the fact that in 1812 the Duke of Bedford sold his 'property' in the borough of Camelford for £32,000.

Winning candidates often showed their appreciation after the election, and not always to just the electors. They often rewarded the citizens in general. After his success at Andover in 1754 Francis Delaval arranged for 500 guineas to be fired into the crowd.[6] Bribery did not end with the passing of the 1832 Reform Act. At Hertford in 1832 the electors accepted bribes from the Tory and then elected the Whig. This caused outrage, not with the candidate who gave the bribes, but with the perfidious electors who could not be trusted to do the honourable thing.[7]

An account of the rotten boroughs is almost bound to include Old Sarum and Dunwich, details of which are given below, but there were many others, far too many to detail in this chapter. Gatton, though, deserves a mention. This borough was in Surrey and returned two members. In 1831 there were only six houses within the borough and they provided seven qualified voters. Elections were almost always uncontested, and in an 1803 by-election the successful candidate was returned by a vote of one to nil. Over a long period control of the borough was bought and sold, often for very large sums of money.

Old Sarum was the original site of Salisbury and in 1295 it was given the right to return two members. Shortly afterwards most of the inhabitants moved to New Sarum, which is now Salisbury. The number of remaining residents dwindled and the houses were progressively abandoned. It was a burbage-borough, which meant that votes attached to properties, in this case abandoned properties. It was not necessary that the burbage-holders lived in the properties or even in the constituency. There were seven burbage-holders who were all under the control of one person, so in practice one man selected two Members of Parliament. For many years the borough was under the control of the Pitt family, and a future prime minister, William Pitt the Elder, sat for the constituency from 1735 to 1747.

Dunwich returned two members from 1298 until 1832. It originally consisted of eight parishes and encompassed a flourishing market town and a port, but the encroaching sea swallowed up all but half a parish. This contained forty-four houses and half a church. In 1709 voting was restricted to resident freemen who were not receiving alms, the maximum number of which was set at thirty-two. Two people each controlled eight votes, so acting together they only needed one other vote to have control.

The words of Philip Francis, shortly after his election for Appleby in 1802, illustrate an extreme example of the working of a pocket borough in practice:[8]

The Fact is that yesterday morning, between 11 & 12 I was unanimously elected by one Elector, to represent this Ancient Borough in Parliament, and I believe I am the very first Member returned in the whole Kingdom. There was no other Candidate, no Opposition, no Poll demanded, Scrutiny, or petition. So I had nothing to do but to thank the said Elector for the Unanimous Voice by which I was chosen. Then we had a great Dinner at the Castle, and a famous Ball in the evening for that part of the Community which mylady calls the Raggamuffins. On Friday Morning I shall quit this Triumphant Scene with flying Colours, and a noble Determination not to see it again in less than seven years.

In the twenty-first century we are accustomed to a variety of candidates contesting each seat at an election. They typically include representatives of the main parties and a range of independents and single issue campaigners. We can be forgiven for not taking some of them too seriously, though we should gratefully acknowledge that it was the Monster Raving Loony Party that pointed out that it was an anomaly to have only one Monopolies Commission. It was not like that before the 1832 Reform Act and to a lesser extent it was not like it afterwards either. Of the seats, 70 per cent were regularly uncontested. The main reason for this was that in tightly controlled seats an election was pointless as it was known in advance who would win. Another reason was that Whigs and Tories sometimes agreed to each put forward only one candidate in a two-seat constituency. They would each get a representative and the cost of a contested election would be avoided. The number of seats contested at the 1761 general election was particularly low – just three English counties and forty-one out of 204 boroughs.[9]

In 1694 the Triennial Act fixed the maximum length of a parliament at three years, but the Septennial Act 1716 changed it to seven years. This remained the position until 1911, but in practice parliaments were usually dissolved more quickly. There were twenty-nine general elections in the years 1701–1831. MPs were not paid and this too lasted until 1911. Voting was conducted in public and this continued until 1872. There were no votes for women and women could not be MPs. This injustice was partially remedied in 1918 and totally remedied in 1928. The Roman Catholic Relief Act 1829 allowed Catholics to be MPs, but only a person willing to swear a Christian oath was able to take his seat in the House of Commons. This did not change until passage of the Oaths Act in 1888. Male suffrage increased progressively and by 1918 almost all men had the vote. Universal suffrage (both men and women) was achieved in 1928.

Party politics as we know it today was absent from the unreformed House of Commons prior to the 1832 Reform Act. There were two very broad groupings, the Whigs and the Tories, but party discipline was nothing like it is now. Many members adopted an independent attitude and were willing to move from grouping to grouping within the 'parties' and occasionally from party to party. They generally did not oppose for the sake of opposing and felt, to some extent at least, an obligation to support an administration that had the confidence of the monarch. The majority of members did not expect or want office, and were content to support the interests that they represented.

We can clearly see, or at least we think we can, that prior to 1832 the unreformed House of Commons was a dreadfully undemocratic institution, ludicrous at times, riddled with corruption and crying out for reform. This was of course true, but before reading further please consider two things. The first is that, like other writing on the subject, this chapter states the facts in bald terms and selects extreme and sometimes entertaining examples. It is rather like some television programmes; everything in them may be true, but the impression that they give is influenced by the editing and what is left out. Secondly, please ponder the implications of the first sentence of *The Go-Between* by L.P. Hartley, 'The past is a foreign country: they do things differently there.' It is a much-quoted sentence and contains a great deal of wisdom.

As detailed in Chapter 3, the clamour for reform grew deafening in the approach to 1832, but for a long time previously, most of the British people were generally satisfied with the mother of parliaments. How could this be? One reason was that many educated people knew that, despite its manifest faults, it compared favourably with the arrangements in numerous other countries. Even the constitution of the democratic United States had significant failings. Many of the men who drafted it in 1787 owned slaves, as did George Washington, the first president. The constitution did not do a lot for Native Americans either.

It can be argued that, in the eighteenth century at least, the House of Commons did to some considerable extent reflect the society of the time. Land was extremely important and the source of much wealth, and it is certainly true that landowners were very well represented. This was one reason why a little later the Corn Laws, introduced in 1815 and repealed in 1846, aroused so much passion in Parliament. There is more about the Corn Laws in Chapter 3. The aristocracy and a relatively small number of powerful families had great power and they were certainly well represented, by themselves and by their nominees. Other interests were also represented, one example being Caribbean plantation owners who opposed the abolition of the slave trade. This was known as the 'sugar interest'. Another was those with investments in the East India Company. This was known as the 'Indian interest'. The changes sparked by the Industrial Revolution and the migration to the cities, especially in the north, progressively made these arguments less true, but it was a valid point for a long time.

It sounds strange today, but in the eighteenth century many accepted that it was not necessary to have the vote in order to be adequately represented, not necessarily by the member for your constituency. We now take the view that MPs have a duty to (and generally do) adequately represent children, persons of unsound mind and prisoners, none of whom have the vote. In the eighteenth century this duty was extended to the representation of all women and the majority of men who also did not have the vote.

In the view of many, a depressing aspect of our modern Parliament is that young men and women often have to spend a considerable period toiling for a party before being elected to the House of Commons. They believe that this may suppress the development of independence and is not the best preparation for life as an MP. Of course not everyone would agree, and the observation may be unfair. Regardless, despite all its faults and because of some of them, this was not the case with the unreformed Parliament. Some talented young men who would give great service to the nation were able to secure election at an early age.

As already noted the future prime minister, William Pitt the Elder, was elected for Old Sarum, the rottenest of rotten boroughs. He was 25 at the time. His son, William Pitt the Younger, was elected for the rotten borough of Appleby at the age of 22. He was Chancellor of the Exchequer at 23 and prime minister at 24, a position he was to occupy for twenty-one of the following twenty-three years. Lord Palmerston (Henry John Temple) entered Parliament as the member for the pocket borough of Newport, Isle of Wight, at the age of 22. He joined the government at the age of 24 and held office for most of the next fifty-six years. He died in office one day short of his 81st birthday, having (with a short break) spent the previous ten years as prime minister. Most remarkable of all was the Whig statesman Charles James Fox. His father bought him the constituency of Midhurst and he entered Parliament before his 21st birthday. Despite all this, Parliament in the early nineteenth century was desperately in need of reform. The clamour for it is described in Chapter 3.

NOTES

1. G.S. Veitch, *The Genesis of Parliamentary Reform*, p.5.
2. Ibid., p.6.
3. Ibid., p.6.
4. Papillon Graphics' Virtual Encyclopaedia & Guide to Greater Manchester.
5. John W. Derry, *Parliamentary Reform*, p.7.
6. Recounted by John W. Derry in *Parliamentary Reform*, p.9.
7. Sean Lang, *Parliamentary Reform 1785–1928*, p.10.
8. G.S. Veitch, *The Genesis of Parliamentary Reform*, p.9.
9. John W. Derry, *Parliamentary Reform*, p.10.

Catholic Emancipation

Prior to Catholic Emancipation Ireland was controlled by the so-called Protestant Ascendancy – the Protestants being the descendants of English and Scottish colonists. Roman Catholics were excluded from power and land ownership by the Penal Laws. Prior to union with Great Britain in 1801 the country was governed by the Lord Lieutenant of Ireland and by the Irish Parliament. The Parliament (from which Catholics were excluded) had the ability to pass or change laws, but not outside the framework of laws already passed by the English Parliament. The Lord Lieutenant ran the country on a day-to-day basis. Catholics suffered a host of restrictions, such as not being permitted to participate in certain professions, the law being just one example. In England, Wales and Scotland Catholics could not vote and could not sit in the House of Commons or the House of Lords.

It is interesting to note that the Duke of Wellington (then Arthur Wellesley) was elected a member of the Irish Parliament at the age of 21. He was an Irish Protestant, born in Dublin in 1769, just 106 days before Napoleon Bonaparte was born in Ajaccio, Corsica, an island that was conquered by France in the year of his birth.

By the middle of the eighteenth century freedom of religious worship had been effectively secured, though the Catholic clergy were still obliged to officiate unobtrusively in private houses or in miserable chapels, both in England and in Ireland.[1] Nevertheless, there was legislative discrimination against Catholics in England and much more so in Ireland. In England it was enforced with a light touch and sometimes not at all, but in Ireland the harsher laws were rigorously enforced. Not surprisingly, there was considerable discontent in Ireland, but the resentment was muted in England. It may have been a factor that the number of Catholics in England was small – much smaller than now – both in absolute terms and relative to the size of the population.

The Catholic Relief Act 1793 considerably advanced the Catholic cause in Ireland, including allowing them to vote. Catholics had high hopes that further measures would follow, including the right to sit in the Irish Parliament. They appeared to have good reason for their optimism because the prime minister, William Pitt, was in favour. Irish Catholics supported Britain in the war against France and provided troops, so it was expected that this loyalty would be rewarded.

Then it all went very sour. The Protestant Irish Parliament and the Protestant Irish Civil Service adopted a hostile attitude and pursued a policy of repression. Pitt changed tack and withdrew his support for full emancipation in Ireland. Some

Catholics turned their eyes towards France[2] and there was growing lawlessness and civil strife. This developed into a rebellion in 1798 – a rebellion that was supported by France and put down with the aid of British troops.

Faced with persecution in Ireland, many Catholics became convinced that full union with Great Britain was their best hope. Pitt and leading members of his government also wanted this, not least because it would secure Irish participation and support in the war with France. Indeed full union had almost certainly been Pitt's aim all along.

Two Acts of Union were passed in 1800, one in Great Britain and one in Ireland. The United Kingdom of Great Britain and Ireland came into being on 1 January 1801. Widespread bribery was used, including the promise of honours, to induce the Protestant Irish Parliament to vote itself out of existence. Ireland gained 100 seats (out of a total of 658) in the House of Commons. It also gained thirty-two seats in the House of Lords, twenty-eight representative peers elected for life, and four clergymen of the (Anglican) Church of Ireland, chosen for each session. To encourage Catholic support Pitt let it be known that full Catholic Emancipation, including the right to sit in the House of Commons and the House of Lords at Westminster, would follow shortly after the Union. This would be for both Irish and British Catholics. It was not a public pledge, but it was a definite understanding.

Pitt's assurances to the Irish Catholics had been conveyed by the Lord Lieutenant, Marquess Cornwallis, and by Lord Castlereagh, the Irish chief secretary. Both men were sincere, but they knew that the cabinet was divided on the issue. Pitt, of course, knew this too, and he knew that George III was opposed, but he believed that his position as a seemingly indispensable war leader would ensure that he could honour his promise. His confidence was, though, mistaken.

The lord chancellor, Lord Loughborough, led the cabinet opposition, and he enlisted the support of, among others, the archbishops of Canterbury, Armagh and London. The king wrote to Pitt in the following terms,[3] 'Lord Cornwallis must clearly understand that no indulgence can be granted to the Catholics further than has been, I am afraid unadvisedly, done in former sessions.' Later the king was heard to say,[4] 'What's this the young Lord (Castlereagh) has brought over from Ireland! It's the most Jacobinical thing I have ever heard of.' He went on to say[5] that he would regard as his personal enemy any man who proposed anything of the kind. Pitt applied to the king, saying that he had majority cabinet support. The king replied that his coronation oath made it impossible for him to even discuss the matter. After seventeen years as prime minister Pitt resigned on 16 February 1801.

Catholics were bitterly disappointed and the succeeding years were exceedingly frustrating for the cause of emancipation. They had learned the lesson that it is not always wise to rely on the promises of politicians. Pitt recommended Henry Addington to the king as his successor. Addington was the Speaker of the House of Commons and had been a childhood friend of his. He led a ministry opposed to the conciliation of Catholics. During his period in office he was overshadowed by Pitt, a state of affairs evidenced by a contemporary rhyme:

Pitt is to Addington,

As London is to Paddington

In 1804 the war with France was going badly and Addington's support in Parliament withered. Pitt returned to office as prime minister, having promised the king that he would introduce no measure in support of Catholic Emancipation. The exhausted Pitt died in 1806. He was 46 years old and had been prime minister for nineteen of them.

Another twenty-three years and six more prime ministers were to pass before emancipation was achieved during the tenure of the seventh, the Duke of Wellington. Most of the prime ministers (including Wellington) were hostile, but two were at least cautiously in favour. Part of the reason for the delay was the antipathy of George III and George IV. The older monarch's long reign lasted until 1820, but his final descent into madness resulted in his son being appointed prince regent in 1811. George IV's opposition was perhaps surprising. At the age of 23 he had secretly married Maria Fitzherbert, six years his senior and a devout, twice-widowed Catholic. The marriage was canonical but illegal. It was followed by a disastrous legal marriage resulting in a legitimate child, several mistresses and several illegitimate children, but he never forgot his Catholic love. Her miniature portrait was hanging round his neck when he died.[6]

Three of the six prime ministers after Pitt opposed Catholic Emancipation. They were the Duke of Portland (1807–09), Spencer Perceval (1809–12) and Lord Liverpool (1812–27). A fourth, Viscount Goderich (1827–28), was completely ineffective and only served for 144 days. The two who supported it were George Grenville (1806–07) and George Canning (1827). For different reasons, their periods in office were short.

George Grenville led what became known as the 'Ministry of All the Talents'. He was Pitt's cousin and succeeded him in office. His support for Catholic Emancipation was the reason that the king called him 'Popish'[7] and demanded his resignation after just fourteen months in office. Canning had been a strong supporter of Catholic Emancipation and it was therefore rather surprising that the king asked him to form a government. In fact it was doubly surprising because he had been a friend and supporter of Caroline, George's estranged queen. There had even been unsubstantiated rumours of a sexual relationship between them. This, if true, was a treasonable offence punishable, in theory at least, by the death penalty. In fact, to the great disappointment of the Catholics, emancipation was not an issue. Canning had the shortest tenure of any British prime minister. He was in bad health when appointed and died after less than four months in the position. Prior to taking office he had promised the king that he would not raise the subject of emancipation.[8]

The ultimate achievement of emancipation had a lot to do with Daniel O'Connell, often known in Ireland as 'The Liberator' or 'The Emancipator'. He was a lively and effective campaigner but, unlike some of his contemporaries, he was always opposed to violence. After practising as a barrister he returned to politics and in 1811 he established the 'Catholic Board'. This campaigned on the single issue of Catholics having the right to take seats at Westminster. In 1823 he set up the 'Catholic Association'. This wanted other reforms as well as the right of Catholics to take seats at Westminster. A decisive event was O'Connell's victory at the County Clare by-election held in June/July 1828. No law prevented him standing as a candidate and being elected, but he could not in conscience take the Oath of Supremacy and take his seat. This was because the wording was a clear rejection of his Catholic faith. There were clear similarities with the position of the atheist, Charles Bradlaugh, who was unable to take his seat in 1880. The circumstances and consequences are recounted in Chapter 14.

The by-election result had come at a time of growing support in England for emancipation, and it placed the government of the Duke of Wellington in a terribly difficult position. If it could happen in County Clare, it could happen in other constituencies too. There was the very real possibility that a general election would see scores of Irish Catholics elected, but unable to take their seats. Ireland was on the brink of disorder and an uprising; the peaceful Catholic Association was in control, but that might change. It was felt necessary to have a large standing army in Ireland, but many of the troops were Catholics and there were worries about how they would act if put to the test.

Both Wellington and Sir Robert Peel, Leader of the House of Commons, opposed Catholic Emancipation. Indeed, Peel's hostility was so great that he had acquired the nickname 'Orange Peel', a reference to the Protestant organisation. Nevertheless, Wellington had been a great general and great generals know when it is wise to retreat. He and Peel reluctantly decided that the very real prospect of civil disorder in Ireland was the greater evil. Emancipation there would have to be.

O'Connell was declared elected on 5 July and Wellington wrote to the king four weeks later. He met the king two months after that and he corresponded with him in November, the delays being caused by the king's ill health. As a result of this activity the following passage was included in the King's Speech, delivered to Parliament on 5 February 1829:

His Majesty laments that in that part of the United Kingdom (Ireland), an association still exists which is dangerous to the public peace, and inconsistent with the spirit of the constitution; which keeps alive discord and ill-will among His Majesty's subjects, and which must, if permitted to continue, effectually obstruct every effort permanently to improve the condition of Ireland. His Majesty confidently relies on the wisdom and on the support of his Parliament; and he feels assured that you will commit to him such powers as may enable His Majesty to maintain his just authority. His Majesty recommends that when this essential object shall have been accomplished you should take into your deliberate consideration the condition of Ireland, and that you should review the laws which impose disabilities on His Majesty's Roman Catholic subjects. You will consider whether the removal of these disabilities can be effected consistently with the full and permanent security of our establishments in Church and State, with the maintenance of the reformed religion established by law, and of the rights and privileges of the bishops and of the clergy of this nation, and of the churches committed to their charge.

To Wellington's irritation the conscience of Sir Robert Peel delayed the next step. He was one of the members for Oxford University and had been elected on the policy of no emancipation. He thought it right to resign and offer himself as a candidate at the by-election. The Oxford electors were intransigent and by 755 votes to 609 they elected an anti-Catholic candidate in his place. The rotten borough of Westbury was then vacated for him and he returned to Parliament unopposed. On 3 March he resumed his position as leader of the Commons.

On 4 March Wellington and Peel met the king at Windsor. Also present were the king's brother, the Duke of Cumberland, Lord Eldon and Lord Chancellor Lyndhurst. Cumberland had previously said, 'If the King gives his consent to the Catholic Emancipation Bill I will leave the kingdom and never return.'[9] Needless to say the threat was not carried out. For five hours the tearful king berated Wellington and Peel, and eventually withdrew the consent that he had previously promised. The two men then resigned and rode back to London. Shortly afterwards Wellington received a letter from the king.[10] It began 'My dear friend' and read:

As I have found the country would be left without an Administration, I have decided to yield my opinions to that which is considered by the Cabinet to be for the immediate interests of the country. Let them proceed as proposed with their measure. God knows what pain it costs me to write these words.
G.R.

In recommending the Catholic Emancipation Bill to the Commons, Peel very generously said:

The credit belongs to others and not to me. It belongs to Mr Fox, to Mr Grattan, to Mr Plunkett, to gentlemen opposite and to an illustrious and right honourable friend of mine who is no more, Mr Canning. By his efforts, and in spite of mine, it has proved successful.[11]

Peel's generosity did not extend to Daniel O'Connell, who had not taken his seat in Parliament. More than any other, he was the man responsible for securing emancipation. Perhaps O'Connell did not mind. He was very capable of speaking for himself. On a different occasion he said of the Duke of Wellington, 'The poor old Duke. What shall I say of him?: To be sure he was born in Ireland, but being born in a stable does not make a man a horse.'[12] It was a splendid joke, capable of infinite adaptation and consequently much used since.

On 30 March the bill passed the Commons by a majority of 320 votes to 142, and on 10 April it passed the Lords by a majority of 213 votes to 109. A distraught George IV gave his Royal Assent on 13 April. He would not look at the parchment, but just scribbled the necessary letters and flung his pen upon the floor. He afterwards said, 'Wellington is King of England, O'Connell is King of Ireland, and I suppose I'm only considered Dean of Windsor.'[13]

Daniel O'Connell, who had done so much to get the measure, did not have the honour of being the first person to take advantage of it. The law was not retrospective and only applied to future elections, so he had to submit to a further by-election. He was returned unopposed. The first Catholics to take their seats did so in the House of Lords. They were the Duke of Norfolk, Lord Dormer and Lord Clifford, followed shortly by Lord Petre, Lord Stafford and Lord Stourton. The Earl of Arundel, the Duke of Norfolk's son, was the first Catholic to take his seat in the House of Commons.

It is almost universally stated that Catholic Emancipation was achieved in 1829. There are obvious reasons for this, but it is not entirely the case. The Catholic Emancipation Act was one of a number of liberating measures. In particular, the Catholic Relief Act 1793 was very important. The 1829 Act still left Catholics with some disadvantages. No Catholic could be lord chancellor of England, lord chancellor of Ireland, viceroy of Ireland or commander-in-chief of the forces. A few niggling, and often ignored, restrictions were in place. For example, priests were not allowed to wear their vestments outside the precincts of the churches.

The year of 1829 did, though, in one important way mark a backward step for the Irish, and in practice for Irish Catholics in particular. In Ireland, the county voting franchise was increased from the 40 shilling freeholder to the ten pound freeholder. As a result county voters in Ireland were reduced from about 216,000 to about 37,000. In some constituencies the electorate was reduced to derisory numbers. This was intended to stop, as the Tories and some others saw it, the prospect of Irish peasants flooding the House of Commons with Catholic MPs. In the short term it did achieve its objective and only a small number of Irish Catholic MPs were elected at the 1830 general election.

The subject of Catholic Emancipation should not be left without mention of its consequences for the Tory Party. Wellington and Peel did not promote emancipation because they wanted to. They did so because they felt that they had to, and it left them feeling resentful. A considerable part of the party felt the same way, and many Tory MPs and peers felt that their leaders should not have conceded. The issue divided the party and weakened the position of its leaders. Wellington and Peel, backed by part of their party, were resolved not to concede on the principle of parliamentary reform. This stance features in the following chapters.

NOTES

1. Denis Gwynn, *The Struggle for Catholic Emancipation*, p.xxiii.
2. Ibid., p.105.
3. Ibid., p.128.
4. Ibid., p.129.

5.   Ibid., p.129.
6.   Elizabeth Longford, *Wellington: Pillar of State*, p.209.
7.   George Malcolm Thomson, *The Prime Ministers*, p.76.
8.   Denis Gwynn, *The Struggle for Catholic Emancipation*, p.239.
9.   Ibid., p.266.
10. Elizabeth Longford, *Wellington: Pillar of State*, p.184.
11. Denis Gwynn, *The Struggle for Catholic Emancipation*, p.275.
12. Shaw's Authenticated Report of the Irish State Trials (1844), p.93.
13. Denis Gwynn, *The Struggle for Catholic Emancipation*, p.274.

3

The Clamour for Reform

'Clamour' is a strong word, and its use is really only appropriate in the run-up to the introduction of the Reform Bill in 1831. As detailed in Chapter 1, it is arguable that for a long time the unreformed Parliament, despite its enormous deficiencies and absurdities, had produced at least tolerable results. For whatever reasons, pressure for reform was for a long time muted. This chapter picks up the story with the efforts of Pitt the Younger, and takes it through to the resignation as prime minister of the vehemently anti-reform Duke of Wellington on 16 November 1830.

In 1782 a number of like-minded people who favoured reform persuaded Pitt, soon to be prime minister, to raise the matter in the House of Commons. He was clearly a coming man, though it is tempting to say that, not yet 23 years old, he was a coming boy. It is ironic that less than eighteen months previously he had been the beneficiary of the unreformed system, and had taken his seat as the member for a very rotten borough. Pitt moved that 'a Committee be appointed to enquire into the present State of the Representation of the Commons of Great Britain in Parliament, to report the same to the House, and likewise what Steps in their opinion it may be proper for Parliament to take concerning the same'. This resolution was defeated by a majority of twenty.

The advocates of reform were disappointed but not too dismayed. They persevered and their actions included the encouragement of numerous petitions to Parliament. In 1783 Pitt tried again and his proposals included more MPs for the counties with larger populations and also more MPs for the more populous towns.[1] This was rejected by a majority of 150.

Pitt's final attempt, introduced as an individual rather than as a government measure, was made in 1785. He wanted to remove the franchise from thirty-six of the most notorious boroughs and redistribute their seventy-two seats to the more populous counties and to London. He envisaged that this would be done gradually and with the consent of the electors in the thirty-six boroughs, and he planned that a fund of a million pounds would be established to enable this to be done.[2] In other words the masters of pocket boroughs and rotten boroughs were to be bribed to give up something that many people regarded as not morally theirs in the first place. It was a big bribe too – a million pounds divided by thirty-six is equivalent to nearly £28,000 for each borough. This was a lot in 1785 money. Leave to introduce the bill was refused by a majority of seventy-four. This shows the strength of parliamentary feeling against reform. Pitt, by this time, was a highly regarded prime minister, who had just won a general election and was backed by a normally secure majority. If he could not pull it off, who could? It appeared that the prospects for reform would be dim for some time to come.

After this 1785 setback Pitt abandoned reform and turned his very considerable talents to other things. His motives in promoting it had probably been a mixture of conviction and a calculation that it was in his interests to do so. The two motives together make a powerful combination. He probably stopped because he thought that the chances of success were slim, and that it was no longer in his interests to pursue it.

After the failure of Pitt's final proposal there was a marked dwindling in the pressure for reform. It is interesting, and perhaps predictable, that the proponents of change were united on the principle but not on the details. There were genuine differences of opinion about the right changes to make, but it was also relevant that the different plans would result in different winners and losers. Vested interests were sometimes a factor. These considerations were not just relevant in the 1780s. They have been a factor right up to and including the twenty-first century.

The impact on opinion of the French Revolution should not be overlooked. Starting in 1789 its aims and progress engendered a lot of sympathy (as well as some hostility) in Britain. However, as it degenerated into excess and licence much of this sympathy evaporated. Subsequent descent into extensive guillotining, including of the French king and queen, pushed the hostility into revulsion.

Supporters and opponents of reform drew different conclusions. Supporters tended to think that well-judged changes would satisfy most potential revolutionaries, and reduce the chances of anything similar happening in Britain. Opponents, on the other hand, took the view that at this of all times it would be dangerous to make concessions. Furthermore, they espoused the 'thin end of the wedge' argument, thinking that moderate changes would inevitably lead to more and more extreme demands.

A number of political societies were established at this time, their aims being to achieve changes similar to those achieved by the French in the early days of their revolution. Two prominent ones were the Sheffield Society for Constitutional Reform (founded in 1791) and the London Corresponding Society (founded in 1792). Skilled working men were prominent in many of them, and their activities included the promotion of numerous petitions to Parliament. They maintained contacts with one another and, alarmingly for the authorities, some of them established contacts with the revolutionaries in France. This provoked a government response and two of the leaders of a Scottish society were convicted of sedition and sentenced to transportation.[3]

Britain went to war with France in 1793. An almost continuous state of conflict then lasted for twenty-two years, only ending with the Duke of Wellington's victory at Waterloo in 1815. Wellington is a name that features prominently later in this chapter, and afterwards too. Wars tend to be accompanied by suppression and the curtailment of freedoms, and this one was no exception. Habeus Corpus was suspended in 1794, which meant that people could be detained without trial. In 1795 Acts of Parliament targeted seditious meetings and treasonable practices. Pitt turned his back on reform and concentrated on winning the war, believing that a certain amount of repression was necessary. In this he had general support, despite the introduction of income tax as a temporary measure in 1799. The tax was indeed terminated soon afterwards, but it was rapidly reintroduced and is very much still with us.

The campaign for reform did not go away during the long course of the wars, but it was greatly subdued. A minor flowering in 1810 saw Thomas Brand introduce a motion in the House of Commons to consider the question of reform.[4] His proposals were modest and the motion was defeated by 234 votes to 115. It was the largest vote for reform since Pitt's motion of 1785. A further attempt by Brand in 1812 was defeated by eighty-eight votes to twenty-seven.[5] Despite this there was no general enthusiasm for reform during the war years, either in Parliament or among the people. This would come later, and it would develop into a clamour.

Agitation for parliamentary reform was greatest at times of economic hardship, and the United Kingdom suffered economic hardship in the years after Waterloo. There was peace, but a distinct lack of prosperity, and the mood of the people hardened very noticeably in the period from 1815 to 1820.

The first of the Corn Laws had been passed in 1804 and a further one in 1815 was a major bone of contention. It gave protection to farmers and land owners by only permitting the import of foreign corn when the domestic price was above a certain figure. The government said that this would give farmers an incentive to expand production, but the people saw it as a way of keeping the price of food (and bread in particular) unnecessarily high. The problem was exacerbated by a very poor harvest in 1816, and the high price of food caused considerable hardship. The Corn Laws were very much to the advantage of the land owners, and the interests of the land owners were excessively represented in the unreformed Parliament. The interests of the hungry masses, on the other hand, were extremely badly represented. This imbalance was a powerful argument for reform. The reformed Parliament would later keep the Corn Laws until 1846, when their repeal would lead to the fall of Sir Robert Peel's government.

Radical publications pressed the case for reform and Parliament was the recipient of numerous petitions on the subject. A number of very large protest meetings were held, including three in Spa Fields, London, in 1816–17. One of them descended into a riot. However, the most tragic and influential of these meetings was held at St Peters Fields, Manchester, on 16 August 1819. What happened rapidly became known as the Peterloo Massacre. 'Peterloo' was a bitterly sarcastic reference to the glorious triumph of Waterloo four years previously.

At St Peters Fields a crowd estimated at 50,000 or more assembled to hear Henry 'Orator' Hunt and other speakers. They were well behaved and not at all riotous. Fearful of what might happen, the local magistrates had taken extensive precautions. Available nearby were infantry, cavalry and 400 special constables. Shortly before the meeting was due to start the magistrates decided that the town was in great danger and took the decision to arrest the speakers. Part of the crowd linked arms to prevent this happening. In the events that followed the infantry and cavalry were used against a tightly packed crowd that could not escape. Several hundred people were injured, many badly, and estimates of the fatalities vary between eleven and nineteen.

Awful as this was, the government made things worse. The home secretary wrote to the magistrates thanking them for their firm action and attempts were made to suppress reports about what had happened. Journalists, the organisers and the speakers were prosecuted, and some of them were imprisoned. Hunt was sentenced to a jail term of thirty months. Parliament was persuaded to pass more repressive measures and collectively they became known as the 'Six Acts'. Peterloo soured the feelings of large parts of the population and the resentment lasted. A modern parallel could be the events in Northern Ireland that became known as 'Bloody Sunday'.

In a gloriously evocative sentence John Cannon memorably wrote,[6] 'In 1820 and 1821 began that tiny shift of pebbles that anticipates the avalanche, as, one by one, members began to announce their conversion to reform.' The mood in Parliament was beginning to move towards the mood in the country. In 1822 Lord John Russell, a name that features prominently in later chapters, tried to remove one of the two seats from the 100 smallest parliamentary boroughs, and redistribute them, partly to large towns with no separate representation and partly to the counties. This was defeated by 269 votes to 164. The parliamentary margin against reform was shrinking.

Things came to a head in 1830, the year which marks the conclusion of events covered in this chapter. The catalyst was the death of George IV on 26 June. Prior to this a number of reform bills had been rejected by Parliament. The first was in February and it was introduced by the unlikely figure of the Ultra Tory, the Marquess of Blandford. The bill was defeated by 160 votes to 57. His main motivation had been the rather ignoble one of trying to reduce the influence of Irish Catholics following Catholic Emancipation. Also in February, Lord John Russell tried to give direct representation to Leeds, Manchester and Birmingham. This was defeated by 188 votes to 140. In May he tried to take sixty seats from the smallest boroughs and give them to the counties and the biggest towns. This failed by 201 votes to 117. Also in May, Daniel O'Connell tried to obtain universal manhood suffrage, the secret ballot and triennial elections. Very predictably this was rejected by the enormous margin of 319 votes to just 13.

George IV had some admirable as well as very regrettable qualities, but he was not a loved monarch. *The Times* obituary included the damning comment, 'the character of which rose little higher than that of animal indulgence'. A little later the paper printed, 'There never was an individual less regretted by his fellow-creatures than this deceased king. What eye has wept for him?' The modern House of Windsor sometimes resents its press coverage, but it does not have to contend with savagery on this scale. The king's passing had political significance, including for reform. His successor had a different character and sometimes saw things differently. George had strongly opposed Catholic Emancipation, which was now irrelevant because it was in the past, but he also opposed parliamentary reform. This did matter because it was very much a live issue. George's death triggered a legal requirement for a general election to be held, and this mattered a lot.

The Duke of Wellington had been prime minister since January 1928 and the Tories, apart from a short interlude, had been the dominant party in Parliament for sixty years. The duke had been a great soldier, and had been, was and would continue to be a great man. However, he was not a great prime minister. He had a pronounced sense of duty, but was not happy in the job. He led a divided party, which makes government difficult and rarely appeals to the electorate. In particular the divisions over Catholic Emancipation had run very deep and a section of his party bitterly resented the volte-face of Wellington and Sir Robert Peel, who led in the Commons. This section of the party became known as the 'Ultra Tories' and they had set their faces against reform. Wellington and Peel, who agreed with them, had 'ratted' once and were determined not to upset them by ratting again.

The general election took place between 29 July and 1 September 1830. The results were poor for the Tories and the Duke of Wellington, but he still had a majority of thirty or slightly more. The results were hard to interpret because the position of some members was fluid and hard to ascertain. However, it was a setback, especially as many of the representative seats with large electorates had moved against the government. Wellington thought that he both could and should carry on, and he resolved to do so.

George's successor William IV opened the 9th Parliament of the United Kingdom on 2 November 1830. Wellington spoke after Lord Grey and some observers hoped or expected that he would make a commitment to modest reform. Any such hopes or expectations were dashed in the most emphatic way possible. In a singularly ill-judged speech the duke repudiated the prospect of any reform whatsoever. His words included the following:[7]

Nay, I, on my own part, will go further, and say, that I never read or heard of any measure … which in any degree satisfies my mind that the state of representation can be improved …

I am fully convinced that the country possesses at the present moment a legislature which answers all the good purposes of legislation, and this to a greater degree than any Legislature ever has answered in any country whatever.

I will go further and say, that the legislature and the system of representation possess the full and entire confidence of the country …

I will go still further, and say, that if at the present moment I had imposed upon me the duty of forming a Legislature for any country, and particularly for a country like this, in possession of great property of various descriptions, – I do not mean to assert that I could form such a legislature as we possess now, for the nature of man is incapable of reaching such *excellence* at once, – but my great endeavour would be, to form some description of legislature which would produce the same results.

Under these circumstances, I am not prepared to bring forward any measure of the description alluded to by the noble Lord.

I am not only not prepared to bring forward any measure of this nature, but I will at once declare that ... I shall always feel it my duty to resist such measures when proposed by others.

Wellington had at least said what he thought, but the reaction of the House of Lords was murmurs of incredulity. He picked up on this and turning to the foreign secretary, Lord Aberdeen, said, 'I have not said too much have I?' 'You'll hear of it,' was the reply. Outside, Aberdeen was asked what the duke had said. 'He said,' replied the foreign secretary, 'that we are going out.'[8]

The prophesy quickly came true. On 15 November the government was defeated in a vote on the Civil List. Wellington resigned the next day.

NOTES

1.   Eric J. Evans, *Parliamentary Reform, c.1770–1918*, p.11.
2.   G.S.Veitch, *The Genesis of Parliamentary Reform*, p.101.
3.   Eric J. Evans, *Parliamentary Reform, c.1770–1918*, p.13.
4.   John Cannon, *Parliamentary Reform, 1640–1832*, p.159.
5.   Ibid., p.163.
6.   Ibid., p.183.
7.   All reported in Elizabeth Longford, *Wellington: Pillar of State*, p.227.
8.   Ibid., p.228.

The First Reform Bill and Its Failure

The death of George IV and the accession of William IV were important to the cause of reform. This was firstly because they were followed by the legally required general election that, after a short interval, led to the resignation of Wellington and the end of his Tory government. At the time monarchs had more power and influence than is now the case, so secondly the different personality and views of the new king were important. The views, personality and influence of William's wife, Queen Adelaide, should also not be overlooked.

Adelaide was queen due to the rush to secure the succession. George III had fifteen children, of which thirteen survived to adulthood. George IV, his eldest son, had a disastrous marriage and one daughter, Princess Charlotte. She would have succeeded her father, but sadly she died giving birth to a stillborn child. Incredibly, this left George III with no legitimate grandchildren, though there were numerous illegitimate ones. The death of Princess Charlotte sparked urgent attempts by George IV's three unmarried younger brothers to provide a legitimate heir.

William was the third son of George III. He had lived for twenty years with the actress Dorothea Jordan. Having already had four children, and whilst working as an actress in her spare time, Dorothea had a further ten children with William. On the death of Princess Charlotte, William hurriedly married Adelaide of Saxe-Meiningen, a tiny German state covering only 43 square miles. At the time of the marriage he was 53 and she was 27. They had two girls together, but one died a few hours after birth and one died after three months. Either would have succeeded William, but instead Victoria, born in 1819 and the Duke of Kent's only child, did so. He had quickly married at the same time as William, and Victoria was the only surviving legitimate grandchild of George III.

William was 64 when he became king. Adelaide was 37 and had suffered three miscarriages as well as giving birth to the two short-lived girls. She had not given up hope of giving birth to an heir who would succeed her husband as monarch. Despite the circumstances of the rushed marriage it was a happy union. Adelaide was a contented and supportive wife, and she was good to William's eight surviving illegitimate children. It is reported that shortly after hearing of the death of his brother he retired to his bed with Adelaide saying, 'I've never been to bed with a queen before.'[1] The story is possibly apocryphal, but if so, like many apocryphal stories it is believable and therefore revealing an underlying truth.

William had joined the Royal Navy at 13 and was often referred to as the 'Sailor King'. He was a bluff, good-natured, friendly man, conscientious, anxious to do his duty and often said to be not notably intelligent. It is perhaps significant that a nickname, often used affectionately, was 'Silly Billy'. Unlike George IV, who had been extremely unpopular, he was a popular king at the start of his reign. Despite reservations and wavering he was willing to accommodate reform, though with objections to some of the details. His attitude would at times be crucial, especially when the dissolution of Parliament was requested and when the need to create new peers became an issue. He was accustomed to listen to the views of his wife and take them into account. Adelaide was Pro-Tory and anti-reform. She was reluctant to express her views in public but she influenced her husband behind the scenes.

Both William and Adelaide had great respect for Wellington and they bade him a sad farewell. Then William asked Lord Grey, the leading Whig elder statesman, to form the next government. The 64-year-old Grey sat in the Lords, but had been elected to the Commons at the age of 22. He had been out of government for twenty-four years. As well as his political career a claim to fame is that Earl Grey tea is believed to have been named after him. Party allegiances were less rigid then, so it is perhaps not surprising that his mainly Whig administration included a number of liberal Tories. His cabinet included his son-in-law (Lord Durham) and his government included two further sons-in-law as well as other relatives. Many of the Whigs had large landed estates and were inter-related. Antonia Fraser wittily called them the cousinship.[2] All but one of the thirteen-strong cabinet had hereditary titles, though some of them sat in the Commons.

Grey's cabinet contained a former Tory prime minister. This was the colonial secretary, Lord Goderich, who had served in this position for just 144 days in 1827/28. His government also contained no fewer than four future prime ministers, three of them in the cabinet. These were the home secretary (Lord Melbourne – prime minister 1834, 1835–41), the foreign secretary (Lord Palmerston – prime minister 1855–58, 1859–65) and the chief secretary for Ireland (Lord Derby – prime minister 1852, 1858–59, 1866–68). Outside the cabinet was the paymaster general (Lord John Russell – prime minister 1846–52, 1865–66). The 38-year-old Russell was the third son of the Duke of Bedford and, unlike many of his colleagues, not wealthy. Prior to Tony Blair he was the last prime minister to become a father whilst the occupant of 10 Downing Street. He was to be the minister who introduced the Reform Bill and was a key person in the story of parliamentary reform. Other prominent cabinet members included Lord Brougham, who was lord chancellor, and Lord Althorp, who was Chancellor of the Exchequer and Leader of the House of Commons.

The coming of the new government did not end protest, discontent and campaigning in the country. In fact it grew rather than diminished. This was sometimes about the need for reform and sometimes an expression of dissatisfaction about such things as wages, food prices and living conditions. Much of it was peaceful, though this did not always prevent it alarming the politicians and other authorities. The activities of the Birmingham Political Union and similar bodies, and also the activities of the early trades union, can generally be described in this way. On 29 January 1831 *The Times* printed 'Unless the people – the people everywhere – come forward and petition, ay, *thunder*, for reform, it is they who betray an honest Minister – it is not the Minister who betrays the people.'[3] By no means all of the protesting was peaceful though, and on 4 December 1830 the cabinet resolved that magistrates should be urged to show no weakness.[4]

The incoming government set to work very quickly and a special committee was formed. Its four members were Lord Durham, Lord John Russell, Lord Althorp and Lord Duncannon. They decided to work in complete secrecy and managed to do so. Anyone who studies politics, then as now, will know what an achievement that was. The same might be said about anyone who has watched the television programmes *Yes Minister* and *Yes, Prime Minister*. This secrecy was a major contributory factor to the incredulity that greeted the subsequent bill's introduction to the House of Commons.

Prompted by each member's personal commitment and by the urgency of the matter, the committee worked at great speed. Looking back one wonders how they managed it. No doubt the small number of members was a factor, and it helped that they had similar but not identical views. The commendable speed did, though, come at a price. The committee's work contained scribbling, crossing out, inconsistencies and mistakes. Rectifications were required before the introduction of the bill and, to the delight of members who opposed it, some were required afterwards. One example was that the Borough of Bewdley was listed to lose one of its two members. In fact it only had one member.[5]

The committee had held its first meeting on 11 December 1830, and it sent its very detailed recommendations to the prime minister on 14 January 1831. The cabinet considered them on 24 January and made amendments. Grey had an audience with the king at Brighton on 30 January and was delighted with his reception. This had been by no means a foregone conclusion, and it was a great relief. Grey advised Lord Durham, his son-in-law and chairman of the committee, that 'the King was particularly pleased with your report and entirely concurred in the statement, so powerfully and clearly made in it, of the necessity of doing something, and that something should be effectual and final'.[6]

The main features of the bill introduced to the House of Commons were as follows. Much of the information (gratefully acknowledged) is taken from John Cannon's *Parliamentary Reform 1640–1832*.

Existing Boroughs

Sixty-one boroughs with a population up to 2,000 were to lose all representation. The smallest of these was Bramber, with a population of ninety-eight. It should be noted that the criterion was population, not qualified voters.

Forty-seven boroughs with a population between 2,000 and 4,000 were to lose one of their two members. Once again the criterion was population, not qualified voters. The largest of these was Bridport with a population of 3,742.

Obvious questions include how can Bramber, with a population of ninety-eight, be the smallest borough to be disenfranchised? What about Old Sarum with its abandoned cottages and seven voters? The answer is that in many cases constituency boundaries were to be adjusted to conform with parish boundaries. This had not been properly thought through and, as explained later in this chapter, was to cause considerable problems.

Allocation of Seats to Urban Areas
Twenty-eight towns were to be enfranchised, twenty-two of them with one member and six of them with two members. Manchester, Birmingham, Leeds and Sheffield were among the towns to have two members.

London
Eight seats were to go to parts of London that had not been previously represented. This included an allocation of two seats to Marylebone.

English Counties
Five counties with populations between 150,000 and 200,000 were to have one extra seat.

Twenty-seven counties with populations in excess of 200,000 were to have two extra seats.

Wales
One extra seat was to be allocated to Wales.

Scotland
Eight extra seats were to be allocated to Scotland and the Scottish representation was to be substantially remodelled.

Ireland
Five extra seats were to be allocated to Ireland, going to Belfast, Limerick, Waterford, Galway and Trinity College Dublin (which already had one seat).

Urban Franchise
The committee had wanted to avoid differences between the existing boroughs and the newly enfranchised towns. It recommended a uniform property figure of £20. This was reduced to a uniform £10 before introduction of the bill. These figures had very significant consequences and the subject is covered in detail later in this chapter.

County Franchise
No changes were proposed. The qualification was to remain with the forty-shilling freeholders.

Secret Ballot
Although Russell was unhappy about it, the committee proposed the introduction of the secret ballot in place of voting in public, but this was reversed by the cabinet and the suggestion was not incorporated into the bill. Grey and some other cabinet members were against it, and so was the king, who saw it as 'inconsistent with the manly spirit and the free avowal of opinion which distinguish the people of England'.[7] A later cynic observed that voting in secret would enable electors to accept bribes from more than one candidate.

Septennial Elections
The committee proposed that the maximum period between elections be cut from seven years to five (quinquennial elections). The king did not agree and a maximum period of seven years (septennial elections) was retained. No change was proposed. In practice parliaments almost never ran the full seven-year term.

Compensation
Incredible as it sounds now, quite a few people took the view that the ability to control an election in a borough, or at least strongly influence the result, amounted to property. They also felt that removal of this property should be compensated. Payment of compensation had been proposed by Pitt in 1785, and it had been paid in Ireland at the time of the union with Britain. The committee did not even consider compensation and it did not feature in the bill. No doubt the potentially enormous cost was a consideration.

REGULATION OF ELECTIONS

Prior to 1828 polling was sometimes open for a matter of weeks. An Act in that year had limited the period in the boroughs to a maximum of eight days, and provided for several polling places if necessary. The bill proposed a maximum polling period of two days in both the boroughs and counties. Provision was to be made for the systematic registration of voters. This was designed to achieve efficiency and fairness, and also to greatly reduce the number of protracted and expensive legal disputes that followed elections. These measures were designed to reduce the cost of elections and would be very popular across the House.

   The work of the committee was rushed and so was the consideration given afterwards. The country was howling for reform, but it would have got a better bill if it had waited a little longer. The cabinet was disastrously late in spotting the implications of the £20 franchise, which means that only persons occupying property capable of being rented at £20 a year had the vote. If implemented, it would have restricted the number of urban voters by catastrophic amounts. 'Repression Bill' might have been a more appropriate title.

Not only would the newly enfranchised boroughs have had very small electorates, the number of voters in existing boroughs would have been reduced in many cases, often drastically so. In Bristol the electorate would have been reduced from more than 5,000 to around 2,700, and the newly enfranchised Manchester with a population of around 180,000 would have had about 1,200 electors. Amersham, which was to retain one member, would have had just seven electors. A few days before the bill was due to be introduced the £20 urban franchise was cut to £10. This reduced the problems, but it did not eliminate them; it still left inconsistencies, some of which would be exposed in the House by the Tories. Also, it left small urban electorates, which of course it was designed to do.

Boroughs were to be adjusted to conform with parish boundaries. This was to give those which were more sparsely occupied a population of at least 2,000, and to move towards some degree of uniformity. Problems with this were only realised at a very late stage. The numbers were based on the 1821 census, which was unreliable, and in any case was ten years out of date. To make matters worse, boundaries were not always adjusted in a consistent way. Frantic last minute changes were made, but inconsistencies remained. These too were pointed out with relish by the Tories.

The bill had very broad support in cabinet and there were no resignations, which was not a foregone conclusion. In particular, the Tory Duke of Richmond might have been expected to leave, but happily for the cause of reform he did not. This acquiescence, and also that of the king, was probably due to the very moderate extension of the franchise, and indeed it was reduced in some areas. It achieved uniformity and it extended some way into the middle class, but the toiling masses were nowhere near to getting the vote. It should be remembered that, unlike now, in 1831 the middle class was small. Much depends on how it is defined, but the middle class is now generally reckoned to be half or more of the population. In the opinion of one writer, 'the bill may seem modest since it promised no secret ballot and a uniform voting qualification in the boroughs designed expressly to ensure that very few of the new voters would be working men'.[8]

As stated earlier it was remarkable that details of the work of the committee remained secret. The fact that the cabinet's deliberations and the content of the bill did not leak was nothing short of miraculous; it must rank with the Virgin Birth in the scale of miracles. How today's ministers must envy the achievement, when not leaking themselves of course. Nevertheless, the secrets were kept and members assembled on 1 March with no forewarning of the thunderbolt that was about to strike.

Lord John Russell had long been a committed advocate of reform, and it was he who introduced the bill to the House of Commons. The chamber could only contain two thirds of the members, and it was completely full and buzzing with expectation. The Duke of Sussex, who was the king's brother, was watching from the gallery. He was in favour of reform and would later vote for it in the House of Lords. The king's other surviving brothers, the dukes of Clarence and Cambridge, were opposed to reform and would subsequently vote against. The great majority of members were expecting Russell to announce moderate measures of reform, and many liberal Tories would have been happy with that. From the standpoint of the twenty-first century many would argue that moderate reform was exactly what was being proposed, but honourable members, especially Tory ones, did not see it that way at the time.

The bill had the title 'Bill for Parliamentary Reform in England and Ireland'. It was intended that there would be a separate Bill for Scotland. Russell's voice was rather quiet and reedy, but his introductory remarks were well-judged and inspiring. His memorable phrases included references to a 'green mount' sending two representatives to Parliament and also to 'a green park with many signs of luxurious vegetation but none of human habitation'. He meant Old Sarum and Gatton respectively. The latter had at one time only had two qualified voters. On a different tack he castigated 'the gross venality and corruption' of a particular election. He then went on to stress the reasonableness and moderation of the bill that he was about to detail.

Russell then proceeded to the detail of the bill, starting with the abolition, redistribution and creation of seats. As he listed them one by one he was greeted with gasps of astonishment, incredulity, cheers, mirth and ironical laughter. It was all way beyond members' expectations. At one point Sir Robert Peel was seen to have his head in his hands. In total 168 members were to lose their seats and many of them were in the House listening to him. He then moved on to the other aspects of the bill and finished with some stirring comments.

When Russell sat down there was disbelief, astonishment and finally a tempestuous reaction.[9] Replying for the Tories Sir Robert Inglis, commenting on the object of the bill, used the words 'cannot be restoration, cannot then be reform, but, in a single word, is and must be revolution'. 'Revolution', however defined, was the fear of a section of the Tories, and in expressing this concern they very much had their eyes on events in France. The Second French Revolution and the overthrow of Charles X were only a few months in the past, and these events would cast a shadow over the debate. They would also influence events up to and beyond the eventual passing of the Reform Act in 1832.

Tory tactics were not to try for the immediate defeat of the bill, but to expose its flaws, get it amended, then have it defeated later. There were quite a lot of flaws to expose, mainly due to the bill's hurried drafting and hasty introduction. Many of the mistakes had been corrected, but by no means all. It did not help the government that many of the inconsistencies appeared to favour the influential Whigs who supported the bill. Cynics might note that this unfortunate tendency has often been manifest after 1831 as well. The bill was given seven days for the first reading and nine days for the second reading. As one might expect, Sir Robert Peel made a good speech for the Tories, and a particularly effective one from the same side was made by John Croker. He pointed out that the population figures of 2,000 and 4,000 were purely arbitrary, and went on to say:

Why was Downton, with only nine £10 householders, to keep one member, while Buckingham, a county town with eight times as many qualified voters, was to lose both? Why was Calne, with fewer than 5,000 persons, to retain two seats, while Bolton, Blackburn, Brighton and Tyneside, with more than 20,000, had to be content with one? Was it not strange that the borough that just made its escape from Schedule B, with a population of 4,005, should be Malton, belonging to Lord Fitzwilliam, a Whig magnate? How could a settlement incorporating such anomalies ever be permanent? No wonder the noble lord [Russell] was so sore last night when we asked him a question or two about returns.[10]

He also remarked that it was strange that Tavistock had survived the cull with its two members intact. This borough was in the gift of Russell's father, the Duke of Bedford, and in the past had been represented by Russell himself.[11]

Not all the opposition came from the Tories. The secretary at war, Charles Wynn, said that he was not prepared for so great a sacrifice and resigned.[12] He thought that the bill was too radical, but a few members thought that, although they would support it, they did not think that it was radical enough. Prominent among them was Henry Hunt.[13] As recounted in the last chapter, he had been a speaker at the so-called 'Peterloo Massacre' in 1819 and had been imprisoned afterwards. Hunt had become the Radical Member for Preston at the 1830 general election.

The debates on the first and second readings lasted for a combined total of sixteen days. It is therefore only possible to mention a fraction of the speeches. It would, though, be remiss not to mention the contribution of Thomas Babington Macaulay,[14] the future renowned historian, who made perhaps the best speech in defence of the bill. At the time he was aged 30 and a Member for Calne, one of the boroughs mentioned by John Croker. He effectively rebutted the claim that the bill would lead to revolution, and compellingly asserted that, on the contrary, by extending the franchise into the middle class and removing justified grievances, the bill made revolution much less likely. What was proposed was the exact opposite to what had been done in pre-revolutionary France. There were no lessons to be learned from Charles X, who had so recently lost his throne.

As the debates progressed two very important and unresolved questions occupied the minds of many members. What would happen next? And would the king agree to the dissolution of Parliament? This is what the government wanted because they were confident that they would sweep the country at the resulting general election, even though it would be held under the unreformed voting arrangements. It was what the Tories did not want, for exactly the same reason – they thought that they would probably lose. The willingness of the king to grant a dissolution was both critical and uncertain.

Minds were concentrated by an event on 18 March. The government was defeated by a majority of forty-six on a vote on the alteration of the Timber Duties. It was a relatively unimportant matter, but it showed the power of the Tories. Grey immediately said that his resolve to press on with reform was not affected, and the king indicated that he and the government still had his confidence. However, very worryingly for them William added that he was resolutely opposed to the dissolution of Parliament.

The vote on the bill was one of Parliament's great dramas. Amid scenes of feverish excitement it took place at 2.57 a.m. on the morning of 23 March. The number of members attending and the number of votes cast were perhaps a record, and it could not have been closer. The bill was carried by 302 votes to 301. The roar of approval carried round London and then around the country. Subsequent analysis of the result revealed that the support of fifty-six Irish members had been essential. English members supporting the bill had been in a minority of three.

The satisfaction and joy was premature, because the bill still had to pass through the committee stage. There was the very real prospect that the Tories would water it down, or improve it as they would see it, or perhaps even wreck it. Despite some dissent, from Lord Palmerston among others, the cabinet decided to keep faith with the bill. There would be no major concessions and it would be taken forward substantially as it had been approved. There were, though, some sensible changes, mainly to deal with anomalies that had been exposed. For example, eight towns with a population of more than 10,000 were given a seat, and eight counties with a population in excess of 100,000 were given another one. The pressure to amend the bill was not exclusively to make it more moderate. Henry Hunt, the Member for Preston and victim of Peterloo, withdrew his support and pressed to have it made more radical. There was no chance whatsoever of this happening. It would either be weakened or go through much as it stood.

After the Easter break matters came to a head on 20 April. The government was defeated on an amendment, moved by the Ultra Tory Lord Gascoyne, which fundamentally altered the bill in an unacceptable way. The vote was taken just before 5 a.m. and the amendment was carried by 299 votes to 291. Shortly afterwards the government was defeated on a bill for supplies. The next forty-eight hours saw devious plotting, high drama, anger and the most dramatic arrival of a monarch into the precincts of Parliament since 1642, when Charles I entered the House of Commons in an attempt to arrest five members on a charge of treason.

It was obvious that Grey would seek the dissolution of Parliament and a general election, and very shortly after the two defeats the cabinet did resolve to ask the king for this. William had previously indicated his strong opposition to the idea, so the request was made without total confidence that it would be successful. However, it was made in the most tactful and persuasive way possible, and it was believed that the king's strong feelings had moderated.[15]

At this point the Tories devised a too-clever-by-half plot. It seemed clever and indeed it was clever, but it backfired. The United Kingdom's unwritten constitution did not make completely clear the circumstances in which Parliament could be dissolved, though it was generally believed that it was the king's prerogative. Like his Hanoverian forebears, this was most definitely William's view. There was, though, a school of thought that held that Parliament could not be dissolved whilst unfinished business was outstanding. Hoping to take advantage of this the Tories planned a vote in the House of Lords opposing dissolution of the House of Commons.[16]

The king replied to the cabinet's request by saying that he had to meet the Prince of Coburg at 11 a.m., but that he would see the prime minister at 11.30 a.m. and hold a Council at 12 p.m. Everyone should be in morning dress. He had been appraised of the Tory manoeuvring, and William was still personally unhappy about dissolution, as well as extremely angry at the plan to deny his absolute discretion. He would probably have agreed to dissolution anyway, but this put it beyond doubt. To use a phrase not in use in the nineteenth century, he would jolly well show them. He immediately accepted the request, but said that any new bill introduced in the new Parliament should not be more radical than the previous one.[17]

Not only did the king agree to dissolution, he bypassed all the usual courtesies and formalities and did it at once. He called for his horses and carriage, then drove out of his palace and headed towards Parliament. The sounding of a cannon signified his arrival. At the time Lord Wharncliffe was speaking in the Lords and Sir Robert Peel was speaking in the Commons. Hansard recorded that in the Commons there were cries of 'To the Bar! To the Bar!' This meant that the members should go to the Bar of the House and await the summons to the Lords. Shortly after this Black Rod appeared and uttered the time-honoured words, 'I am commanded by his Majesty, to command the immediate attendance of the honourable House in the House of Lords.'

The astonished members complied amid scenes of pandemonium. They were headed by the Speaker, Charles Manners-Sutton, who was said to be red-faced and quivering with rage.[18] Both Houses were in uproar and numerous altercations included Lord Lyndhurst, the former Tory lord chancellor, shaking his fist at the Duke of Richmond, a Tory who was serving in the government.[19]

There was some confusion about whether the as yet uncrowned king was entitled to wear the Crown. William had not wanted to have a coronation but, if it really was required, he had wanted to have a simple and inexpensive ceremony. William was not in a mood to debate the point. He called for the Crown and placed it on his own head. Then turning to Grey he said, 'Now my Lord, the coronation is over.'[20]

Some of the more thoughtful MPs might have recalled the coronation of Napoleon Bonaparte as emperor in 1804. He had unexpectedly taken the Crown from Pope Pius VII and placed it on his own head. Some of the anti-Catholic members might even have remembered that Pius's leading role in the coronation of Europe's most feared despot (as they saw it) might have been one of their reasons for opposing Catholic Emancipation. Perhaps this is rather far-fetched, but it is an interesting thought.

William's words could not have been more favourable to Grey and the cause of reform: 'I have been induced to resort to this measure for the purpose of ascertaining the sense of my people, in the way in which it can be most constitutionally expressed, on the expediency of making such changes in the representation as circumstances may appear to require.'[21] William had spoken, William had acted and the matter moved back to the people – though only to the small number of people permitted to vote in an election for a still unreformed Parliament.

NOTES

1.   Antonia Fraser, *Perilous Question: The Drama of The Great Reform Act 1832*, p.6.
2.   Ibid., p.57.
3.   Ibid., p.76.
4.   Ibid., p.61.
5.   John Cannon, *Parliamentary Reform 1640–1832*, p.212.
6.   Ibid., p.213.
7.   Ibid., p.211.
8.   Eric J. Evans, *Parliamentary Reform, c.1770–1918*, p.24.
9.   Antonia Fraser, *Perilous Question: The Drama of The Great Reform Act 1832*, p.80.
10. Recounted by John Cannon, *Parliamentary Reform 1640–1832*, p.216–7.
11. Recounted by Antonia Fraser, *Perilous Question: The Drama of the Great Reform Act 1832*, p.89.
12. Recounted by John Cannon, *Parliamentary Reform 1640–1832*, p.216.
13. Ibid., p.217.
14. Ibid., p.215–6.
15. Antonia Fraser, *Perilous Question: The Drama of The Great Reform Act 1832*, p.107.
16   Ibid., p.107.
17. John Cannon, *Parliamentary Reform 1640–1832*, p.220.
18. Antonia Fraser, *Perilous Question: The Drama of The Great Reform Act 1832*, p.109.
19. Ibid., p.109.
20. Ibid., p.110.
21. Ibid., p.110.

5

The Second Reform Bill and Its Failure

Following the failure of the first Reform Bill King William dissolved Parliament on 22 April 1831. The House of Lords voted down its replacement, the second Reform Bill, 169 days later. The vote was taken at 6.40 a.m. following an all night sitting. Their lordships displayed great stamina.

After the dissolution on 22 April most supporters of reform were buoyant and optimistic. They were confident that even though the forthcoming election would be fought on the unreformed constituencies and franchise, a majority for reform was almost inevitable. Events would shortly show that this confidence was justified. They also believed that the majority of the disenfranchised citizens were overwhelmingly on their side, which of course was unquestionably true. Furthermore, they were confident that the very popular King Billy could be relied on to do the right thing. For a time at least this was the view of the prime minister. Grey wrote to Lord Anglesey, 'The King has behaved like an angel. There is no extent of gratitude that we do not owe him for the confidence and kindness with which we have been treated.'[1] In the face of all this, many just could not believe that the Lords would not acquiesce when presented with a second bill. This belief turned out to be mistaken.

Celebrations of the dissolution included the ordering by the lord mayor of London of illuminations on the evening of 27 April. This meant the placing of candles in the windows of fine houses. Crowds celebrated this but then showed their displeasure at families that had not complied. A mob surged up Piccadilly, breaking windows that were not lit up. Nathan Rothschild was one victim and the destruction culminated in the storming of Apsley House, the London residence of the Duke of Wellington.

It was a terrible time for Wellington. As well as his political setbacks and dismay about national events, he had just suffered a personal tragedy. After a debilitating illness lasting several months his wife had died on 24 April, just two days after the dissolution and three days before the attack on his house. Wellington had not enjoyed a happy marriage, but he had grown close to his wife during her final illness. It is safe to assume that he would in no circumstances have illuminated his windows, but at the time he was in Hampshire making arrangements for his wife's funeral. The body of the dead Duchess was resting in the house at the time of the attack.

The mob smashed a number of windows and pulled up some railings in preparation for an assault. Further damage was forestalled by one of the Duke's servants, who fired two blunderbusses, loaded with gunpowder only, over the heads of the crowd. Wellington later wrote, 'I think my servant John saved my House or the lives of the Mob – possibly both – by firing as he did. They certainly intended to destroy the house, and did not care one pin for the poor Duchess being dead in the House.'[2]

Wellington's windows were to be broken again during a further assault on 12 October. Following this he put up iron shutters in order to protect them. This is believed to be one of the reasons why he is often called 'The Iron Duke'. It is not, as is commonly supposed, a tribute to his military triumphs.

Violence and disorder were not on anything like the scale of the events that would take place after the rejection of the Second Reform Bill, but it did exist and so did the fear of it, with or without good reason. The Ultra Tory General Gascoyne was pelted in his constituency and he went on to lose the seat that he had held since 1796. This was the man whose amendment had been instrumental in the failure of the first Reform Bill.

The future Lord Lytton advised his Tory mother, 'I see great reason why for your own sake you should not even quietly and coldly oppose Reform. The public are so unanimous and so violent on the measure, right or wrong, that I do not hesitate to say that persons who oppose the Reform will be marked out in case of any disturbance. It is as well therefore to be safe and neutral, especially when no earthly advantage is to be gained by going against the tide.'[3]

During the election campaign a Tory candidate, Wellington's nephew Lord Worcester, almost drowned as a consequence of the actions of a mob that favoured reform.[4] Wellington himself was made aware of a plan to waylay his coach. He kept a brace of double-barrelled pistols in his carriage and his servant on the carriage's box was armed. Wellington was, as always, imperturbable. He had with insouciance defied danger in numerous battles, and in addition to fighting a duel he had survived several assassination attempts.

Strong feelings over the bill sometimes divided families and strained friendships. In this it had something in common with the 1956 Suez Crisis in more modern times. Another possible analogy is the Second Iraq War of 2003. The son of the first Lord Carrington was a supporter of reform and had been an MP for ten years. His father, well known as an amiable man, opposed reform and wrote to his son in the following terms: 'My Dear Bob ... It would be as well for you not to come to this house for sometime as I would be tempted to use language which you would never forget, and which I myself might never forgive myself.'[5]

Polling in the general election took place on different dates and over different periods. The first poll opened on 28 April, just six days after the dissolution, and the last poll closed on 1 June. During this period there was a groundswell of support for reform, but also a palpable fear among some that the country was moving into uncharted waters and that there would be dire consequences. These consequences could vary from mild disorder, through a breakdown in authority right up to possible revolution. Needless to say those with the most to lose tended to be among the most fearful. Nevertheless, the predominant mood was one of optimism.

As explained, earlier party allegiances were much looser then than is the case now, so it is not possible to give the exact size of the government's majority. However, it was reckoned to be somewhere between 120 and 150 in favour of reform, a huge swing from the previous general election. The Tory-controlled rotten boroughs continued to elect Tory members, but where there was anything like an open election there was an avalanche of support for the Whigs and for reform. In the counties the Tories were almost annihilated.

There were two crumbs of comfort for the Tories. One was the failure to defeat Lord Chandos in Buckinghamshire, but a more substantial setback was the failure of the foreign secretary, Lord Palmerston, to hold the seat at Cambridge University that he had held for twenty years. He was quickly found a seat at Bletchingley, for which a payment had to be made. This was a rotten borough and was due to be disenfranchised when the bill was enacted.

There was no doubt that the re-elected government would introduce another Reform Bill, and there was no doubt that it would be endorsed by the Commons. What was in doubt was whether the unelected House of Lords with its inbuilt Tory majority would accept the will of the people and pass it. Also in doubt was whether or not, if the bill was rejected by the Lords, the king would be willing to create new peers in order to get it through.

The cabinet had to consider whether or not to modify the bill in order to increase the chance of it being accepted by the Lords. The king, for one, thought that they should. On 28 May he wrote to Grey urging him to consider modifications which, while not affecting the principle of the bill would indicate a 'disposition to conciliate'.[6] Grey's reply was both swift and brisk; he said that, 'frankness forced him to observe that, in his judgment, no concessions that could be made, short of a total destruction of all the beneficial effects of the bill, would satisfy those by whom it has hitherto been most violently opposed'.[7]

Despite this a faction of the cabinet, including Palmerston, Goderich and Lansdowne, did want to make a concession, suggesting a return to a higher franchise. This suggestion did not carry the day and the hesitation passed off without resignations. Grey, Althorp and Durham took the view that the concession would be more likely to alienate the Commons than mollify the Lords.[8] A few minor and sensible amendments were agreed. A damaging change was reversed after it was realised that it would significantly reduce the number of voters. This was the proposal that the £10 franchise voters be limited to those who paid their rates at six monthly intervals or longer.

It was to be 'the Bill, the whole Bill and nothing but the Bill'. This was what Lord John Russell, newly promoted to the cabinet, presented to the Commons on 14 June. The bill's passage through the Commons provided less drama than that of its predecessor. This was because the initial shock was absent and because it was known in advance that its success in the Commons was assured. Success in the Lords was another matter. The debate took place against the backdrop of stiflingly hot weather and the alarming arrival of cholera in the country. The bill's second reading was obtained on 6 July by 367 votes to 231, a majority of 136. Once again the number of MPs voting was very high.

The activities of William Gladstone at around this time deserve a mention. This is the future Liberal prime minister and a man who was to be a great friend of parliamentary reform. However, in 1831 he was a reactionary Tory with some decidedly unprogressive views. He was a very committed but intolerant Anglican and an opponent of the Reform Bill. At 21 years old he was a student at Oxford University and President of the University Debating Society.

On 17 May he made a vehement forty-five-minute speech to the Society in opposition to the Reform Bill. According to Roy Jenkins, 'It was hardly a moderate speech. Its thesis was that the Reform Bill, if carried, would break up the social order not merely in Britain but throughout the civilised world.'[9] His speech was extremely well received and his side of the argument won by ninety-four votes to thirty-eight. Later he took time off from his studies and spent fifty hours over five days listening to the debate on the Reform Bill in the House of Lords.

Gladstone was shortly to be the 22-year-old MP for Newark. He won the seat at the general election following the 1832 Reform Act, his precocious candidacy owing much to the influence of the Duke of Newcastle. It was a rumbustious campaign and he wrote that stones thrown at him missed his head by three inches. Roy Jenkins reported that 'there had been the distribution of far more money on Gladstone's behalf than he was aware of or subsequently approved. However, it was not quite scandalous enough to lead to a petition against corrupt practices.'[10] The future Grand Old Man, who would be four times a Liberal prime minister and an MP for more than sixty-three years, was on his way. Shortly after his victory he said, 'I was born Red, I live Red and I shall die Red.' Red, unlike now, was the Tory colour at the time.

After a sometimes tedious forty days the bill completed its Committee stage in the Commons on 7 September. A succession of members made special pleading on behalf of their constituency and constituents and a number of unsuccessful legal challenges were mounted. Croker had embarrassed ministers by pointing out anomalies in the first bill and he did so again with the second. For example, why did Sunderland with a population of 33,000 merit two MPs, but Bolton with 44,000 merit only one? It was a good question, and one of several good questions that he asked. Wales was given an extra MP and Stroud and Ashton-under-Lyne were enfranchised.

Two major issues were raised and the government gave way on one but held firm on the other. It was proposed that the 1831 census, the results of which were becoming available, should be used instead of the 1821 one as the basis of calculating populations. This had a lot of merit, but it also had the potential to cause endless delays, arguments and legal challenges. The government did not give way on this and the out of date census was used.

The second issue concerned the county franchise. It was proposed that tenants at will renting property of £50 p.a. be given the vote. A tenant at will occupied a property with the consent of the owner, but without an agreement that specified a definite rental period. The government was opposed to this because it believed that it would greatly increase the influence of landlords. However, the amendment was carried by a majority of eighty-four votes, and in view of this the government found it expedient to give way.

As soon as the bill was finished in the Commons attention switched to the Upper House. What would the Lords do? There were four possibilities:

1. They might accept the will of the people and of the elected House and pass the bill, perhaps with a few improving amendments.
2. They might seek a genuine compromise.
3. They might accept the principle of the bill, then cut it to shreds with wrecking amendments.
4. They might reject the bill outright.

It is hard to see that a compromise was available and, if it was, it must have been heavily weighted towards keeping almost all of the bill. The government was committed to 'The Bill, the whole Bill and nothing but the Bill' and this was clearly the will of the people. Rejection of the bill would provoke a Lords v Commons clash and a constitutional crisis.

Looking back from the twenty-first century and with the benefit of hindsight very few people would argue that the Lords should have rejected the bill, but this did not seem so obvious in the first third of the nineteenth century. Many Tories sincerely thought that the bill was dangerous and would have all sorts of consequences that were damaging to the country. Some even feared revolution, recent events in France being in their minds. The counter argument was that on the contrary dealing with legitimate grievances would make revolution much less likely. Subsequent events would show that fears of revolution were unfounded and that the removal of legitimate grievances did reduce the risk. Thrones around Europe fell in 1848, but not the throne of the United Kingdom.

There was also the thin end of the wedge argument. Opponents of reform thought that the bill would inevitably be a staging post towards later and more fundamental changes. This of course did happen, though it was not the government's intention. Whether this was a bad thing is another matter; most of us would say that it was not.

What was the point of the Lords if it could not take a different view from the Commons? Croker put it very well by saying, 'In what crisis of public affairs will it ever be permitted to the peers to exercise their deliberative functions if it be denied to them now? Or are they henceforward to understand that they must confine their independence to amending a Turnpike Act?'[11]

In addition to these principled fears there was of course naked self interest. It was baldly expressed by the Duke of Newcastle who said, 'May not I do what I like with my own?'[12] He meant that he owned a number of seats and that he was entitled to sell them or use them as he saw fit, rather as he was entitled to do what he liked with a prize bull that he owned. It does not seem an attractive argument now, and it was not an attractive argument in 1831 either.

A Tory dinner party was held at Wellington's house on 21 September, the tone being lowered by lords Kenyon and Eldon who arrived drunk from a dinner given by the king's brother and anti-reformer the Duke of Cumberland. At the dinner party it was decided that the Tories would take a hard line and try to vote down the bill on its second reading. This was despite the Lords receiving a barrage of petitions and other advice urging acceptance.

Lord Grey rose on 3 October to move the second reading in the Lords. Like Wellington he had recently suffered a family bereavement and it affected him deeply. On 24 September and after a long illness his much-loved grandson had succumbed to tuberculosis. This boy was Charles Lambton, the son of his cabinet colleague and son-in-law Lord Durham. The dead boy had some time previously been immortalised as the subject of a painting titled *The Red Boy* by Sir Thomas Lawrence. The distraught Lord Grey had to sit down shortly after starting his speech, but after a short break he was able to continue. He then made a long and effective speech, though whether it changed minds that were already made up must be open to question.

Part of Grey's speech was an appeal to the Lords Spiritual. These were the twenty-three bishops of the Church of England who sat in the Lords. The only one of them to speak was the Archbishop of Canterbury and he was listened to with special attention because it was assumed that he was speaking for most or all of his colleagues. The subsequent vote showed that this assumption was correct. The archbishop spoke against reform. In the twenty-first century it is often felt that the clergy in general, and the Church of England in particular, hold left wing views. If this is true now, and it probably is, it was not always the case. Within the lifetime of many readers of this book the Church of England was often referred to as The Tory Party at Prayer. So it was in 1831, and it made the bishops unpopular.

Wellington was relatively muted because of his previous implacable and what many regarded as absurd opposition to any reform whatsoever. He did though make it clear that he was still totally opposed to reform. Lords Wharncliffe and Harrowby took leading roles for the opposition and there was a flutter of excitement because they seemed to indicate that they were open to a compromise. Then they shut the door and made it clear that they opposed the bill.

By far the most memorable speech was made on the last day by Lord Brougham, the lord chancellor. It was more than three hours long and he made it whilst fortified by a not inconsiderable amount of alcohol, mulled port being mentioned. He implored his listeners to accept the bill with words both passionate and eloquent, and his manner of delivery was decidedly eccentric. This magnificent piece of parliamentary theatre ended with the following peroration:

Raise not the spirit of a peace-loving but determined people – alienate not the affections of a great empire from your body. As your friend, as the friend of my country, as the servant of my sovereign, I counsel you … For all these reasons, I pray and beseech you not to reject this Bill. I call upon you by all that you hold most dear, by all that binds every one of us to our common order and our common country – unless, indeed, you are prepared to say that you will admit of no reform, that you are resolved against all change, for in that case opposition would at least be consistent – I beseech you, I solemnly adjure you, yes, even on bended knees my lords I implore you not to reject this Bill.[13]

After five days of debate Lord Grey commenced his effective winding up speech at 5 a.m. and the House divided at 6.30 a.m. Despite all the arguments in favour and despite Brougham's impassioned eloquence it rejected the bill by the decisive majority of forty-one. It was noted that twenty-one of the twenty-three bishops had voted with the majority in not accepting it. Had they all voted the other way the bill would have passed with a majority of one. Two of the king's brothers, the royal dukes of Cumberland and Gloucester, were among the majority who had voted down the bill.

The young William Gladstone thought that 'it was an honourable and manly decision'.[14] Be that as it may, the Lords had voted the country into a constitutional crisis.

NOTES

1. Antonia Fraser, *Perilous Question: The Drama of The Great Reform Act 1832*, p.111.
2. Elizabeth Longford, *Wellington: Pillar of State*, p.268.
3. Antonia Fraser, *Perilous Question: The Drama of The Great Reform Act 1832*, p.121.
4. Elizabeth Longford, *Wellington: Pillar of State*, p.268.
5. Antonia Fraser, *Perilous Question: The Drama of The Great Reform Act 1832*, p.112.
6. John Cannon, *Parliamentary Reform 1640–1832*, p.221.
7. Ibid., p.222.
8. Ibid., p.222.
9. Roy Jenkins, *Gladstone*, p.23.
10. Ibid., p.35.
11. John Cannon, *Parliamentary Reform 1640–1832*, p.224.
12. Antonia Fraser, *Perilous Question: The Drama of The Great Reform Act 1832*, p.119.
13. Ibid., p.148.
14. John Cannon, *Parliamentary Reform 1640–1832*, p.225.

Success at Last: The Third Reform Bill

The *Morning Chronicle*'s edition of 9 October 1831, one day after the rejection of the Second Reform Bill by the House of Lords, was edged in black. To some extent this indication of mourning summed up the feelings of much of the country, but fear and anger were also very much to the fore. The nation had been simmering for some time, but the response to the failure of this bill was much more riotous and violent than the response to the failure of the first one. Over the next few months parts of the country were subject to considerable disorder, including serious loss of life.

The burning of effigies has a long and some would say inglorious tradition in Britain. Celebration of the failure of the 1605 gunpowder plot to blow up Parliament is the origin of the practice of placing an effigy of Guy Fawkes on bonfires on 5 November. It was a pro-Catholic plot and in some places Fawkes was joined by an effigy of the Pope. On 5 November 1831 an effigy of the firmly Protestant Bishop of Exeter also suffered this fate. The bishop had been a strong opponent of the bill. Shortly after the House of Lords vote effigies of Wellington and the Duke of Cumberland had been burned at Tyburn. Cumberland was much despised by many and additionally suffered the fate of being splattered by mud.

Apsley House, the London residence of the Duke of Wellington, was stoned for the second time on 12 October. This time Wellington was inside and he reacted with his customary courage and fortitude, calmly writing a letter as glass shattered around him. The Duke of Newcastle's Nottingham Castle was burned down and in Derby the houses of opponents of the bill were attacked. Also in Derby the gaol was destroyed. Trouble erupted in many parts of the country, but nothing matched the events in Bristol.

Bristol had a history of riots and eleven people had died in 1793,[1] though on that occasion the issue had nothing to do with reform. The spark in 1831 was the arrival in the city of Sir Charles Wetherell. As well as being an Ultra Tory and strong opponent of reform he was the Recorder of Bristol. His appearance was greeted by expressions of anger and he had to be protected by the police and by special constables. Shortly afterwards his house was attacked and set on fire. The situation developed into a ghastly riot with much drunkenness and many casualties. Also burned were the Mansion House, the Bishop's Palace, the Toll House, the Excise House, the Customs House and three gaols.[2]

The rioting lasted four days until 2 November. The official number of people killed was twelve though Antonia Fraser puts it at around 400, including those burnt to death drunk.[3] In all, 102 prisoners were taken and 83 of these were subsequently convicted. Thirty-one of the convictions were on capital charges and four people were subsequently executed. Seven were transported.

Predictably, the riots in general and the events in Bristol in particular often confirmed the opinions of both the supporters and opponents of Reform. Responsible supporters, although strongly deprecating the riots, felt that they reinforced the need for moderate and justified Reform. The opponents saw the riots as a foretaste of things to come, and even of a possible revolution. They asked why such a disgusting rabble should have the vote, and shuddered to think what they might do with it. This, of course, missed the point that virtually none of the rabble stood to get the vote. Middle-class potential voters made their feelings known in more civilised ways.

As Grey and his cabinet assessed their defeat on 8 October all this was to come, and they had to decide whether to resign or abandon reform. Their decision was to do neither, but instead prepare a further Reform Bill. Grey rapidly communicated this to the king. In many minds was the question of whether or not, and distasteful as it would be, the king would ultimately create the necessary number of new peers if it became necessary.

Numerous people continued to have high hopes of the king, but they believed that the queen was opposed to reform and had links to the Tories. These beliefs were justified and Adelaide did try to influence her husband, sometimes with some success. Furthermore, the Court contained many Tories. The queen was decidedly unpopular. The fact that she came from a tiny German state and spoke with a German accent was rather unfairly held against her. Prince Albert, Queen Victoria's husband, would later suffer from the same disadvantages. So great was the feeling that in some places streets and pub signs with images of Wellington and Adelaide were removed.[4]

Despite his affection for his wife the king, on two occasions at least, felt compelled to assert himself. The queen's Lord Chamberlain, to whom she was close, was Earl Howe, a Tory who had voted against the bill. Grey felt justified in asking the king to have him dismissed from the Lord Chamberlain's role because it was not right that a man holding the position should openly disagree with government policy. The king agreed, but allowed the earl to resign rather than be dismissed by Grey. The resignation was requested and accepted without Adelaide being told in advance. When the queen found out she was furious and felt very bitter towards Grey, a state of affairs that continued for a long time. On another occasion an angry king had told his wife, 'Madam, English politics are not to be understood by any German.'

Not all the protests were violent – some were peaceful and responsible. On 12 October a very big march in London was well planned and passed off without disorder. The banning of alcohol by the organisers probably had much to do with this. On the same night Grey received a delegation in Downing Street. He was pressed to demand the immediate creation of peers, which he refused to do, but the meeting was conducted in a civilised way. Ominously, but still peacefully, a well attended meeting of the Birmingham Political Union resolved to pay no taxes if the next bill was defeated.[5]

Prior to the introduction of the next bill the cabinet considered what if any concessions might be made to appease moderate opponents in the Lords. Discussions were held with some peers who became known as 'The Waverers'. Prominent among them were lords Lyndhurst, Wharncliffe and Harrowby. The term 'Waverers' was apt because they wavered backwards and forwards. A significant problem was that it was not known how many votes they could deliver, even if they were satisfied. Quite possibly it was only a very few. Nevertheless, the new bill did address some of their concerns.

Lord John Russell introduced the new bill to the Commons on 12 December 1831. The following details of the main changes from the failed bill draw on John Cannon's book *Parliamentary Reform 1640–1832*:

♦ The number of towns to lose one member was reduced from forty-one to thirty.
♦ Ten of the newly enfranchised towns were awarded a second seat.
♦ The 1831 census was taken as the basis of the population calculations rather than the 1821 census.
♦ The freeman qualification in the boroughs was continued.

The first two points, taken together, pleased the Tories who disliked single-member boroughs. Radicals, on the other hand, liked the increase in the urban representation.

The fate of the bill in the Commons was never in doubt. It was noted that Peel, whilst stating his continued opposition, added the following qualification which gave hope of future flexibility: 'On this ground I take my stand, not opposed to a well considered Reform of any of our institutions which need reform, but opposed to this Reform.' The House divided on 17 December and the bill was given a second reading by 324 votes to 162, a majority of 162.

Following this very solid vote on the second reading, problems at the committee stage in the Commons were not expected. What was expected were continued problems in the Lords and minds were concentrated on the possible, or indeed probable, need to create new peers. There was a solid inbuilt Tory majority in the House of Peers, partly the result of a gradual flow of creations during the previous sixty years of almost exclusive Tory rule.

The king and almost the whole of the aristocracy found the idea of large-scale creation for the purpose of passing a particular bill at the least distasteful, and to be avoided if possible. Grey himself felt this and so did many of his Whig colleagues. The problem was that it appeared that it might be the only way of securing the passage of the measure to which they were committed. They hoped that it would not be necessary and that the threat alone would be sufficient. A practical problem was that no one knew how large-scale the creation would have to be. The second bill had failed by forty-one votes, so perhaps forty-two new peers would be sufficient. On the other hand it might not and it would be absurd to create new peers and still be short of a majority. Perhaps some previous opponents would abstain this time and a smaller number would do. No one knew.

A cabinet meeting on 2 January 1832 discussed the options and two days later the prime minister met the king at Brighton. Grey explained that he had little reason to believe that the bill would be passed and he asked the king for a 'demonstration of his confidence'.[6] William made it very clear that he did not want to permanently change the Upper House. Accordingly, all peers created should be the eldest sons of existing peers, childless men of a certain age who could be expected to die without begetting heirs or Irish peers who counted as members of the aristocracy. Irish peers did not have a seat in the Lords. There were a number of Whig eldest sons of peers sitting in the Commons who would be obvious candidates. Although his name was not mentioned Palmerston was an example of an Irish peer sitting in the Commons.

Grey suggested a partial creation in the hope that this would induce a sufficient number of opponents to modify their positions. This suggestion was rejected by the king. If creation was necessary, he wanted it to be done at once. Grey reported back to the cabinet that he had the king's qualified assurance. A subsequent cabinet minute to the king stated that the cabinet believed that the exercise of the king's prerogative could be justified, but no particular number was mentioned.

The bill went through the committee stage without serious difficulty and the Commons gave its third reading at 1 a.m. on 23 March. The period was a testing time for ministers, some of whom, Lord Althorp in particular, were showing signs of weariness. Ominously the queen was known to be using her influence against the bill, and against the Whig administration. This continued to annoy the public who were being informed by a hostile press, which infuriated both the king and the queen. In all this time Wellington did not waver from his line of uncompromising opposition, which was to be significant when he was later asked to form a government.

After the bill's successful completion of its passage through the Commons, attention turned to the Lords where the ultimate challenge lay. The Waverers could be crucial and continued attempts to influence them were made. Worryingly for the government the king was exhibiting signs of distress at the situation in which he was likely to find himself.

Debate on the second reading lasted four nights and Wellington was as obdurate as ever. He forecast dire consequences if the bill was passed, and said that he intended to vote against it. The Bishop of Exeter, he whose effigy had been burned alongside that of Guy Fawkes, spoke against the bill and raised an alarming and disruptive constitutional point. He wondered if the king's coronation oath might prevent him giving Royal Assent to the Irish Reform Bill. Adelaide told the king that she approved of the bishop's speech, but William would not entertain the idea. 'Madam,' he said, 'It may be clever or eloquent, of that I am no judge; but though the peers may occasionally be factious, By God, the Bishops are in that house to defend my crown and not to follow vagaries of their own.'[7] Unlike today, it was a time when men called their wives 'Madam'.

After four exhausting nights the vote was taken at 7 a.m. on 13 April and it was 184 for the bill and 175 against, a government majority of 9. Lord Wharncliffe had led sixteen Waverers to switch and fifteen Tories who had opposed the previous bill were absent.[8] This time nine bishops including the Archbishop of York had voted in favour. Ten bishops, led by the Archbishop of Canterbury and of course including the Bishop of Exeter, had voted against.

The favourable vote was welcome but the government knew that much further trouble lay ahead. Seven votes in favour were proxies, which were permitted but could not be used in the committee stage. The Waverers would probably return to the Tory fold and could well demand further concessions from the government, concessions that the government would not be able or willing to give.

The worst fears were quickly realised and what happened took the government by surprise. The bill went into committee on 7 May and the Tories almost immediately inflicted a crushing defeat. Wellington once again expressed his adamant opposition and the Waverers returned to the opposition fold. It was a disaster, but a disaster that triggered events leading to the ultimate triumph of the bill.

On 8 May the cabinet decided that the government would tender its resignation unless the king agreed to create the necessary number of peers. That afternoon Lord Grey and Lord Brougham travelled to Windsor in order to meet the king and deliver a cabinet minute to this effect. William was very dismayed and expressed his horror at the prospect of creating fifty or more peers. In fact such was his distress that he neglected to offer his visitors any refreshments. He sent them away with the promise that he would give them a written reply shortly. This arrived the next day and said that he would not make such a large addition to the peerage, and that he would therefore accept the resignation. He asked the present government to continue to discharge its functions until the replacement had been appointed; it would be what we now call a caretaker government.

The king had few options and the one that he chose had almost no prospect of success. Using the services of Lord Lyndhurst as an intermediary he asked the Duke of Wellington to form a new administration, and he expressed the wish that the Duke of Richmond and Lord Brougham, the lord chancellor, would continue to serve. Realising that the country was in a turbulent and dangerous condition, and that reform was required, William made it clear that any government must undertake an extensive measure of reform.[9]

In deciding whether or not to accede to the king's request Wellington must have considered his personal position and the very severe practical difficulties. On the face of it his record should have made it almost impossible. He was personally opposed to any reform whatsoever. This stance had triggered his loss of office and the Tory calamity in the ensuing election. He had maintained this view consistently, including very recently.

How could he possibly serve and introduce a significant level of reform? The answer was his very pronounced feeling of duty to his monarch. He had shown it in his service to George IV – even acting as executor of his will – he felt it to William and in due course he would feel it to Victoria. There was a precedent for him supporting a measure that he had previously opposed. This was Catholic Emancipation, which had been secured by his government despite his personal belief that it was wrong. Wellington put his duty as he saw it first, cast aside other considerations and tried to form a government.

The obstacles were enormous and in the end proved insurmountable. There was the lamentable state of the Tory party in the House of Commons. The Lords had blocked Grey and in the same way the Commons could and probably would block Wellington. On the other hand it could be wondered if Whigs who wanted reform would really block reform, even if it was not their measure and even if it was not as much as they wanted.

Personnel for the suggested government were very thin on the ground. Brougham refused the king's request to serve and the key figure of Peel also said no. He had switched on Catholic Emancipation and once was more than enough. He intended to be consistent. His support would have made a big difference. Other prospective ministers sided with Peel, but two military comrades were loyal to Wellington. These were Sir George Murray and Sir Henry Hardinge, who had lost a hand at Quatre Bras just before Waterloo. The latter had acted as Wellington's second in his duel with the Earl of Winchelsea, and his disability had prevented him loading Wellington's pistol. His continued devotion was later shown when he was one of eight pallbearers at Wellington's funeral.

The people had lost their faith in King Billy and William was hissed on 12 May as his carriage was driven through a crowd. The press stepped up its attacks on Queen Adelaide and some of the criticism was vitriolic. The belief that she had used her influence on the king was well founded. Financial pressure was used and there was a move to withhold taxes. The campaigner Francis Place came up with a brilliant placard:

TO STOP THE
DUKE
GO FOR
GOLD

The posters appeared initially on London walls and then around the country. A run on the banks was something to fear. It was not the first or last time that financial pressure was used to influence political events. In 1956 President Eisenhower's refusal to use American money to ward off a run on sterling was a key factor in persuading Sir Anthony Eden's government to change policy during the Suez Crisis.

During a debate in the Commons on 14 May a number of Tories who had opposed the bill on its second reading criticised Wellington for his reversal. Davies Gilbert said that although he had opposed the bill it was perfectly absurd that the Whigs should not pass it.[10] Charles Wynn, who had been approached to take office in the new administration, said that the management of the bill should stay with its authors.[11]

Shortly after this Wellington's attempt to form a ministry, not necessarily with him at the head, collapsed. The king negotiated with Grey, still hoping that he would make concessions on the bill and avoid the creation of peers, but Grey had the upper hand and held fast. One Tory MP said that, 'The King must either recall Grey or start for Hanover.'[12] On 18 May the king capitulated and gave Grey the assurance that if the bill was blocked, he would create sufficient peers to ensure its passage.

In the end the threat was enough and the creation of peers was not necessary. Most Tory lords recognised the inevitable and to the relief of the king, Grey and almost all of the Whigs, the aristocracy was not enlarged. Wellington and most of the other opponents absented themselves from the final vote. Wellington had tried to justify his behaviour by saying that he still believed that reform would be 'most injurious' to the country. He had continued, 'I cannot help feeling that if I had been capable of refusing my assistance to His Majesty – if I had been capable of saying to His Majesty "I cannot assist you in this affair" – I do not think, my Lords, that I could have shown my face in the streets from shame of having done it – for shame of having abandoned my Sovereign under such circumstances.'[13] On 4 June the bill was carried by 106 votes to 22.

Although it was not a requirement, it was the king's usual practice to give the Royal Assent to Bills in person in the Lords. This time he made an exception and Assent was given in his absence. Furious at the invective of the press and others, and furious at the way that his plans had been thwarted, he wrote to Lord Brougham, the lord chancellor, 'he will not go down to pass the Reform, for that after the Manner he and his Queen have been treated by the people he should feel himself disgusted and degraded by their applause'.[14] It seemed petulant and it was not a wise decision. The unpopular William needed to build bridges to his subjects and this had the opposite effect.

Royal Assent was given on 7 June and the separate Irish Reform Bill, Scottish Reform Bill and the Boundary Bill received Royal Assent on 27 June. Parliament was dissolved on 3 December 1832 for the first general election to be held under the reformed rules. The new Parliament which met on 29 January 1833 included William Gladstone, 22 years and 32 days old, who had been sponsored by the Ultra Tory Duke of Newcastle and returned as the Member for Newark.

Needless to say there were expressions of celebration and jollification through much of the land, though of course not everyone was happy. Wellington, for one, was decidedly unhappy and he continued to forecast calamitous consequences, his mood not being improved by yet another distressing and dangerous experience on 18 June. He was surrounded by a mob and was abused and threatened during the 5-mile drive to his home. Brave and stoical as ever, he declined offers of help from women who offered him refuge in their homes. On arriving at Apsley House he raised his hat to Lord St Germans who had joined him for the last part of the ride and said, 'An odd day to choose. Good Morning.'[15] The seventeenth anniversary of the Battle of Waterloo occurred on 18 June 1832 and was generally known as Waterloo Day.

King William and Queen Adelaide were also not happy. Whilst attending Ascot races William was hit on the head by a stone thrown at him. Fortunately the padding in his hat provided protection.

On 16 October 1834 the Houses of Parliament burned down. There were those who sincerely believed that it was an act of divine punishment for the passage of the Reform Act. If this was the case, the Almighty waited quite a long time before showing His displeasure. It is sometimes said that Queen Adelaide was among those who considered the fire to be God's punishment. Her husband, who disliked living in Buckingham Palace, saw it as an opportunity to build a new palace and parliament on the site. As we know his ambition was not realised.

The belief in divine retribution persists in some quarters to this day. A much more recent example was the lightning strike on York Minster resulting in a serious fire. This happened on 9 July 1984, and three days earlier the controversial Dr Jenkins had been consecrated Bishop of Durham in the building. Some thought that the lightning was a mark of God's displeasure; Dr Jenkins had expressed controversial views, including some that appeared to cast doubt on the truth of the Virgin Birth and the Resurrection.

NOTES

1.   Antonia Fraser, *Perilous Question: The Drama of the Great Reform Act 1832*, p.167.
2.   Ibid., p.168.
3.   Ibid., p.169.
4.   Ibid., p.153.
5.   John Cameron, *Parliamentary Reform 1640–1832*, p.227.
6.   Antonia Fraser, *Perilous Question: The Drama of the Great Reform Act*, p.190.
7.   Ibid., p.213.
8.   John Cannon, *Parliamentary Reform 1640–1832*, p.233.
9.   Ibid., p.234.
10. Ibid., p.237.
11. Ibid., p.237.
12. Antonia Fraser, *Perilous Question: The Drama of the Great Reform Act 1832*, p.242.
13. Ibid., p.244.
14. Ibid., p.255.
15. Elizabeth Longford, *Wellington: Pillar of State*, p.277.

An Assessment of the 'Great Reform Act'

Just how significant was the 1832 Reform Act? And how much change resulted from it? It is often referred to as the *Great Reform Act*, but to what extent is this justified? This chapter assesses the three Reform Acts. There was not just one – something that is sometimes overlooked. In order to do this it is helpful to start by listing the main provisions of the Acts. A study of appendices A and B would also be useful. These list the constituencies just before and just after the redistributions.

PARLIAMENTARY REFORM ACT (ENGLAND) 1832

A register of voters was established for the first time. This was a factor in the reduction of corruption and it would be one of the causes of the increasing influence of political parties.

Distribution of Seats

There was an expansion in the number of county seats and a reduction in the number of borough seats. County seats increased from 80 to 144 and borough seats reduced from 405 to 323.

Fifty-six boroughs lost both their two members and a further thirty boroughs lost one of their two members. Twenty-two new two-member and twenty new one-member constituencies were created. This went a long way towards eliminating the notorious rotten boroughs, or at least making them considerably less rotten than previously. The biggest gainers were major towns such as Manchester, Birmingham and Sheffield.

In the counties Yorkshire gained two extra seats, making six in all. Twenty-six counties were each given two extra seats, making four in all. The Isle of Wight, which had previously been grouped with Hampshire, was given a separate seat.

Voting Franchise

In the boroughs adult males owning or occupying property worth £10 a year were given the vote. This was provided that they had been in possession of the property for at least a year, had paid all relevant taxes on it and had not received poor relief in the previous year. Adult males entitled to vote before the passage of the Act continued to be able to do so, but the right died with them and did not pass to their heirs.

In the counties there were three voting qualifications:

+ adult males owning freehold property worth 40 shillings
+ adult males with copyhold land worth £10 a year
+ adult males renting land worth £50 a year.

Copyhold tenure meant that the land was held according to the custom of the manor. This mode of landholding took its name from the fact that the 'title deed' received by the tenant was a copy of the relevant entry in the manorial court role. A tenant who held land in this way was known as a copyholder.

The extra seats went some way towards reducing the inequality between the more heavily populated counties and the much less populous ones. However, tiny Rutland retained its two members.

It is difficult to be precise but it is generally reckoned that the overall number of people eligible to vote in England and Wales increased by very slightly less than half. A total of 49 per cent is often quoted. It sounds a lot but it was building on a small base. After the Act about 20 per cent of adult males were entitled to vote. Antonia Fraser puts it at about 18 per cent.[1]

PARLIAMENTARY REFORM ACT (SCOTLAND) 1832

Distribution of Seats
Scotland was given a total of fifty-three MPs. Edinburgh and Glasgow each returned two members and five other burghs returned one member. A further fourteen burghs each returned one member, based on grouped districts. There were thirty county members, twenty-seven of them allocated to single counties and three of them allocated to paired counties.

Voting Franchise
In the boroughs the main voting qualification was occupation of property worth £10 a year. Electors voted directly, rather than indirectly via town councils as before.

In the counties the voting qualifications were:

+ owners of property worth £10 a year
+ leaseholders with leases over fifty-seven years of property worth £10
+ leaseholders for nineteen years whose property was worth £50
+ leaseholders who had paid £500 for their lease.

According to Eric J. Evans one inhabitant in twenty-seven had the vote in the boroughs and one in forty-five in the counties.[2] It should be stressed that inhabitants include all women and girls, and all males under voting age. At the time the ratio of minors to people of voting age was much higher than is the case now; large families and early death were much more common. Again according to Eric J. Evans, the number of voters in Scotland increased from about 4,600 to 64,500.[3] About 12 per cent of the adult male population had the vote.

PARLIAMENTARY REFORM ACT (IRELAND) 1832

Distribution of Seats

Ireland, which means the whole of the island of Ireland, was given a total of 105 MPs. This was an increase of five. The boroughs of Belfast, Waterford, Limerick and Galway were each given an extra member, and the University of Dublin was given a second seat. There were no changes in the counties. As had been the case since the Act of Union in 1800, thirty-two counties each elected two members.

Voting Franchise

In the boroughs adult males entitled to vote before the passage of the Act continued to be able to do so, but the right died with them and did not pass to their heirs. In addition the vote was given to occupiers of property worth £10 a year, and in places designated 'counties of cities' owners and occupiers of property worth £10 a year could vote.

In the counties owners of property worth £10 a year could vote, and so could leaseholders to the value of £10, provided that the leases were for twenty years or more.

Ireland was treated less favourably than England; the £10 ownership franchise was retained, though it was 40 shillings (two pounds) in England and Wales. In the counties the addition of leaseholders increased the franchise, but eligible voters in the counties were few and far between. According to Eric J. Evans one in twenty-six inhabitants in the boroughs had the vote, and in the counties it was one inhabitant in 116.[4] As with Scotland 'inhabitants include women, girls and males below voting age'. This makes a big difference, but it is not hard to see that the mainly Catholic citizens of rural, Irish counties were not well treated.

Let us be very critical and consider the limitations and anomalies of the three Acts. For a start it is reasonable to ask the basic question of why the voting qualifications in the boroughs should differ from the voting qualifications in the counties. The requirements for an adult male citizen living in say Weston Turville in Buckinghamshire were not the same as for his friend an adult male citizen living in Aylesbury, just 3 miles away. Many people thought it sensible at the time, but it is hard to see it that way now.

Voting qualifications in different parts of the United Kingdom were not the same. Once again there appeared to be reasons at the time, especially if you were English, but from the perspective of the twenty-first century we can ask why. Of course history was a major factor. It was thirty-two years after the Act of Union with Ireland and 125 years after the Act of Union with Scotland.

The size of the electorate expanded to about 18 to 20 per cent of adult males in England and Wales, 12 per cent in Scotland and less in Ireland. It was a step forward, but there was no hint of votes for women and it was still a very long way from universal suffrage – that would not come until 1928.

County representation increased and the more populous counties were given extra seats, but there were still anomalies. Tiny Rutland had just 800 electors, which were dominated by two aristocratic families.[5] This was seriously out of kilter with say Yorkshire, even though it now returned six members.

The rotten boroughs had gone, but there were still discrepancies. At one extreme Westminster had two members and 50,000 electors.[6] On the other hand a host of smallish towns returned one or (more usually) two members. Large cities like Manchester and Sheffield were enfranchised separately, but only with two members each.

The Acts did not abolish the requirement that an MP own property. Since the 1711 Property Qualifications Act membership of the Commons had been restricted to those receiving an income of £600 a year from land for county MPs and £300 a year from land for borough MPs. Abolition had been in the original bill, but it had not survived the turmoil in Parliament. The rules were amended in 1838 to include income from personal as well as landed property. Abolition came in 1858.

Two further matters should be mentioned. There was no serious suggestion that MPs should be paid – that would not happen until 1911. Furthermore, voting in public was not abolished – that would have to wait until the Ballot Act 1872.

So far so negative, but let us look at it from a more positive point of view. The elimination of the rotten boroughs was a really major step forward. A glance back to the first chapter of this book is a reminder of just how dreadful things were before 1832. No more Old Sarum, where two MPs, including from 1735 to 1747 a future prime minister, were returned by seven electors, all of them under the control of one person. No more Dunwich, where much of the constituency had slipped into the sea. No more Appleby, where in 1802 Philip Francis had been chosen by just one elector. These three cases were among the most notorious examples of rotten boroughs, but there were very many others where, though not so bad, the position was ridiculous.

The 1832 distribution of boroughs left much to be desired, but the improvement was considerable. Manchester, Birmingham and Sheffield deserved more than their two members each, but they did not have any at all previously and the new arrangements were a big step forward. Similarly, the new distribution of seats went some way to recognising the consequences of the Industrial Revolution. Industrial towns in the north and Midlands were better represented. The movement of seats from the boroughs to the counties was justified and, Rutland notwithstanding, the balance within the counties was better.

The voting qualifications were not the same in the different parts of the United Kingdom, and they were not the same in the counties as in the boroughs. However, the enormous and illogical variations that existed before 1832 were swept away. Once again a glance back at Chapter 1 would be instructive.

Within England, prior to the 1832 Reform Act, the voting qualifications varied enormously. There were scot and lot boroughs, potwalloper boroughs, freedom boroughs and burbage boroughs. The most bizarre of the latter gave the vote to shareholders in a disused salt pit. In some boroughs residence was not a requirement and some people were able to vote in more than one constituency. On the other hand, Preston at one time had something close to adult male suffrage. The 1832 Reform Act stipulated voting requirements that were consistent and almost always more sensible than the nonsense that they replaced. The United Kingdom was still a very long way from universal male suffrage, but the increase in the number of voters was a notable step along the way.

In conclusion let us return to the three questions posed at the beginning of this chapter, one of which has already been answered. This was, 'how much did it change?' Another was, 'just how significant was the 1832 Reform Act?' It has to be a matter of judgment, but in the opinion of your writer it was very significant. Some of the criticisms of its limitations are valid, but the changes for the better were very significant indeed.

It is often called 'The Great Reform Act'. The final question was 'to what extent is this justified?'. Its passage was greeted with joy. Some radicals were not satisfied and some diehards were displeased, but numerous citizens at the time would have been happy with the designation. It was the first of the Reform Acts and it set the United Kingdom firmly on the road towards further reform measures. As Sir Winston Churchill said at another time and in another context (in 1942 after success in the Battle of Egypt), 'Now this is not the end. It is not even the beginning of the end. But it is, perhaps, the end of the beginning.' Yes, most certainly, its unofficial title is justified. It was indeed The Great Reform Act.

NOTES

1.   Antonia Fraser, *Perilous Question: The Drama of The Great Reform Act 1832*, p.269.
2.   Eric J. Evans, *Parliamentary Reform, c.1770–1918*, p.130.
3.   Ibid., p.130.
4.   Ibid., p.131.
5.   Antonia Fraser, *Perilous Question: The Drama of The Great Reform Act 1832*, p.269.
6.   Ibid., p.269.

8

The Rise and Fall of Chartism

Chartism was a movement of working class people that demanded implementation of the six points in its Charter. These points, if enacted, would have gone a very long way to achieving the form of democracy that we enjoy today. It bubbled up in the late 1830s and then waxed and waned over a period of a little more than ten years. The high points were the presentation of three petitions, each with a very large number of signatures, to Parliament in 1839, 1842 and 1848. During the life of the movement, and to a greater or lesser extent at different times, agitation, public meetings, newspapers and various forms of campaigning kept the issues alive and in front of government, Parliament and the people. There was always tension between peaceful forms of campaigning and threatened or actual violence. Many crimes were committed, and many Chartists were imprisoned or transported. Governments and the property-owning classes were at times seriously alarmed. The word 'revolution' was at times mentioned, especially in 1848 when revolutions erupted in various places in Europe.

Chartism failed and in the short term none of its objectives were achieved, though later all but one of the Charter's six points were enacted. For almost a century we have taken five of the points for granted. The sixth, annual elections, is wanted by hardly anyone. It is debatable how much Chartism kept reform in the minds of Parliament and the people, and thus paved the way for later changes. Although it failed, Chartism was a massive movement; its story is interesting and deserves to be told. Just how big the movement was can be illustrated with three revealing quotes:

'The greatest movement of popular protest in British history.'[1]

Asa Briggs

'The world's first broad and politically organised, proletarian-revolutionary movement of the masses.'[2]

Vladimir Ilich Lenin

'The first working man's party the world ever produced.'[3]

Karl Heinrich Marx and Friedrich Engels

Most Whigs, let alone most Tories, thought that the 1832 Reform Act finished the job. Nothing, or at least not much, remained to be done. The rotten boroughs had gone and there had been some degree of sensible redistribution of seats. The right to vote had been extended deep into the middle classes, but not into the working classes. Most Whigs, let alone the Tories, thought that letting the working classes have the vote would be dangerous and highly undesirable. So the incoming Whig government that took office after the general election held shortly after the passage of the Act set about governing untroubled by thoughts of further reform. The country at large also seemed generally satisfied. Lord John Russell, speaking in Parliament in 1837, ruled out further reform. He almost certainly did not mean it but, if he did, he must subsequently have changed his mind. As told in the next chapter, he would consequently introduce further measures of reform into Parliament. His words in 1837 led to him acquiring the nickname 'Finality Jack'.

Despite all this, just a few years later the country was in turmoil. Within six years of the passage of the Great Reform Act the People's Charter had been published and Chartism was gathering strength; shortly afterwards the first of the Chartists' massive petitions was presented to Parliament. There was no single reason for this turn around, but the following are believed to be the main causes.

Although the Reform Act was acclaimed, some significant people, both inside and outside Parliament, were very far from satisfied. As a matter of principle they wanted more, much more. A prominent example was Henry Hunt, who had been a speaker at St Peter's Field, Manchester during what became known as the Peterloo Massacre. He was subsequently imprisoned but was an MP in 1832. He refused to support the Reform Bill because, in his view, the reforms were grossly inadequate. He lost his seat at the next general election. Others supported the bill on the grounds that half a loaf was better than no bread, but they did so with the intention of pressing for more later.

A few MPs and more than a few working class citizens nursed grievances from a long way back. These included the Peterloo Massacre and the repressive Six Acts, both dating from 1819. There is a saying that revenge is a dish best served cold. It is of modern origin, but the principle behind it was just as valid in the 1830s. Some seriously disgruntled people were in a mood to spite Parliament and politicians, Whig and Tory alike.

These working class people, and some middle class ones too, were joined by many others in being very unhappy with the performance of the reformed Parliament. The post-1832 governments and parliaments frequently acted in ways that were repressive and not, as they saw things, in their interests. There are a whole string of examples, an early one being the Irish Coercion Act of 1833. Another strongly-held grievance was the stamp duty on newspapers. It was reduced from 4d to 1d per copy in 1836, but the public at large thought that it was a tax on knowledge and the expression of opinion, and should not exist at all. Almost all of us would sympathise with this point of view. We are very widely taxed but there is no VAT on books or newspapers, not yet anyway.

The biggest grievance of all was the Poor Law Amendment Act of 1834. This very harsh measure abolished outdoor relief and established workhouses for the poor. These were feared and loathed by the working classes, and were a cause of great resentment. Families were separated and children kept apart from their parents. The workhouses rapidly acquired the derogatory unofficial name of 'bastilles'. Desperate people thought that if a reformed Parliament could do this, something a lot better was needed.

Another cause of working class discontent was the limitation and then prohibition of trade union activity. In 1834 the 'Tolpuddle Martyrs' were convicted and then transported to Australia. They had sworn a secret oath as members of the Friendly Society of Agricultural Labourers, an organisation deemed to have some of the features of a trade union. Around the same time a wave of strikes were unsuccessful and the collapse occurred of Robert Owen's recently formed Grand National Consolidated Trades Union.

Over a long period, prosperity, or the lack of it, had a pronounced effect on the extent of working class discontent. During much of the 1830s there was a series of good harvests. There was also a general pick-up in economic conditions which fed through to the benefit of the workers. As is so often the case though, the effect of this was patchy and some groups of workers did not benefit. Indeed the position in some trades worsened and wages were cut. The general improvement came to an abrupt end in 1836 and slightly later a financial crisis caused a panic. Hard times continued and the trough of the depression was reached in 1842, the year of the second Chartist petition. A little later the Irish potato famine which started in 1845 caused great distress and discontent in Ireland. This was probably a factor in the revival of Chartism and the presentation of the third and final petition in 1848.

A large and important meeting was held at the Crown and Anchor Tavern in the Strand, London on 28 February 1837. It had been called by the London Working Men's Association (LWMA) and was chaired by Robert Hartwell. The meeting considered a petition containing five of the six points that would later be incorporated into the Charter. Further meetings were called and a committee of six radical MPs and six LWMA members was formed to draft a bill to legislate for the points in the petition.[4] However, several of the MPs lost their seats in the election called after the death of William IV. As a result the Charter was drafted by William Lovett and Francis Place, both LWMA members. It was published on 8 May 1838.

The London Working Men's Association had been formed in 1836. Its aims included 'to seek by every legal means to place all classes of society in possession of their equal, political and social rights'. It was a respectable body committed to the use of non-violent, legal means. Although LWMA was instrumental in calling the meeting and drafting the Charter, it was a very long way from being the sole parent of Chartism. A plethora of societies and individuals joined in, both before and after the meetings. The aims of some of the societies and individuals were not always consistent and neither were their methods. Although most were law-abiding, some were much more willing to resort to what we call direct action, or even violence.

Some of the leaders were personally antagonistic and found it hard to work together, both at the beginning and during the life of the movement. This is often said to be one of the reasons that Chartism did not succeed. A quick review of some of the societies and leaders is instructive.

During 1835 various Working Men's and Radical Associations were formed in Scotland and the north of England.[5] The National Radical Association of Scotland was formed in August 1836[6] and in 1837 various other radical associations followed, especially in the textile districts of Lancashire and Yorkshire.[7] Their main purpose was to protest against the New Poor Law, but they rapidly associated themselves with Chartism.

The locations were significant because Chartism was always strong in Scotland and the north of England, more so than in London. Despite this, and as its name suggests, the London Working Men's Association was based in the capital. So too was the East London Democratic Association. This was formed in 1837, but changed into the London Democratic Association in 1838.[8] This body had strong disagreements with the London Working Men's Association. Thomas Attwood's Birmingham Political Union had been formed in 1829 and campaigned for the Reform Bill. In 1838 he re-formed it and positioned it in the fight for Chartism.[9]

It is a long list and probably tedious to read. Many more examples could be given. Space prohibits the description of the numerous leaders, though it is worth mentioning that many of them are today not highly regarded. Furthermore, it is worth reiterating that they sometimes had conflicting aims and methods, and that they sometimes badly failed to pull together. Having said that, an exception must be made for Feargus O'Connor, who was a proficient rabble-rouser, forceful and prone to quarrel with the other leaders. He was the most prominent leader and at times effective; he was particularly important because of his association with the newspaper *The Northern Star*.

Feargus O'Connor did not come from the classes in whose interests he strived. He was born into a prominent Irish Protestant family in 1794, his father being an Irish politician with landed estates. Feargus became a lawyer and was elected to the House of Commons as a Member for County Cork in 1832. He was re-elected in 1835, but was disqualified on the (disputed) grounds that he lacked the necessary property qualifications. This made Chartism personal because abolition of the property qualifications for MPs was one of the Charter's six points. He was elected as a Member for Nottingham in 1847 and became the only Chartist MP.

O'Connor was the most effective Chartist speaker, his style of oratory being loud and aggressive. He intimidated the authorities with his leadership and methods. He believed in the power of the weight of numbers, both in the form of signatures on petitions and attendance at meetings and demonstrations. He was feared and in May 1840 he was convicted on the charge of seditious libel. His career and his life both ended sadly. Chartism failed and he quarrelled with other Chartist leaders, by no means for the first time. In 1852 he struck three MPs in the House of Commons and was arrested. His behaviour was caused by the onset of mental illness, probably brought on by syphilis. He died in an asylum in 1855.

O'Connor founded the newspaper, *The Northern Star*, in 1837, and it was published weekly for fifteen years until 1852. It was a great success and played an important part in the story of Chartism. He wrote a weekly article and a host of other Chartist and radical writers also contributed. One of them was a young Friedrich Engels, who was working in Manchester at the time.

At its peak the newspaper's circulation was 50,000 copies a week, but this figure greatly understates the number of people informed and influenced by it. It was normal for each issue to be passed round and read by many people. Most of the readers were poor and for them at least the newspaper was expensive. A major reason for this was the hated stamp duty that had been reduced from 4*d* to a still oppressive 1*d* per copy. Paper was taxed too. Many members of the working classes were illiterate, and for this reason public readings were arranged. It seems rather touching and brings to mind modern Christians, almost entirely literate of course, drawing inspiration from Bible readings. It is also sad to reflect that for most of these poor people their hopes would not be realised in their lifetimes.

As stated earlier the Charter was published on 8 May 1838 and agitation, large meetings and the formation of new societies continued apace. The Charter was in the form of a draft of an Act of Parliament and it was divided into thirteen sections.[10] The wording was rather flowery. The first section was the preamble and read as follows:

> Whereas the Commons House of Parliament now exercises in the name and on the supposed behalf of the people the power of making the laws, it ought, in order to fulfil with wisdom and with honesty the great duties imposed on it, to be made the faithful and accurate representative of the people's wishes, feelings and interests.

The famous six points, expressed in up-to-date language were:

1. All adult males should have the vote.
2. Members of Parliament should be paid.
3. Each parliamentary constituency should have roughly the same number of voters.
4. Voting should be by secret ballot.
5. There should not be a property qualification for MPs.
6. General elections should be held annually.

All the first five points were achieved between 1858 and 1918. The Charter did not demand that all adult women should have the vote, though it had been considered; votes for all women came in 1928.

Annual general elections never happened and most of us would almost certainly say 'thank goodness'. Wouldn't it be awful if we had to suffer perpetual electioneering? What happens now is bad enough. Elections for the House of Representatives in the

USA are held on fixed dates every two years, and many of our American friends feel that this is too often. Perpetual electioneering risks turning MPs into our delegates rather than our representatives, something that would have dismayed the great parliamentarian Edmund Burke.

Many people feared that Chartism could lead to a revolution, and they also feared the potential and actual violence associated with it. At this point in the story it is instructive to consider to what extent these fears were justified.

To fully understand the fear of a possible revolution it is necessary to remember the times and the recent history. The French Revolution had taken place only half a century earlier. Previous chapters in this book tell how much it worried the ruling classes and how much it influenced opposition to the Reform Act. There were also revolutions and unrest elsewhere in Europe. Chartism's last hurrah was the presentation of the third and final petition on 10 April 1848. This was only two months after another revolution in France, and 1848 was the year of revolutions all over Europe. Why should Britain be unaffected? It is easy to see why the ruling classes were nervous.

In order to understand the fear of revolution it is necessary to say what we mean by the term. It means different things to different people. At one extreme it meant blood on the street, Queen Victoria despatched to Hanover and the system of government overthrown with something else put in its place. Chartism did contain some republicans, but it is fair to say that virtually no one wanted all this.

At the other extreme revolution could mean the government being taken out of the hands of the aristocracy, the landed gentry and the ruling classes. It could mean that, whilst the framework of government was retained, there would be massive changes. In particular the ruling classes especially feared that the much more numerous working classes would all have votes and that their votes would carry the same weight as their own. This would mean that people they regarded as dangerous or unworthy, or at least unready, would acquire power and have the opportunity to swamp them with legislation that was against their interests. To make matters worse, all the changes would come at once, not be phased in over a period. This was exactly what the Chartists did want, so to this extent their fears were justified.

Of course the new masters might have exercised their power in the wider interests of all and not abused it. We shall never know. It should be noted that there were no plans to change the parliamentary framework, and no plans to abolish the monarchy or the House of Lords. There were not even any plans to curtail the powers of the House of Lords, though this might have come later. A mature judgment must be that fears of a revolution were largely unjustified; the British working man (and woman) was and is far too sensible.

Revolution and violence often go hand in hand. The authorities were perpetually worried by threatened and actual violence, and they were right to be so. There was always the threat of violence, sometimes actual violence, occasionally serious violence and on one occasion very serious violence. Even when it was not evident, as was usually the case, force of numbers was intimidating.

The two wings of Chartism are often rather simplistically called 'Moral Force' and 'Physical Force'. The Moral Force leaders and followers were committed to using only peaceful and legal means. Thomas Attwood of the Birmingham Political Union was a leading Moral Force leader. Others included William Lovett, Henry Hetherington and John Cleave.

Physical Force Chartists felt that their cause was just and that only force would achieve their aims. Feargus O'Connor is often associated with this, though he usually trembled on the edge of it. Physical Force Chartist leaders included James Stephens and George Harney.

Most Chartists were between these two extremes, probably veering towards the moral end of the scale. However, most of them were prepared to make their point by weight of numbers, shouting and the like. Many of them were prepared to fight fire with fire; the religious among them thought that God was on their side and they all thought that right was on their side. They were prepared to meet violence with violence, and perhaps also to meet unreasonable banning and restrictions with violence. They regarded this as legitimate self defence. A Chartist slogan is very revealing, 'Peacefully if we may, forcibly if we must.'[11]

During the years 1839 to 1848 more than 3,500 Chartists were arrested and tried, some of them more than once.[12] Many of those found guilty were bound over, but a significant number were imprisoned and some were transported. One of them, a young man called Samuel Holberry, died in prison, which inflamed feelings. He became known as the Chartist Martyr.

By far the most serious incident was the so-called Newport Rising on 4 November 1839. It was planned, though the outcome was most definitely not foreseen. It involved serious violence by a large number of people, many of whom were armed, including some with firearms. It is an illustration of the strength of the Physical Force Chartists. Some details are not fully clarified, but it is probable that twenty-two demonstrators were killed and more than fifty were wounded. It was the biggest loss of life in a civil disturbance in the nineteenth century.

The authorities had anticipated a riot and were well prepared. Around 500 special constables had been sworn in. Newport already contained about sixty troops and the mayor sent for more. Thirty-two soldiers were in the Westgate Hotel where Chartist prisoners were being held. The crowd stormed the hotel to try and get their comrades released. Some of their number did get into the hotel and it is claimed that a Chartist fired the first shot. The troops were heavily outnumbered, but in their favour were discipline and superior firepower. The attackers were driven off having suffered the casualties already mentioned. No defenders died but serious injuries were suffered by one soldier and the mayor of Newport. Two special constables were also injured.

Following the Newport Rising twenty-one Chartists were charged with high treason. The main leader, John Frost, and two other leaders, Zephanian Williams and William Jones, were sentenced to be hanged, drawn and quartered, the last people in Britain to face the prospect of this grisly punishment. Frost had been mayor of

Newport four years previously, and he was a former town councillor, magistrate and justice of the peace. A massive Chartist campaign for clemency was mounted and the sentences were commuted to transportation for life. Frost was sent to Van Diemen's Land (modern-day Tasmania) where he was immediately sentenced to two years' hard labour for making a disparaging remark about the colonial secretary. He then worked as a storekeeper, a clerk, and then for eight years a schoolteacher. In 1856 he was pardoned and he returned to Britain. He died in 1877 at what at the time was the remarkably advanced age of 93. John Frost Square in Newport is named after him. He lived long enough to see the end of the MP's property qualification, the introduction of the secret ballot, an extension of the franchise and progress towards constituencies of equal size.

The government was surely wise to commute the punishments to transportation. Executing the three, let alone having them hanged, drawn and quartered, would have created martyrs and martyrs are always trouble. There would have been bitterness way beyond what already existed and what would exist in the future. History gives many examples. Following the 1916 Easter Rising fifteen Irish leaders were executed by firing squads. One of them, James Connolly, had been injured in the fighting and he was shot whilst tied to a chair. Their crime, from the British point of view at least, could hardly have been more serious – they led an armed insurrection in the middle of a war. A significant part of the Dublin public was initially hostile to the rebels and some of them had to be protected from the crowd after their surrender. However, the executions caused a sea change in sentiment and to a greater or lesser extent we have lived with the consequences ever since. Australia would not have made Van Diemen's Land available, but transportation to a very remote spot might have been a better alternative.

The Newport Rising took place 115 days after the presentation to Parliament on 12 July 1839 of the first of the three great petitions. Its rejection no doubt inflamed the tempers of the rioters. The petition contained just under 1,300,000 signatures[13] and on 7 May it was 3 miles long.[14] As well as containing the six points, it lamented the many wrongs inflicted on the nation by its rulers. The petition included the following words:

> Heaven has dealt graciously by the people … but the foolishness of our rulers has made the goodness of God of none effect. The energies of a mighty kingdom have been wasted in building up the power of selfish and ignorant men … The few have governed for the interest of the few, while the interests of the many have been sottishly neglected, or insolently and tyrannously trampled upon. It was the fond expectation of the friends of the people that a remedy for the greater part, if not for the whole of their grievances, would be found in the Reform Act 1832 … They have been bitterly and basely deceived. The fruit which looked so fair to the eye, has turned to dust and ashes when gathered. The Reform Act has effected a transfer of power from one domineering faction to another, and left the people as helpless as before …

In case the word is not immediately familiar (it was not to the writer) the dictionary defines 'sot' as a habitual or chronic drunkard. 'Sottishly' was not a term likely, in the immortal words of Dale Carnegie, to win friends and influence people.

Thomas Attwood MP of the Birmingham Political Union presented the petition to Parliament. Very quickly and very predictably it was rejected by 235 votes to 46. Disillusioned and in poor health, Attwood resigned his seat. It gives cause to reflect that had the petition been accepted in full, 200 parliamentary constituencies would have been in Ireland. This must have affected Ireland's relationship with the rest of the United Kingdom.

The Chartists' leaders had expected the petition to be rejected, but they had made few plans about what they would do next. Furthermore, there was little co-ordination concerning what few plans there were. The Physical Force Chartists thought that they should continue the intimidation and the Newport Rising was the most extreme manifestation of this. In the winter of 1840, 476 men and women Chartists were in prison, some of them for offences committed before the rejection of the Charter.

A National Charter Association was formed in July 1840 and this had no fewer than 350 branches by April 1842. Economic conditions were very poor, which gave impetus to the movement. Sir Robert Peel replaced Lord Melbourne as prime minister on 30 August 1841. Peel had developed liberal tendencies, and this was shown with the passage of the Factory Act in 1844 and the abolition of the Corn Laws in 1846. His government, however, was no more likely to accept the Chartists' demands than that of his predecessor.

A Chartists' convention had initiated the first petition and a second convention was convened to launch the second one. This convention had less middle class influence than the first and it was now very clearly a working class movement. The second was the largest of the three petitions, and the number of signatories was said to be 3,315,752. It weighed six hundredweight (305kg) and was on 6 miles of paper. Seven bands accompanied it to Parliament where it was formally presented by the radical MP Thomas Slingsby Duncombe. The second petition fared no better than the first and was quickly rejected by 187 votes to 49.

The rejection of the 1842 petition was followed by what Asa Briggs calls a summer of discontent.[15] The country was hit by a wave of strikes, mainly in Lancashire, Cheshire, Yorkshire, the Midlands and the Strathclyde region of Scotland. The strikers, often supported by Chartists, failed to achieve their objectives, and in late August and September they returned to work. The strikes were in some cases accompanied by violence and arson, and in some cases the Chartists were blamed.

The strikes and the violence were followed by prosecutions and punishments. In Staffordshire, for example, there were 154 sentences of imprisonment and 54 sentences of transportation. In 1843 a number of Chartists, including Feargus O'Connor, were charged with seditious conspiracy. The charges failed and Prince Albert wrote to Peel, 'I am sorry that Feargus escaped.'

O'Connor did not neglect Chartism but proceeded to divert some of his prodigious energy into an ambitious Land Plan. It was a far-reaching scheme to enable workers to buy small plots of farm land, and six estates were purchased and divided up. Demand greatly exceeded the supply of available land and the successful applicants were chosen by ballot. They had to pay for the land, plus interest over a period. The Land Plan was very popular and vastly oversubscribed, but unfortunately it was badly run. In 1848 it was declared to be an illegal scheme. On top of all this activity O'Connor ran for Parliament again, and in 1847 he became an MP for Nottingham.

After 1842 the economy picked up and relative prosperity ensued. The railway boom of the 1840s was a big contributory factor. Ireland, though, suffered the terrible potato famine of 1845–47. The boom was good for everyone, including the working classes, but it did nothing for Chartism. Discontented, hungry people were more likely to campaign for it.

Sir Robert Peel's government fell after the repeal of the Corn Laws and in 1846 he was replaced by Lord John Russell. 'Finality Jack' was a friend to moderate reform, but not a friend to Chartism. Unfortunately for him the prosperity soon came to an end. There were two bad harvests and the railway boom came to a shuddering stop. Hard times were back with a vengeance and the stage was set for Chartism's third and final great push – this was the 1848 petition, the one that is best remembered.

The Chartists set to work collecting signatures, the third Chartist National Convention was called and a demonstration on Kennington Common on 10 April was planned. It was intended that following the demonstration the crowd would accompany the petition to Parliament.

Lord John Russell's government acted firmly and sensibly. Its policy was to have an iron fist in a velvet glove. The demonstration at Kennington Common was allowed, but the march on Parliament was banned. The 78-year-old Duke of Wellington was put in charge of the London garrison and 8,000 troops were at his disposal. Wisely they kept a low profile – but they were there. Wellington said that he would provide plenty of space into which the crowd could retreat. The absence of space had been a major contributory factor to the disaster of 'Peterloo' in 1819. A large number of special constables were on standby and their number included William Gladstone and the future Emperor Napoleon III of France.

The whole day was a great disappointment to the Chartists and to Feargus O'Connor in particular. Estimates of the crowd on Kennington Common varied from 15,000 to 50,000, but whatever the true number it was vastly less than they hoped for and expected. O'Connor addressed the crowd and then just four coaches took the petition and him to Parliament. The crowd dispersed and there were no deaths or serious injuries. O'Connor had used his influence to prevent violence and, what is more, he had tipped off the authorities about a plot to assassinate Lord John Russell.[16]

Feargus O'Connor MP claimed that the petition had 5,700,000 signatures. On 13 April Mr Thornley for the Commons Committee on Public Petitions said the following:

Upon the most careful examination of the number of signatures in the committee, with the assistance of thirteen law stationers' clerks, who acted under the superintendence of the various clerks of the committees, the number of signatures attached to the petition does not, in the opinion of the committee, exceed 1,975,496. It is further found, that a large number of the signatures were consecutively written in the same hand. It was also observed that a large number of the signatures were those of persons who could not be supposed to have concurred in its prayer; among those were the name of her Majesty, signed Victoria Rex, the Duke of Wellington, Sir Robert Peel, &c, &c. There was also noticed a large number of names which were evidently fictitious, such as 'Pugnose', 'Longnose', 'Flatnose', 'Punch', 'Snooks', 'Fubbs', and also numerous obscene names, which the committee would not offend the house of its dignity by repeating but which evidently belonged to no human being.

An outraged O'Connor stuck to his claim of 5,700,000 and said that it was not possible that thirteen clerks could have made the count in just three days. This is of course absolutely right. Let us assume that the thirteen clerks each worked for thirteen hours on each of the three days. This is after breaks for food, calls of nature etc., and what is more they did it without computers or other aids that we now take for granted. 182,520 seconds would have been spent counting 1,975,496 signatures, which is an average of 10.8 signatures per second. It is an obvious nonsense. Never mind though, O'Connor was discredited and the false names attracted disgust and mirth in the country at large. Only fifteen MPs voted in support of the petition.

Many books state or imply that Chartism finished with the rejection of the 1848 petition, and many books claim that Chartism failed. The first claim is not true and the second claim should be a matter for debate. Chartist activity continued at an intense level through the summer of 1848. There was an upsurge in violence at this time, with the consequence that there was also an upsurge in arrests and the imprisonment of Chartists. The movement then went into a steady decline with periodic short increases in activity. The leaders continued to fall out and have different views. The last Chartist National Convention was held in 1858. It was very badly attended and it is probably fair to count this year as the end of the story.

Did Chartism fail? Most people say yes because its aims were not achieved in its lifetime. On the other hand it kept the cause of reform alive and in front of Parliament and people. It had influence and the cause was later successfully pursued by others. All but one of its aims were eventually achieved and there was and is no demand for the last one. Did Chartism fail? Thoughtful answers might include 'yes, but' or 'perhaps'.

NOTES

1. Asa Briggs, *Chartism*, p.1.
2. Ibid., p.7.
3. Ibid., p.81.
4. Ibid., p.42.
5. Eric Evans, *Chartism*, p.5.
6. Ibid., p.5.
7. Ibid., p.5.
8. Ibid., p.5.
9. Asa Briggs, *Chartism*, p.58.
10. Ibid., p.33.
11. Ibid., p.13.
12. Ibid., p.75.
13. Eric Evans, *Chartism*, p.11.
14. Asa Briggs, *Chartism*, p.67.
15. Ibid., p.86.
16. George Malcolm Thomsom, *The Prime Ministers: From Robert Walpole to Margaret Thatcher*, p.121.

1848–1866: A Developing Head of Steam

The last chapter reviewed Chartism, a movement that after 10 April 1848 declined rapidly. The next chapter reviews the Second Reform Bill of 1867, which significantly extended the franchise and made other important changes. The main part of this chapter reviews the increasing pressure for further reform and the five failed reform bills between 1852 and 1866. Two of the failures led directly to changes of government and a third was one of the reasons that a government fell. The pressure for reform was not great to begin with, but built up very considerably in the 1860s. Before doing this, however, it is right to look at two other measures implemented in the period.

The first was the Irish Franchise Act of 1850. The Parliamentary Reform Act (Ireland) 1832 had treated Ireland less favourably than the rest of the United Kingdom, and since then death and emigration caused by the famine of 1845–47 had considerably reduced the number of voters. The 1850 Act discontinued the 'certification' system and replaced it with a system based on occupation of property. The main beneficiaries were voters in the counties. The size of the electorate tripled from about 50,000 to about 150,000.

The second measure was the Property Qualification for Members of Parliament Act, which became law in March 1858. This abolished the property qualification for MPs, and was the first of the Chartists' demands to be conceded. The Property Qualifications Act 1711 required county members to be receiving £600 a year from land. For borough members it was £300 a year. The requirement had been relaxed in 1838 to allow personal as well as landed property to be included. Notwithstanding this, it was a serious hurdle for many prospective members.

The property qualification was abolished whilst Edward Glover was awaiting trial on a charge of making a false declaration in respect of the requirement. He was elected for Beverley at the 1837 general election. At the time of the vote it was rumoured that he could not meet the property requirement, and there was a demand that he state his qualification. He did so in front of a magistrate.

A committee of the Commons decided that he had made a false declaration and he was arrested on 23 December 1837. He spent Christmas in jail, but was later released on bail. He was convicted in April 1838 and sentenced to imprisonment, but was released on health grounds in August.

During the hullabaloo of Chartism the Commons had a small group of members continuously in favour of further reform. They were swimming against the tide – but they were there. As mentioned in the last chapter, forty-six members voted to accept the 1839 petition and forty-nine members voted to accept the 1842 petition, but just fifteen members voted to accept the derided 1848 one. Eric J. Evans says that pressure for reform slackened after the Chartist humiliation of 1848, but did not disappear.[1] He also says that a reform party was in continuous existence at Parliament. Radicals and reformers numbered between forty and fifty in the late 1840s and early 1850s.[2]

The radicals and reformers did not all have the same objectives, and they did not all want to move at the same speed. The elderly (75 in 1852) Joseph Hume was particularly prominent in pressing the case, and he produced Bills for reform in every parliamentary session between 1848 and 1852.[3] The great radicals, Cobden and Bright, are two further names worth mentioning.

Of great significance was the fact that various leaders began to modify their objections to reform. Early and prominent among them was Lord John Russell, he whose comment in 1837 had earned him the nickname 'Finality Jack'. Of course, as made clear in the last chapter, he probably had not meant his dismissive remark. Be that as it may, speaking in the House in 1848 he said that 'the time for some reform was near, if not at hand'.[4] The hero of the Great Reform Act was on the move, or at least thinking about being on the move. He would play a major part in the abortive steps taken before the 1867 Act.

Later (1860) and on the other side of the House, Benjamin Disraeli referred to Gladstone as the 'mechanic' whose 'virtue, prudence, intelligence and frugality, entitle him to enter the privileged pale of the constituent body of the country'.[5] The name of Disraeli is very often linked with that of William Gladstone. They are grouped together like fish and chips or Laurel and Hardy; on the other hand, perhaps chalk and cheese would better describe their relationship. They were opponents for a quarter of a century and their rivalry was based on personal antagonism as well as political differences. Disraeli is often said to have been Queen Victoria's favourite prime minister and Gladstone is known to have been one of her least favourite ones. She once complained that 'he speaks to me as if I was a public meeting'.

Gladstone had been implacably opposed to the 1832 Reform Act, but over the years his views slowly mellowed. Both Gladstone and Disraeli thought that the vote was a privilege and not a right, but that it was a privilege that should be more widely distributed. Neither believed in universal manhood suffrage. The two men were to be responsible for the Second and Third Reform Acts and they feature prominently in the forthcoming chapters of this book.

The widespread movement in sentiment in favour of reform was not shared by one key person. This was Lord Palmerston, who was prime minister for just under ten years during the period under review. He did not want reform and it led to tension between Lord John Russell and himself. Palmerston was a remarkable man, not least because he died in office just one day short of his 81st birthday and three months after winning a general election. He had a sense of humour and was perhaps the most English of prime ministers. 'If I were not a Frenchman, I should wish to be an Englishman,' said the Frenchman. 'If I were not an Englishman, I should wish to be an Englishman,' said Palmerston.[6] Queen Victoria was having a run of prime ministers with whom she did not get on. She once referred to Palmerston and Russell as 'those two dreadful old men' and Gladstone completed the trio. It is interesting, but perhaps inconsequential, to note that all three were Whigs or Liberals.

The period 1848–66 featured many changes of government and prime minister. The party system was very fluid and Lord John Russell is often said to be the last Whig prime minister. There were frequent coalitions between different factions. Reform was a major issue during this time and Russell's failure to carry a Reform Bill was the cause of his resignation in 1866. The prime ministers were:

30 June 1846 to 23 February 1852	Lord John Russell
23 February 1852 to 19 December 1852	Lord Derby (Disraeli was Leader in the Commons)
19 December 1852 to 30 January 1855	Lord Aberdeen (Lord John Russell was Leader in the Commons)
6 February 1855 to 19 February 1858	Lord Palmerston
20 February 1858 to 11 June 1859	Lord Derby (Disraeli was Leader in the Commons)
12 June 1859 to 18 October 1865	Lord Palmerston
29 October 1865 to 28 June 1866	Earl Russell (He had sat in the Lords since 30 July 1861. Gladstone was Leader in the Commons)
28 June 1866 to 27 February 1868	Lord Derby (Disraeli was Leader in the Commons)

It would be good to think that principle and a sincere regard for what they saw as the good of the country was the motivation of the politicians. This was no doubt true for a few, but probably only a few. It was probably to a greater or lesser extent just one of the factors for most of the others. Self-interest and party-interest loomed very large. They always had an eye on which way newly enfranchised citizens would be likely to vote, and on such things as the effect on their party and themselves of a proposed redistribution of seats. Perhaps nothing else could be expected, and self-interest continued to influence decisions for a long time afterwards. It was, for example, a major factor when votes for women were being considered. It more than doubled the electorate and politicians agonised over which way the new votes would be cast.

It continues in the twenty-first century. On 5 May 2011 a referendum rejected the Alternative Vote (a form of proportional representation) in favour of keeping 'first past the post'. Following this the Liberal Democrats did not give their support to a redistribution of seats that would probably have benefited the Conservative Party.

Proposals to make changes to the House of Lords have regularly foundered, partly at least because of calculations of party advantage.

As mentioned earlier in this chapter there were five failed reform bills between 1852 and 1866, and Lord John Russell (Earl Russell after 30 July 1861) introduced four of them. Lord John was the third son of the Duke of Bedford and sat in the Commons. On 30 July 1861 he took an earldom in his own right and moved to the Lords. The first of Russell's reform bills was in 1850 when he was prime minister, and the second was in 1854 when he was Leader in the Commons in the government of Lord Aberdeen.

The main plank of the 1852 Bill was that the vote would be given to householders owning property of lower value. It was to be £20 in the counties and £5 in the boroughs, these figures being reductions from £50 and £10 respectively. The definition of the value was to be rateable value, something that dismayed Disraeli. He objected because of the inequalities in different parishes.[7] The bill never got as far as a vote in the Commons. Russell's government was a coalition of different factions, formed after Peel's downfall following the repeal of the Corn Laws, and by 1852 it was rapidly running out of steam. Russell could not get sufficient support from his colleagues and the bill was withdrawn. It was not the only measure to fail in this way.

The catalyst for his loss of office was a difference with Lord Palmerston (sitting in the Commons), the other of Queen Victoria's two dreadful old men. They were rivals over a long period and generally did not get along, though sometimes making up the quarrel. Russell supported reform and Palmerston did not. The issue was that Palmerston, who was secretary of state for foreign affairs, had unilaterally congratulated Louis Napoleon on his *coup d'état* in France. Louis was the nephew of Napoleon Bonaparte and he was the man who had served as a special constable when the third Chartist petition was presented. Palmerston acted without consulting the queen and without involving the rest of the government. Under pressure from Victoria, Russell sacked him. A few months later Palmerston got his revenge by colluding with Disraeli and bringing down Russell's government.

After a short-lived Lord Derby government, the leadership baton passed to Lord Aberdeen. Palmerston was home secretary and Russell was Leader in the Commons. He tried again. With just one change Russell's 1854 property qualification was the same as the bill's 1852 predecessor. The difference was that the borough property franchise was to be £6 rather than £5. There was, though, a very significant new idea – consideration was given to what became known as 'fancy franchises'. This was recognition that owning or occupying property of a certain value should not be the sole criterion. For example, consideration was given to people qualifying because of an income of £10 from certain dividends, the payment of 40 shillings in direct taxes, deposits of three years standing in a savings bank or the possession of an academic degree from a university.[8] Most of these people would already qualify, but it marked a step away from an exclusively property-based qualification. Like its 1852 predecessor Russell's 1854 Bill never got as far as a vote, though the reason was different. On 28 March 1854 Britain entered the Crimean War. An unhappy cabinet, containing an unhappy Palmerston, decided that to avoid distraction the bill should be withdrawn. A disappointed Russell had been confident that he could get it through this time.

The Crimean War was in many ways and especially in its early stages a disaster for Britain. The Light Brigade charged on 25 October 1854 and things were not going well. It was another divided and unhappy cabinet and Russell resigned in January 1855. This was a major factor in the collapse of Aberdeen's government shortly afterwards. His replacement was Lord Palmerston, popular and an opponent of reform. He was thought to be the man to win the war, rather as Lloyd George was regarded when he replaced Asquith sixty-one years later. Palmerston did win the war, or at least it is fair to say that he was in office when it finished. Sevastopol fell on 8 September 1855, and the Treaty of Paris that ended the war was signed on 30 March 1856.

Palmerston resigned on 19 February 1858 after his Conspiracy to Murder Bill was defeated in the Commons, and the Derby/Disraeli duo returned for a further brief period (just under sixteen months). It was time for another Reform Bill, this time from the Conservatives. The Derby/Disraeli offering had some similarities with Russell's 1854 attempt. In particular, it proposed recognition for the so-called 'fancy franchises'. It gave the vote to persons who had £60 in a savings bank, ministers of religion, graduates, members of the learned professions and persons who had £20 pensions in the naval, military or civil services. There was to be a uniform £10 borough and county franchise and a £20 lodger franchise. Unlike Russell's bill the borough franchise was not reduced, but the county franchise was. The £10 qualification had to include a residence or building with an annual value of £5. There was to be a redistribution of seats, mainly in favour of the counties.

The failure of reform bills had become commonplace, but this time it came to a vote. The bill was rejected by 330 votes to 291 in a remarkably full House of Commons. Derby asked for and was granted a dissolution, and the popular, 75-year-old Lord Palmerston won the ensuing general election and returned to Downing Street. A surprisingly cheerful Russell agreed to serve and prepared yet another Reform Bill, this time for 1860. It was similar to his previous one. He wanted to extend the vote to £6 borough and £10 householders, and he wanted a redistribution of seats.[9] Palmerston did not want reform, but lack of backbench support was the reason for the bill's withdrawal without a vote.

After a short illness Palmerston died in office three months after winning another general election. He was 80 years and 364 days old, which made him Britain's second oldest prime minister. This was 176 days older than Sir Winston Churchill, but three years and sixty-three days younger than William Gladstone. Attributed last words are notoriously unreliable, but his are reported to be, 'Die my dear doctor, that's the last thing I shall do.' It ranks with (disputed) reports of the last words of William Pitt the Younger. He is reputed to have said, 'I think that I could eat one of Bellamy's pies.'

The queen had no hesitation in appointing the 73-year-old Russell to serve as her prime minister. Perhaps this had something to do with the fact that Gladstone was the only realistic alternative.[10] Earl Russell, as he now was, sat in the Lords and appointed

Gladstone as Leader in the Commons. Russell set about planning yet another Reform Bill to be introduced in the Commons by Gladstone. The following summary of the bill draws on Charles Seymour's book *Electoral Reform in England and Wales*.

The bill reduced the property franchise in the boroughs from £10 to £7, which was £1 higher than the figure in Russell's previous bill. This was because the government was nervous about enfranchising too many artisans. It believed that £6 would enfranchise about 240,000, whereas £7 would limit it to about 145,000. The bill also gave the vote to lodgers with an annual value of £10 and there were changes in the registration system. All qualified occupiers would be registered, even though they did not themselves pay rates.

The £50 tenant franchise in the counties was reduced to £14. This was more cautious than the 1860 Bill, which had it at £10. Depositors with £50 in a savings bank were to be given the vote. The bill left the middle classes with a clear superiority in numbers. It was believed that taking the measures as a whole the bill would have left the artisans with slightly more than a quarter of the electorate; this roughly doubled the proportion, which at the time stood at about an eighth.

The total electorate would increase from about 1,050,000 to 1,450,000. An increase of almost 40 per cent sounds a lot, but it was taken from a low base figure. The government regarded the bill as being cautious, and they thought that this increased the chance of it getting through.

The bill proposed a minor redistribution of seats.[11] The main beneficiaries were the counties, and the main losers were the smaller boroughs. There would be six entirely new boroughs. London would get four more seats, and there would be five more for large English boroughs. Large Scottish boroughs would get three.

The government's confidence was misplaced. The Conservatives were of course out to wreck the bill and they were joined by a group of about forty Liberals. Brilliantly led by Robert Lowe, they had been elected to support Palmerston, were hostile to reform and alarmed by the proposed increase in the franchise. They became known as the 'Adullamites' or sometimes the 'Cavers'. The terms originated with John Bright, who had a memorable turn of phrase; in describing the group he brought in a biblical reference to the cave of Adullam, where David and his allies sought refuge from Saul.[12] Adullam's cave was said to be a refuge for the discontented and the name stuck.

Lowe had spent nine years in Australia, where he had worked in the law courts and sat in the New South Wales Legislative Council. The union system in Australia was well developed and he had been shocked by the activities of the unions. As he saw it, though others would disagree, the weight of numbers was used to achieve undesirable objectives, and he thought that an extension of the franchise would result in the same thing happening in the UK. In his view this should wait until the advance of education had made the working classes ready for it. Lowe's persuasive oratory was a big factor in the failure of the bill and the termination of the Russell/Gladstone ministry. Showing a remarkable absence of rancour Gladstone, when prime minister in a subsequent government, made him Chancellor of the Exchequer and then home secretary. Furthermore, when he later moved to the House of Lords

Gladstone secured for him the rank of viscount. This was despite the objections of Queen Victoria, who favoured the more usual rank of baron.

The management of the bill was not Gladstone's finest hour. He did, though, make one notable speech in proposing an amendment. Like many of his great orations it was long (lasting more than two hours) and delivered late at night (starting at 1 a.m.).

His speech contained a number of Latin quotations, which he did not think it necessary to translate. The lack of translations is a good indication of the classical education of many members. It would not happen now. It is amusing to recount a rhetorical trick of Sir Winston Churchill many years later. One of his parliamentary speeches included a Latin quotation, which he followed by saying, 'I will provide a translation for the benefit of …' At this point he was interrupted by furious interjections from Labour members who thought that they were about to be patronised. This happened more than once, but the Harrow-educated Sir Winston finally managed to say, 'I will provide a translation for the benefit of … Honourable Members educated at Eton.'

Despite Gladstone's great speech the government was humiliated by a majority of only five. After this Gladstone chose to make an amendment on a not very fundamental point a vote of confidence. Forty-four Liberals voted with the Conservatives and it was carried by 315 votes to 304. It was the end of the Russell/ Gladstone bill. It would have enfranchised an extra 400,000 voters.

The prime minister could have asked for a dissolution, but it was less than a year since the last general election. So Russell resigned: the end of a long and distinguished career. He is remembered above all for his commitment to reform.

It was time for Derby and Disraeli to pick up the torch. What they did next is told in the following chapter.

NOTES

1. Eric J. Evans, *Parliamentary Reform, c.1770–1918*, p.37.

2. Ibid., p.37.

3. Ibid., p.37.

4. Charles Seymour, *Electoral Reform in England and Wales*, p.240.

5. John W. Derry, *Parliamentary Reform*, p.42.

6. George Malcolm Thomson, *The Prime Ministers: From Robert Walpole to Margaret Thatcher*, p.132.

7. Charles Seymour, *Electoral Reform in England and Wales*, p.243.

8. Ibid., p.243.

9. Eric J. Evans, *Parliamentary Reform, c.1770–1918*, p.125.

10. Roy Jenkins, *Gladstone*, p.252.

11. Eric J. Evans, *Parliamentary Reform, c.1770–1918*, p.125.

12. Old Testament references are 1 Samuel 22:1, 2 Samuel 23:13 and 1 Chronicles 11:15.

Disraeli's Triumph: The Second Reform Act

The Second Reform Act reached the Statute Book on 15 August 1867, and it was followed in 1868 by Reform Acts for Scotland and Ireland. It was a large and important advance that, among other things, enfranchised around a million new voters and increased the size of the electorate by about 90 per cent. It was said to be a 'Great Leap Forward' but Lord Derby called it 'A Leap In The Dark'. Following the third reading of the bill in the House of Lords he said:

> No doubt we are making a great experiment and taking a leap in the dark but I have the greatest confidence in the sound sense of my fellow-countrymen, and I entertain a strong hope that the extended franchise which we are now conferring on them will be the means of placing the institutions of this country on a firmer basis, and that the passing of this measure will tend to increase the loyalty and contentment of a great proportion of Her Majesty's subjects.

Both expressions were justified. It really was a great leap forward and it was a leap in the dark because the consequences, which some feared, had yet to be seen. A famous *Punch* cartoon was captioned 'A Leap In The Dark'. It showed a horse ploughing into a fence labelled 'REFORM'. The horse is carrying Britannia with her arm across her face obscuring her vision.

It is probably fair to say that there were two main reasons why the Act was passed in 1867 and why it was so significant. The first was that the public and many of the politicians were ready for it. Its time had come. The second was that the Conservatives, and Disraeli in particular, grasped the nettle, made the original intentions more ambitious and drove it through.

Although there is some doubt about it, Harold Wilson is believed to have said that a week in politics is a long time. Be that as it may, a third of a century certainly is. Lord Derby took office on 28 June 1866 and this is the period that had elapsed since the Great Reform Act of 1832. During this time Chartism had flared up and died away, then between 1852 and 1860 no fewer than four reform bills had failed. The public had been relatively restrained in the 1850s and early 1860s, but the mood changed after the death of Lord Palmerston. The public wanted reform and they thought that the Liberal Bill of 1866 would give them a moderate measure of it. It was by far the most serious attempt since 1832, but it did not succeed. In defending his 1866 Bill Gladstone used the following words:

> You cannot fight against the future. Time is on our side. The great social forces which move onward in their might and majesty and which the tumult of your debates does not for a moment impede or disturb ... are against you. They are marshalled on our side. And the banner which we now carry in this fight, though perhaps at some moment it may droop over our sinking heads, yet it soon again will float in the eye of Heaven, and it will be borne by the firm hands of a united people of the three kingdoms, perhaps not to an easy, but to a certain and to a not far distant victory.

He was both eloquent and right, and the first sentence was particularly apt. You cannot fight against the future. The time for more reform was at hand.

The public mood was shown by meetings and demonstrations called by the Reform League. There was sometimes disorder, but nothing on the scale of events around the 1832 Reform Act or the Chartist riots. One event is particularly remembered. On 23 July 1866, shortly after the failure of the 1866 bill, a great meeting was to be held in Hyde Park. It was declared illegal by the home secretary and a large contingent of police barred the entrances. The demonstrators tore down the railings along much of Park Lane, forced their way in and went ahead with the meeting.

The Reform League had been founded in the autumn/winter of 1864/65 with the aim of campaigning for manhood suffrage and the secret ballot. Support grew very rapidly and a considerable number of branches were opened – after just over two years there were a hundred of them in London alone. Charles Bradlaugh, whose remarkable story is told in Chapter 14, was a prominent supporter and so was the radical MP John Bright. The demonstrations continued after the events in Hyde Park. Some were very big and another mass demonstration in Hyde Park led to the resignation of Spencer Walpole, the home secretary. He had banned the meeting, then been forced to retract and let it go ahead. After passage of the Second Reform Bill, support for the League dwindled and it was dissolved in March 1869.

On both sides of the House there was a hardcore of MPs opposed to any reform, or at least opposed to any major reform. Chapter 9 referred to the activities of the forty or so Liberal Adullamites who adopted this stance, and there were others on the Conservative side who held similar views. However, it is probably correct to say that the personal convictions of the majority on both sides now favoured some degree of reform. Unsurprisingly they did not agree on the desired amount of it, nor on the particular measures that they wanted. A further factor was that like nearly all politicians, then as now, they wanted outcomes that were favourable to them and their parties. This goes some way to explaining why a House with a majority of members favouring reform voted down the moderate Russell/Gladstone bill.

The name of Benjamin Disraeli will forever be linked with the 1867 Reform Act. It is right that his name features in the heading of this chapter, a distinction that this book only otherwise accords to Charles Bradlaugh. It was Disraeli's bill. Lord Derby was prime minister, but it was Disraeli, Chancellor of the Exchequer and Leader in the Commons, who shaped the bill, changed it, introduced it, presided over the massive widening of its scope, and finally passed it on to the Lords and hence to the Statute Book. Disraeli almost doubled the size of the electorate.

Why did he do it? In 1866, just one year earlier, he had led the opposition to the Liberal Bill that was much less far-reaching than the one that he now espoused. As with many issues it is hard to be sure where his convictions really lay, but he probably did favour reform, though he had a formidable record of acting in his own interests as he saw them. This 'slipperiness' was one of the reasons that Gladstone disliked him. Most notably, twenty years earlier he had played a major part in bringing down the government of Sir Robert Peel over the repeal of the Corn Laws. This was done to further his own career and not because he favoured continued tariffs. He certainly made no attempt to bring them back when he was in a position to do so.

What Benjamin Disraeli did undoubtedly favour was the career of Benjamin Disraeli, and to a much lesser extent the success of the Conservative Party. He had a very high opinion of his abilities, and was right to do so. He was 61 years old and had been dominant in the Commons for a score of years, but despite this he had only held ministerial office for two short periods. These were as Chancellor of the Exchequer for nine months and fifteen months in earlier governments led by Lord Derby. He was now Chancellor of the Exchequer and Leader in the Commons for the third time, but in a minority government. The Liberal Party had a nominal majority of seventy-seven and there was no reason to think that a dissolution would make much difference.[1] He was very aware of the advancing years. Lord Randolph Churchill once said that Gladstone was an old man in a hurry. Perhaps 61 should not be considered old but the remark, which was made some years later, might be applicable to Disraeli as well. He needed to do something dramatic to change the mindset of the electorate and make the Conservatives the party of power. Lord Derby's health was ailing and he was the heir presumptive.

It was generally thought that extending the franchise would benefit the Liberal Party, but Disraeli was not sure that this was correct. He thought that the party and person that gave the new voters what they had demanded would be rewarded accordingly. In any case he had little to lose. His parliamentary tactics were unprincipled but dazzlingly successful. It is now hard to understand just why, but his performance eclipsed Gladstone's, and invigorated his party. He pulled it off. Afterwards it was widely expected that he would be prime minister for years to come.

Due to divisions in the cabinet the incoming Conservative government at first moved cautiously and interestingly it seems that Derby was ready to grasp the nettle before Disraeli. On 22 December 1866 he wrote to his Leader in the Commons. He was clear that the Conservatives should present a bill and should offer more than the Liberals, or at least appear to do so.[2] He proposed a borough household franchise, which would sound very radical and very attractive. However, he wanted to drastically water down its effects. This would be done by limiting it to those who paid poor relief, paid their rates directly and satisfied a two-year residence qualification.[3] Furthermore, he wanted 'fancy franchises'. This meant an additional vote in the same constituency for such things as a university degree and a certain level of savings. John Smith, a graduate of Oxford University with £50 in the bank and living in Kidderminster, would have three votes in the Kidderminster constituency. The effect of all this would be that the new votes of the working class householders would be largely balanced by the extra votes of the middle classes. It was rather cynical, but there was a lot of cynicism around.

From this point onwards it was Disraeli who was very much in charge. On 12 February 1867, without involving the cabinet he committed the government to an immediate bill, and on 25 February he produced it. This became known as the 'Ten-minutes Bill'. It was called this because it had been agreed upon just ten minutes before Derby presented it to a Conservative Party meeting.[4] It was a modest measure that provided for a £6 franchise in the boroughs, a £20 franchise in the counties and fancy franchises. The bill was criticised in the Commons for being too timid, and as a consequence Disraeli withdrew it and announced a more radical one.

A consequence of this was the resignation of three cabinet ministers, who wanted very little reform and preferably none at all. They were Lord Cranborne (sitting in the Commons and heir to the Marquess of Salisbury), the Earl of Carnarvon and General Peel (younger brother of the late Sir Robert Peel and owner of the 1844 Derby winner). Cranborne (as the next Marquess of Salisbury) served as secretary of state for India and then foreign secretary in Disraeli's 1874 government. He went on to be prime minister for a little over thirteen years. Disraeli shrugged off the resignations and did not let them deflect him from his course of action.

Roy Jenkins makes the perceptive observation that the three resignations have much in common with the resignations of the three Treasury ministers in 1958.[5] In this case an implacable Enoch Powell strengthened the resolve of Nigel Birch and Chancellor of the Exchequer Peter Thorneycroft. In 1867 Cranborne was the one with the iron resolve, and he influenced his two colleagues who might have weakened. Jenkins does not make the point that in neither case did the resignations have much effect. In 1958 Prime Minister Harold Macmillan referred to 'little local difficulties' and departed on an extensive Commonwealth tour.

The revised bill as introduced gave the vote in the boroughs to any man who had occupied a house for two years, had been rated to the relief of the poor and had paid his rates. Also to be enfranchised were men who paid 20 shillings (£1) annually in direct taxes, and if they were householders as well they had a double vote.[6] 'Fancy franchises' were also included – a university degree, membership in a learned profession or a certain sum in a savings bank or government funds. There were though a number of conditions that restricted the number who would qualify under the property-related provisions. Furthermore, no voting rights were given to the very large number of compound householders who did not pay their own rates. These were men who paid a sum to their landlords that was inclusive of both rent and rates, the landlord then being responsible for paying the rates.

The bill was primarily about the boroughs, but as introduced the county rental qualification was put at £15. This high figure was intended to preserve propertied interests and stop them being swamped by new voters.[7] County boundaries were to be redrawn with the effect of putting more voters into borough constituencies.

With Gladstone's agreement the bill was given a second reading on 25 March without a division. He and most of the Liberals wanted reform and accepted the principle, but of course not necessarily the details. It then moved to Committee where the drama took place. The bill that left Committee was very different and much more far-reaching than the one that went into it.

Disraeli wanted a more radical bill and he got it. His tactic was to benignly preside over a series of amendments that drove it in this direction, and he was prepared to take them from all quarters of the House, Liberal as well as Conservative. There was, though, a major exception. He would not take them from Gladstone. It had to be seen to be a Conservative bill, not a Liberal one, and it had to be seen to be a Disraeli triumph, not a Gladstone one. The country had to know that it should thank him for what was being done for them, not the leader of the opposition. This led to some curious outcomes. On more than one occasion he rejected a Gladstone amendment, then later accepted one that was more extreme from another person on the same topic. Arguably this sometimes caused him to go further than he really wished. Of course not all radical amendments got through. Very predictably one from John Stuart Mill to enfranchise women did not pass. That would have to wait another fifty-one years. The voting against the amendment was 196 votes to 73.

The main effect of the amendments was to remove the safeguards put in to limit the consequences of the increased franchise in the boroughs, which meant that there would be more voters. These amendments included a reduction in the residence qualification from two years to one year. 'Fancy franchises' were dropped, so there were to be no extra votes for such things as a university degree or money in the bank.

The original bill had provided for some redistribution of seats. Amendments changed the details, with the consequence that about 100,000 voters would be transferred from county to borough seats. This would leave many counties representing a larger proportion of genuinely rural residents. The bill did not do much for rural dwellers – that would have to wait until the Third Reform Act masterminded by Gladstone in 1884.

The effect of one amendment dwarfed all the others. It became known as the 'Hodgkinson Amendment' and was named after the rather obscure Liberal MP for Newark who moved it. Gladstone unattractively called him 'a local solicitor little known in the House'.[8] His amendment followed the pattern of Disraeli rejecting a Gladstone amendment, then accepting one from someone else on the same subject. Gladstone had attempted to help compounders – tenants compounding their rates and rent in a single payment to the landlord, but thanks to Disraeli Gladstone's amendment was rejected by 322 votes to 256.

The obscure Grosvenor Hodgkinson secured his place in the history books by going much further than Gladstone, his leader, and proposing that in the boroughs compounding be banned by law. Tenants would be required to pay their rates directly and not through their landlord. This would remove the problem and, providing that they otherwise qualified, give compounders the vote. To the amazement of all, Disraeli accepted the amendment. In fact it had been badly drafted and was withdrawn, with a government replacement put in its place. This amendment alone had the dramatic consequence of adding nearly half a million voters in the boroughs.

With the acquiescence of a rather sore Gladstone the third reading took place on 25 July and the bill transferred to the Lords. More than a third of a century previously the Great Reform Act had floundered and sunk in this place, before finally getting through in the midst of a constitutional crisis and the threat of the large-scale creation of new peers. There had been the very real possibility that the Lords would reject it and that the consequences would be desperate. There was no such trouble this time.

The Upper House had a few Adullamites and a selection of opponents and doubters, but it was not in the mood for a fight and Lord Derby was able to manage a successful passage without too much difficulty. Some amendments came back to the Commons, but only one significant one was not reversed. Baron Cairns succeeded in preventing electors using more than two votes. The bill gave some of the largest urban constituencies three MPs, but the amendment meant that the electors were restricted to voting for two. This change was likely to favour the Conservatives because it made it more likely that the minority party would gain one of the three seats. In the constituencies affected the minority party was likely to be the Conservatives. The amendment caused quite a bit of unease on both sides in the Commons and it was strongly opposed by Gladstone. This resulted in Disraeli giving it his backing and it got through.

The Reform Act (England and Wales) 1867, better known as the Second Reform Act, passed into law less than two years after the death in office of Lord Palmerston. The great statesman and opponent of reform would have been horrified. Many others were too, or they were at least worried. Lord Derby called it a leap in the dark, and so it was. The provisions of the Act went way beyond anything realistically envisaged when Palmerston was alive and in a position to discourage or prevent them. The main provisions were as follows.

Voting in the Boroughs

The vote was given to all householders who had been resident for a year, and to all lodgers who paid rent of at least £10 a year and who had been resident for at least a year.

In seats that returned three MPs, each elector only had two votes. In seats that returned four MPs each elector only had three votes. Electors with more than one vote had to cast them for different candidates.

Voting in the Counties

In addition to persons already entitled to vote, the franchise was given to owners (or lessees on sixty-year leases or longer) of property worth £5 a year, and occupiers of lands with a rateable value of £12 a year, who had paid poor rates on the property.

Size of the Electorate

The overall electorate of England and Wales increased by about 90 per cent to 2 million or very slightly less. John W. Derry puts the increase at 88 per cent.[9] The greatest increase was in the boroughs where the number of electors more than doubled. According to the 1861 census the population of England and Wales, including women and children, was 20,066,224. The 1871 census puts it at 22,712,266.

Redistribution of Seats

The redistribution of seats was relatively modest. The two main themes were the transfer of seats from the boroughs to the counties, and the transfer of seats from boroughs with low population to areas with high population. Major discrepancies remained. Full details are given in Appendix C.

Other

It was no longer necessary to hold a general election following a change of monarch.

This last point could be very important, as with the general election following the death of George IV in 1830. The significance of this to reform is explained in Chapter 4. Had the requirement not changed there would have been three general elections in fifteen months in the 1930s. A general election was held on 14 November 1935. King George V died on 20 January 1936 and Edward VIII abdicated on 11 December 1936.

The Reform Act (England and Wales) 1867 was followed by the Reform Act (Scotland) 1868. The franchise principles were similar to those in England and Wales, but no lodger franchise was necessary. This was because Scottish law categorised lodgers as tenants. The net effect was that the number of electors in the boroughs almost tripled. Redistribution gave Scotland a net increase of seven seats, the number increasing from fifty-three to sixty. Full details are given in Appendix C. If the allocation had been proportionate to the size of Scotland's population, there would have been ninety Scottish seats.[10]

The third and final act in the trio was the Reform Act (Ireland) 1868. In the boroughs the vote was given to occupiers of property worth more than £4 per year, and the vote was given to lodgers. There was no change to the voting qualifications in the counties. There was no redistribution of seats but some voters were reallocated from the counties to the boroughs. The net effect was a net increase of about 50 per cent in the number of voters, the new total being about 45,000.

The so-called 'leap in the dark' was one of the major milestones on the road to reform. Its assessment deserves and gets a separate chapter.

NOTES

1. Roy Jenkins, *Gladstone*, p.268.
2. Eric J. Evans, *Parliamentary Reform c.1770–1918*, p.50.
3. Ibid., p.50.
4. Roy Jenkins, *Gladstone*, p.270.
5. Ibid., p.270.
6. Charles Seymour, *Electoral Reform in England and Wales*, p.258.
7. Eric J. Evans, *Parliamentary Reform c.1770–1918*, p.51.
8. Roy Jenkins, *Gladstone*, p.272.
9. John W. Derry, *Parliamentary Reform*, p.46.
10. Eric J. Evans, *Parliamentary Reform c.1770–1918*, p.53.

11

An Assessment of the Second Reform Act

As explained in Chapter 10, Disraeli's motives in pursuing the Second Reform Act were probably a mixture of self-interest, some would say cynical self-interest, and a belief in what he was doing. Many would say that self-interest was by far the dominant factor, but let us be charitable and first look at the case for principle.

The terms 'Tory democracy' and 'one-nation conservatism' are often approvingly quoted today, especially the latter, and both originated with Disraeli and his philosophy. One-nation conservatism is associated with a rather paternalistic way of governing and Disraeli, when he became prime minister in 1874 with a Conservative majority, did govern in this way. The Act probably went further than he wanted to go, and in some ways further than Gladstone wanted to go, but one-nation government did depend on a significant extension of the franchise. The Act provided this, so disregarding the hard-to-ignore fact that the next government was Liberal, a consequence was that it paved the way for one-nation conservatism. You could also say that a consequence was that it paved the way for one-nation government. To this extent, and assuming that we think that this is desirable, Disraeli deserves our thanks.

Putting this aside it is undoubtedly true that a big part of Disraeli's motivation was a wish to boost the prospects of the Conservative Party and himself. He thought that the Act would do this, but many disagreed, including many Liberals. This was one of the reasons why, with a big majority, the Liberals did not stop him. He must have been dreadfully disappointed with the result of the 1868 general election, which he lost badly, but it could be said that in the longer term he was to some extent vindicated. It is tempting to see Disraeli's election victory in 1874 as a delayed thank you for the Second Reform Act, but it would probably be a mistake to do so. Gladstone's administration was in deep trouble and the tired prime minister had made the mistake of acting as his own Chancellor of the Exchequer. The 1874 vote was surely, in part at least, a recognition of this. Nevertheless, prior to the Act the Liberals had been the natural party of government, their domination being periodically interrupted by short-lived, minority Conservative administrations. There were Conservative prime ministers in twenty-one of the thirty-one years from 1874 to 1905. For thirteen years and ten months of this time it was Lord Salisbury (Cranborne), the man who had resigned in protest at the prospect of the 1867 Act.

On 27 February 1868, not long after the passage of the Act, Lord Derby resigned. He was ageing and in poor health, with gout being a particular problem. He was 68 and had only just over a year to live. He remains the longest serving leader of the Conservative Party, though his three periods as prime minister were all at the head of brief, minority governments. He was not short of other interests, both before and after his retirement. He had a passion for horse racing and was a member of the Jockey Club – the classic race at Epsom had been named after his grandfather. His translation of the *Iliad* ran to six editions.[1] It is hard to imagine a modern prime minister doing that for fun in his or her spare time. His resignation left the field clear for Disraeli to take office. He had, in his own words, finally climbed to the top of the greasy pole.

Disraeli was prime minister at last, but he headed a minority government; the Liberals had a majority of about seventy-seven. It was time to test his belief that the newly enfranchised voters would reward the Conservatives and him, so a general election was called. The result was absolutely clear – they would not. The Liberals were returned with an increased majority of about 116. After 277 days in office Disraeli departed and handed the reins of government to Gladstone. The future 'Grand Old Man' started the first of his four administrations and said that his mission was to pacify Ireland.

The 1868 general election was the last at which representatives of only two parties were elected, although both the Conservatives and Liberals were fairly loose coalitions. Sources give slightly different figures but the following analysis is taken from www.historylearningsite.co.uk:

England	Conservative	803,637 votes	211 seats
	Liberal	1,192,098 votes	244 seats
Wales	Conservative	29,866 votes	10 seats
	Liberal	52,256 votes	23 seats
Scotland	Conservative	23,985 votes	7 seats
	Liberal	125,356 votes	51 seats
Ireland	Conservatives	38,767 votes	37 seats
	Liberal	54,461 votes	66 seats
	Others	188 votes	0 seats
Universities	Conservative	7,063 votes	6 seats
	Liberal	4,605 votes	3 seats
Total	Conservative	903,318 votes	271 seats
	Liberal	1,428,776 votes	387 seats
	Other	188 votes	0 seats

The boroughs were a catastrophe for the Conservatives, but they took 60 per cent of the county seats.[2] The transfer of voters from the boroughs to the counties meant that the counties now had 42 per cent of both the voters and the seats.[3] The Conservatives did rather well in London and its suburbs and also in Lancashire. As can be seen from the figures, they did better in England than in Wales, Scotland and Ireland. Their performance in Scotland was particularly bad – in fact the use of the word dreadful would be justified.

A very important consequence of the 1868 Act was a big and rapid build up of party activity and organisation. This was made necessary by the increased number of voters. The National Union of Conservative Associations was founded in 1867, and the National Federation of Liberal Associations followed in 1877. Elections were fought more on a national party basis, and less with reference to the personal records and beliefs of the candidates. Members of Parliament became more beholden to their parties and the number of government defeats in the Commons reduced. This trend had been discernible before 1867, but the Act accelerated it. In the 1850s it was normal for governments to lose ten or more votes in a session. By the 1890s it was down to just one or two.[4]

Parties and MPs found it more necessary to present themselves to the electorate and take account of public opinion. It could be said that some power moved from Parliament to the people. We are now usually confronted with a ballot paper listing many candidates and parties, but in the nineteenth century many seats were uncontested. This was especially true before the 1867 Act. It was 58 per cent in 1859, but down to 32 per cent in 1868. It was even lower in 1885 at 7 per cent.

The right to vote depended on being listed on the electoral register, and at the time of the 1868 election the registers were a long way from being up to date. This was partly because it was a big job to bring in all the newly enfranchised voters, but it was also because the task was approached with some indolence and more could have been done. Unfortunately the parties tried to manipulate the process and numerous unjustified challenges were mounted. Sadly this behaviour continued after 1868.

The drawing up of the registers was greatly hindered by the difficulties caused by the prohibition in the boroughs of the compounding of rates. Compounding was the practice of a lodger paying a single sum to his landlord to cover both rent and rates; the landlord would then pay over the rates element. Hodgkinson's amendment had banned compounding, thus requiring tenants to pay rates directly; this had the consequence of enfranchising the tenants. The amendment was badly drafted and it had been withdrawn, with a government amendment substituted. However, even this one ran into all sorts of practical difficulties, many of which had been foreseen.

The end of compounding in the boroughs was unpopular in many quarters. Some landlords tried to avoid reducing the amount collected by not lowering it to take account of the portion accounted for by the rates. Not surprisingly this was greatly resented by the tenants. The difficulties and costs of collecting the rates were increased. If a landlord had say six tenants, the parish authorities had to deal with six individuals instead of one landlord, and it was often much harder to get the money out of a defaulting tenant than a defaulting landlord. Landlords had the sanction of eviction, which the parish authorities did not. Tenants had to make two payments instead of one, which was more time-consuming and perhaps troublesome.

Non-compliance was widespread and violence was sometimes threatened against persons trying to collect rates directly from tenants. Some tenants just refused to pay directly.[5] In Birmingham 25,000 summons were issued for non-payment in October 1867, and a further 15,000 in May 1868.[6] A consequence of not paying directly was that the tenant forfeited the right to vote, but it appeared that quite a few tenants did not value the vote particularly highly. The turnout at the 2010 general election was 65.1 per cent, so it seems that this was not just a nineteenth-century phenomenon. In some places where compounding had not been the custom it was introduced in defiance of the law. Practices varied; in some places the law was enforced – in Tynemouth for example. There, more than 2,000 were disqualified after their names had been put on the register. In other places a blind eye was turned and the names of compounding ratepayers were entered on the register. It was very unsatisfactory. The problem was addressed in Gladstone's ministry and the law was changed. From that point the names of all compound ratepayers were required to be entered in the rate book and on electoral lists.

Unsurprisingly there were no votes for women and a little more surprisingly there was no secret ballot. That was now close and would be obtained five years later during the tenure of the succeeding Liberal government. The story of the secret ballot is told in the next chapter of this book.

The franchise was based exclusively on property, which may be considered to be a good thing or a bad thing, but probably a bad thing. The case for it was that men with a stake in property were likely to be solid, sensible citizens. The same argument was applied to jury service. Right up until 1972 in order to sit on a jury a person had to own property.

The property franchise excluded a range of citizens including live-in servants, though they were predominantly female and already barred for that reason. Also excluded were adult sons living with their parents, recipients of poor relief, people in between owning properties and itinerant workers who frequently moved from job to job. The one year residence requirement was more restrictive then, it seems, at first sight. This was because the residence requirement was fixed at a given date each year. So a person who bought a property ten months before the date had to wait twenty-two months before qualifying. Had fancy franchises got into the Act, some citizens who did not own or rent property would have qualified. People with university degrees or money in a savings bank were likely to be solid citizens, though nearly all of them would have qualified on property grounds.

The franchise qualifications for the boroughs and the counties remained different, and most of the new voters were in the boroughs. With a viewpoint from the twenty-first century this seems hard to understand, though a lot of people thought at the time that it made sense. Scotland and Ireland continued to be less favourably treated than England.

The transfer of some voters from the boroughs to the counties seems sensible. The redistribution of seats was a step in the right direction, but only a small step; enormous discrepancies remained. John Derry puts it very well in his book *Parliamentary Reform*:

> The distribution of seats was still uneven and unjust. 70 boroughs had a population of less than 10,000; 40 a population of more than 200,000; yet both types returned two MPs. Thus, Tiverton with 10,000 inhabitants sent two MPs to Westminster, while Marylebone with 477,000 sent the same. The south and west were over-represented. Wiltshire and Dorset returned a total of 25 MPs for both borough and shire: their population totalled 450,000. The West Riding of Yorkshire with 2,000,000 inhabitants returned 22 MPs, while London with a population of 3,000,000 was represented by 24 MPs.

There was much still to do concerning the redistribution of seats. The House of Commons was still dominated by landowners.

NOTES

1. George Malcolm Thomson, *The Prime Ministers*, p.124.
2. Eric J. Evans, *Parliamentary Reform c.1770–1918*, p.56.
3. Ibid., p.56.
4. Ibid., p.59.
5. Charles Seymour, *Electoral Reform in England and Wales*, p.354.
6. Ibid., p.354.

The Secret Ballot and the
Reining-In of Corruption

The linking of corruption and the secret ballot in the heading of this chapter is apt. Open voting was one of the factors that facilitated corruption, though by no means the only one. The arrival of the secret ballot in 1872 diminished corruption, but by no means stopped it. Corruption never has been totally eliminated, but eleven years later the Corrupt and Illegal Practices Prevention Act 1883 was successful in massively reducing it.

Corruption is interesting and makes a good story, so it is important not to exaggerate it and quote too many true but untypical examples. Nevertheless, until the latter part of the nineteenth century corruption was very widespread and shocking. The first chapter of this book gives a number of blatant examples, and an undemanding search will easily find many others. At its worst, corruption involved the buying of votes or even seats. The practice of 'treating' the electors was very common; many electors expected and received copious amounts of food and drink at the time of an election. The more cynical among us may, perhaps wrongly, think that they see a parallel with modern bidding for the right to host football's World Cup. Some electors ran up debts in the expectation that a candidate would pay them off. Elections were often, to put it mildly, boisterous, though many found them enjoyable. Without a secret ballot, workers could be dismissed if they voted the wrong way, and tenants could be evicted for the same reason. There was sometimes intimidation and violence.

Contemporary fiction is a source of information about how elections were viewed, a good example being Anthony Trollope's *Ralph the Heir*. Trollope had been an unsuccessful Liberal candidate for the corrupt borough of Beverley at the 1868 general election. Every election since 1857 had been followed by a petition alleging corruption and it was believed that 300 of the 1,100 electors were willing to sell their vote. Following the 1868 election a petition was filed and it led to the disenfranchisement of the borough in 1870. Trollope's novel was about the fictitious Percycross election, but it was based on what had happened in Beverley.

Trollope's novel was based on fact, but Charles Dickens' *Pickwick Papers* was entirely fiction. It would, though, not have been so successful had it not chimed with readers' knowledge of how elections were conducted. The book was published in 1836/37 when Dickens was only 24, and part of it describes an election in the fictional constituency of Eatanswill. The following is an extract:

'You have come down here sir to see an election – eh? Spirited contest my dear sir, very much so indeed. We have opened all the public houses in the place. It has left our opponent nothing but the beer shops, masterly policy, my dear sir, eh?' The little man smiled complacently, and took a large pinch of snuff.

'And what is the likely result of the contest?' inquired Mr Pickwick.

'Why, doubtful, my dear sir, rather doubtful as yet' replied the little man. 'Fizkin's people have got three-and-thirty voters in the lock-up coach house at the White Hart.'

'In the coach-house' said Mr Pickwick, much astonished.

'They keep 'em locked up there till they want 'em' resumed the little man. 'The effect you see, is to prevent our getting at them. Even if we could, it would be of no use, for they keep them very drunk on purpose. Smart fellow, Fizkin's agent, very smart fellow indeed.'

'We are pretty confident though' said Mr Perker, his voice sinking almost to a whisper. 'We had a little tea party here last night, five-and-forty women, my dear sir, and gave every one a green parasol when she went away. Five-and-forty green parasols, at 7/6d each. Got the votes of all their husbands, and half their brothers. You can't walk half a dozen yards up the street, without encountering a half a dozen green parasols.'

The secret ballot was so important because it prevented a person paying a bribe knowing that the person who had accepted it had actually voted in the way instructed. Similarly, a person threatening a voter with unpleasant consequences could not be sure that the person threatened had acted as instructed. An example was a landlord threatening to evict a tenant. Conversely it provided an opportunity for a person willing to take a bribe. He could accept inducements from rival candidates and neither would know how he actually voted.

The secret ballot divided opinion for a long time. Some radicals, and others too, had wanted it included in the first Reform Bill presented to Parliament in 1831, and the idea had been supported by lords Durham and Althorp,[1] though not by Lord John Russell and many other Whigs. The king's disapproval had ensured its exclusion.[2] Not long afterwards it had been one of the six demands of the Chartists. Speaking in 1842 Lord Macaulay, the great historian and parliamentarian, had said that although he rejected Chartism the secret ballot was one of its two points that he could support.

Almost everyone now thinks that the case for the secret ballot was overwhelming, even unanswerable, but in the nineteenth century a surprisingly large body of opinion thought differently. Some took the view that it was unmanly to cast a vote in secret, not unwomanly because women did not have the vote. A man should have the courage of his convictions and not be afraid to show them openly, and the spirit that won the empire was not consistent with operating in the shadows. It sounds silly now but many people did think like that. Even more remarkably some people thought that employers, country squires and the like had a legitimate interest in the votes of their employees and people dependent on them. It was a paternalistic view of how society operated.

At the time of the first Reform Bill Sydney Smith had made a witty observation that perhaps should not be taken too seriously. He opposed the secret ballot because 'people would want to know who brought that mischievous, profligate villain into Parliament. Let us see the names of his real supporters.'[3]

Although he was a key figure in the march of parliamentary reform, Lord John Russell was one of the politicians who opposed the secret ballot. As already recounted he did not want it in the Reform Bill that he introduced in 1831, and he maintained his opposition right through to 1872. In 1871 he told the Duke of Richmond that he must oppose the ballot 'not only as a change from publicity to secrecy in the performance of a great public duty, but as an obvious prelude to a change from household to universal suffrage'.[4]

The issue of the secret ballot came to a decision during William Gladstone's first term as prime minister, starting in 1868. The general election held in that year was widely regarded as being particularly corrupt, and this had the effect of concentrating a lot of minds. Furthermore, there were fears that some of the newly enfranchised working men were especially vulnerable to pressure and needed the protection of the secret ballot. Sometimes the demands were made discreetly but sometimes openly. The following words are from the splendidly named MP for Wareham, Mr John Samuel Wanley Sawbridge-Erle-Drax:

Electors of Wareham! I understand that some evil-disposed person has been circulating a report that I wish my tenants, and other persons dependent on me, to vote according to their conscience. This is a dastardly lie; calculated to injure me. I have no wish of the sort. I wish, and I intend, that these persons shall vote for me.[5]

The key figure was the prime minister, William Gladstone. Since his early days as an MP his position on the secret ballot, as on many other issues, had changed. In the 1830s he had told the readers of the *Liverpool Standard* 'that the fall of the Roman Republic was to be attributed to the corruptions of secret voting'.[6] He had moved a vast distance from this absurdity, but he was cool on the Ballot Bill that became law in 1872.[7] Nevertheless, he was somewhat reluctantly persuaded and his government introduced the legislation. It is believed that John Bright had a hand in the persuading. Gladstone's ambivalence is illustrated by one of his diary entries:

Spoke on ballot and voted in 324-230 with mind satisfied and as to feeling a lingering reluctance.[8]

The Commons spent no fewer than eighteen days on the bill before sending it to the Lords, where it was rejected. With an extraordinarily low turnout for such an important measure, the voting was ninety-seven to forty-eight against. The Lords acted in this way on the incongruous grounds that the measure had not been adequately considered. Despite his lack of enthusiasm for the bill, Gladstone responded with great firmness. He said that the next time round the bill would be presented with an 'authoritative knock', and he threatened an autumn session and then a dissolution if necessary.[9] The Lords gave way and the bill became the Ballot Act in July 1872. The secret ballot was to run to 1880 and it then required annual renewal. It was renewed annually and was made permanent in 1918.

The secret ballot was first used at a by-election held in Pontefract on 15 August 1872. The ballot box used is today preserved in a local museum, and it is still marked with the seal used to ensure that there was no tampering with the votes. Rather charmingly the seal was made with a liquorice stamp used to make Pontefract cakes at a local liquorice factory. It was noted that the atmosphere at the election was markedly different from what had in the past been normal. The following is an extract from an issue of *The Times* published on 16 August 1872:[10]

No bands of music paraded the town. No colours or banners were seen in procession. The church bells were silent ... Both at Pontefract and Knottingley the topic was the dullness of the election. 'It hardly seemed like an election' the tradespeople said; and they were right.

This absence of boisterous behaviour (at best) or drunkenness, or even intimidation (at worst) was regarded as a decided blessing by many upright Victorian citizens. Its passing was though mourned by some.

The secret ballot helped the cause of the Nationalists in Ireland. This was because it enabled tenants to vote as they saw fit, without fear of reprisals by their landlords. For the same reason it probably, on balance, marginally damaged the Conservatives in the counties. It is, though, right to point out that not all landlords and employers exerted pressure, and that not all voters submitted to it anyway. It is also fair to say that some tenants and workers, perhaps many or most of them, respected their landlords and employers, and thought it right to take their views into account. Just how much influence a landowner could have is illustrated by the election for South Lincolnshire in 1841. Thirty-two out of the forty-one parishes owned by one landowner voted unanimously for his choice of candidate.[11]

Quite often following an election, unsuccessful candidates would petition on the grounds of alleged corruption. Some constituencies were notorious and petitions were almost routine. Mention was made earlier in this chapter of Anthony Trollope's experience at Beverley. Petitions concerning this borough followed every election between 1857 and 1868, and it was disenfranchised in 1870. Other notorious boroughs included Bridgwater, Lancaster, St Albans and Great Yarmouth. In connection with the ten general elections between 1832 and 1868, 346 petitions for corruption were presented. In assessing the significance of this number it should be remembered that a significant number of constituencies were uncontested. In 1852 twenty-three seats were declared vacant because of corruption. William Gladstone's victory at Newark in 1832 came close to being challenged on petition. According to Roy Jenkins[12] far more money was spent on his behalf than he was aware of or subsequently approved.

Corruption was very widely practised by both parties, which did not stop it being regularly noted and lamented by both sides in Parliament. Palmerston, not a man easily shocked, once said to his fellow members, 'I speak it with shame and sorrow, but I verily believe that the extent to which bribery and corruption was carried at the last election, has exceeded anything that has ever been stated within these walls.' It was reported in *The Times* that 'in the General Election of 1865 there was more profuse and corrupt expenditure than was ever known before'.

A person looking for examples of corruption is spoilt for choice. An examination of books and the Internet will provide an abundance of them. Following are some noteworthy examples:

In the Irish borough of Cashel Henry Munster paid the very large sum of £30 to each of 25 of the town's 26 butchers to secure their vote in the 1868 election.[13]

At a by-election held in 1880 in Sandwich the agent for the Conservative candidate booked 350 public houses as 'committee rooms'. The Royal Commission that reported on the by-election damned very extensive bribery and the fact that numerous electors were ready to accept bribes. It reported that 'we cannot doubt that electoral corruption had long and extensively prevailed in the borough of Sandwich'.[14] The seat had for many years been held by the Liberals, which supports the view that corruption was not confined to one party.

At Beverley a sub-agent went into the market place and asked electors how much they wanted for their votes. The electors were waiting for the highest bidder and money was openly paid over.[15] At Totnes there was great disappointment when a candidate withdrew. The wives of the electors had come to the Conservative hotel to collect the money that was to be distributed and sadly departed without it.[16] Also in Totnes tenants of the Duke of Somerset were paid between 60 and 150 pounds to vote against his wishes, a phenomenal sum at the time for a bribe. They faced the consequence of certain eviction, but calculated that it was worth it.[17]

At Gloucester and Macclesfield more than half the electors were directly bribed.[18]

Corruption was sometimes more subtle than the direct payment of money. In 1881 The Chester Bribery Commission reported that the Chester Conservatives had taken 2,281 persons on a picnic. They had only been charged a nominal amount for the refreshments[19]. The Commission also reported that 'a general notion appears to have been abroad in the city [Chester] that the Liberal Association might bribe and treat freely, without endangering the seats of the candidates'.[20] This is another confirmation that bribery was not confined to just one party.

Laws to prevent corruption had been in place since the late seventeenth century, but as can be gauged from this chapter they had very little practical effect. Parliament began to deal with the problem in 1854 when the Corrupt Practices Act reached the Statute Book. It did not go nearly far enough and it was in practice largely ineffective. It failed to stop intimidation, though it possibly had a slight effect in reducing direct bribery. The Act required candidates to publish their expenses and file them with an election auditor. However, it did not impose spending limits or impose harsh penalties for non-compliance. In practice accounts were frequently not accurate and the auditors did not do a good job.

What the 1854 Act did do was point the way forward. Twenty-nine years later, in 1883, another act did go far enough and was very effective. In the meantime another step had come in 1868 when Disraeli's Conservative government legislated to transfer the decision on election petitions from the Commons to the courts.

Neither the 1854 Corrupt Practices Act nor the 1872 Ballot Act had stopped corruption. Indeed, by some measures it was getting worse; elections were getting more expensive, and legitimate expenses were rising as well as illegitimate ones. The increase in the electorate brought about by the 1867 Act created the need to spend more money. There were more people to canvass honourably, as well as more people to bribe dishonourably. This had the very unfortunate consequence of making it difficult for men of limited means to stand as candidates.

After 1867 and especially after 1880 MPs increasingly came to the view that something had to be done, even though some of them owed their seats to corrupt practices. The 1880 general election had been particularly expensive and particularly corrupt. Mr Gladstone's second government grasped the nettle and it had a lot of support from the Conservative opposition. Despite this, individual MPs had concerns and objections and Bills introduced in 1881 and 1882 foundered. In 1883 it was different and the Corrupt and Illegal Practices Prevention Act became law.

The following were the main terms of the Act.

Limitation of Election Expenses

The amount of money that could be spent was limited. In the boroughs the figure was £350 if the number of electors did not exceed 2,000. If the number of electors exceeded 2,000, it was £380 plus £30 for every additional 1,000 electors. In the counties the figure was £650 if the number of electors did not exceed 2,000. If the number of electors exceeded 2,000, it was £710 plus £60 for every additional 1,000 electors.

Legitimate Expenses

Legitimate expenses were closely defined. All expenses were allocated to one of five categories.

The number of employees was strictly limited and paid employees were not allowed to vote.

One committee room was allowed for each 500 electors.

The expenses of public meetings, postage, advertising and similar items was included.

Miscellaneous expenses of £200 were allowed, and each candidate was allowed £100 for personal expenses.

Agent
Each candidate was required to name a single agent. This person alone had the right to settle expenses.

Returns and Accounts
Within thirty-five days the agent was required to send to the returning officer a certified statement of all money spent, together with receipts. Receipts were required for all items of expenditure over £2.

Members were not allowed to take their seats until they had made a declaration certifying the truth of the accounts.

Treating
Treating was identified as a corrupt practice. The penalty was the same as the penalty for bribery.

Different Kinds of Corrupt Practice
The categories were bribery, treating, undue influence and personation. The punishment was the same for all four categories.

Punishment for Corrupt Practice
If personally guilty, the candidate could never sit for that constituency.

If guilty by his agent, the candidate, he could not sit for that constituency for seven years.

Corrupt practice might invalidate the result for the constituency in question. On conviction the maximum penalty was one year's imprisonment, with or without hard labour, and a fine of not more than £100.

An elector convicted of corrupt practice could not be registered to vote for a period of seven years. Furthermore, he could not hold any public or judicial office during that period.

Illegal Practices
These were the payment of travelling expenses, or the hiring of conveyances, banners, ribbons, bands or any marks of distinction. They also included surpassing the sum of expenses allowed by law and the payment of any sum not directly authorised.

Punishment for Illegal Practices
There was a distinction between corrupt practices and illegal practices.

If personally guilty, the candidate could not sit for the constituency for seven years.

If guilty by his agent, the candidate was disqualified for the life of the Parliament.

An elector guilty of illegal practice could not exercise his political rights for a period of five years.

In addition there could be a fine of up to £100.

Enforcement

There was a new official to be known as the Director of Public Prosecutions. This person was to attend the trial of any petitions. He was also to follow any directions given to him by the court for the examination of witnesses and the prosecution of alleged offenders. He was entitled to prosecute on his own authority.

The Act was a success and the instance of corruption diminished by an enormous amount. The figures for petitions bear this out. In 1880 thirty-three petitions were presented and twelve members were unseated. In 1885 seven petitions were presented, but only one member was unseated. In 1892 two members were unseated and in 1895 it was one.[21]

By 1883 the Ballot Act and the Corrupt and Illegal Practices Prevention Act were on the Statute Book. Another Great Reform Act was shortly to follow. This is described in the next chapter.

NOTES

1. Antonia Fraser, *Perilous Question: The Drama of the Great Reform Act 1832*, p.102.
2. Ibid., p.102.
3. Ibid., p.102.
4. Eric J. Evans, *Parliamentary Reform, c.1770–1918*, p.62.
5. Ibid., p.107.
6. Roy Jenkins, *Gladstone*, p.354.
7. Ibid., p.314.
8. Ibid., p.356.
9. Ibid., p.356.
10. Eric J. Evans, *Parliamentary Reform, c.1770–1918*, p.109.
11. Ibid., p.29.
12. Roy Jenkins, *Gladstone*, p.35.
13. Eric J. Evans, *Parliamentary Reform, c.1770–1918*, p.66.
14. Ibid., p.111/112.
15. Charles Seymour, *Electoral Reform in England and Wales*, p.393.
16. Ibid., p.393.
17. Ibid., p.395.
18. Ibid., p.396.
19. Ibid., p.438.
20. Ibid., p.440.
21. Ibid., p.449.

The Twin Acts of 1884 and 1885

The first of the two reforms referred to in the title of this chapter is the Representation of the People Act 1884. This is often called the Third Reform Act, following the first in 1832 and the second in 1867. Its main measure was a large increase in the franchise in the counties. The second one is the Redistribution of Seats Act 1885, its long title being 'An Act for the Redistribution of Seats at Parliamentary Elections and for other Purposes'. This says it exactly. The redistribution of seats was very extensive, very thorough, very necessary and very overdue. It badly needed doing and, although the constituency boundaries have been subsequently amended several times, it left them in a form that is recognisable today. The two Acts were very closely linked, and indeed the first one may well not have got through without a government commitment to the second. It is right that they are both examined within a single chapter of this book.

After the Second Reform Act in 1867 very few people thought that parliamentary reform was complete – to use a very modern expression that it was the 'end of history'. Some wished that it was, and a tiny number regretted that it had ever started. This had been the Duke of Wellington's position, but his views had mellowed somewhat with age and he had departed this life in 1852. Many, almost certainly most, wanted further reform at some stage, and almost everyone recognised that whether they approved or not, further reform was bound to come. Predictably, numerous politicians were anxious that reform would not damage them or their parties. It would be even better, they thought, if further reform benefitted themselves and their parties, and damaged their opponents. It was ever thus, though there were of course honourable exceptions. Then as now some politicians were men of honour, who put principle before self-interest. Then as now politicians were happiest when they were in the fortunate position of self-interest, principle and the national interest, all requiring the same action.

The most obvious next measure was to extend the franchise in the counties, in order to bring dwellers in the counties in line with dwellers in the boroughs, who had benefitted in 1867. Also at the front of the queue was the need for a major redistribution of seats. This was desperately needed – the existing distribution being a scandal or a farce, depending on your point of view. Your opinion will probably be that it was both a scandal and a farce. Ireland had a very strong claim for early attention; it was severely disadvantaged, both before and after 1867. The acts of 1884 and 1885 addressed all these issues.

Left for another day, or for the following century as it turned out, was manhood suffrage – which meant votes for all adult male citizens, rather than those who qualified on the basis of property. Also left for the following century were reform of the House of Lords, votes for women and universal suffrage. It should, though, be mentioned that a doomed attempt was made to insert votes for women into the Third Reform Act. Among other things left were the position of the university seats and a move to proportional representation. This last one has never been implemented for parliamentary elections, and is very much a live issue in the twenty-first century. Rumblings about proportional representation were heard in 1884, but there was no serious prospect of it being implemented at that time.

As mentioned in Chapter 11 Disraeli and the Conservatives lost the 1868 general election heavily, and the Liberals took office with William Gladstone becoming prime minister for the first time. He favoured more parliamentary reform, but did not see it as an issue for the near future. Some radicals were keen for more reform and the sooner the better, but many in both the Liberal and Conservative parties agreed with the prime minister. The secret ballot was a live issue and as recounted in Chapter 12 the Ballot Act was passed in 1872, but otherwise not much happened.

Gladstone's government faltered badly in its last two years and a triumphant Benjamin Disraeli led the Conservatives back to power in 1874. It was the first Conservative majority government since 1841. When he had taken office in 1868 he had said that he had at last climbed to the top of the greasy pole. This time he said, 'Power, power at last, but it has come too late.' Disraeli was 69 and very conscious of his health and of the advancing years.

A study of the votes cast and the seats won is relevant to the pressing need for the redistribution of seats, and also to the issue of proportional representation. Gladstone's Liberals contested 489 seats, obtained 1,281,519 votes and got 242 MPs. Disraeli's Conservatives contested 507 seats, obtained 1,091,708 votes and got 350 MPs. The apparent anomaly is partly explained by the fact that the Conservatives were victorious in more uncontested seats. In Ireland Home Rulers obtained 60 of the 101 seats, their first representation in the UK Parliament. It was an ominous indicator of trouble to come.

The incidence of a party getting more seats but fewer votes has happened in more recent times. In 1951 Clement Attlee's Labour Party got 13,948,883 votes and 295 seats. It was the largest total number of votes ever obtained by the Labour Party. The Conservative and National Liberal parties, in alliance but effectively the Conservatives, got 13,717,850 votes and 321 seats. Despite a shortfall of 231,033 votes Sir Winston Churchill became prime minister and launched what Harold Wilson would later call thirteen years of Tory misrule. The Liberal Party has featured very prominently in this book and will continue to do so, but in the 1951 general election it got 730,546 votes and just six seats. How the mighty are fallen. The Liberals got 2.56 per cent of the votes but only 0.96 per cent of the seats, a discrepancy which helps explain their continuing advocacy of proportional representation.

In early 1974 the country was crippled by a devastating miners' strike and the consequent three-day week. The Conservative prime minister, Edward Heath, called a general election to ask the country 'Who governs Britain?'. He is popularly supposed to have received the answer 'Not you mate', and the Labour Party took power with Harold Wilson as prime minister. However, the voting figures deserve close scrutiny. The Conservative Party got 11,872,180 votes and 297 seats. The Labour Party got 11,645,616 votes (226,564 fewer) but 301 seats (four more). Analysis is complicated by the fact that a recovering Liberal Party got 6,059,519 votes, but just fourteen seats. Had their share of the seats been the same as their share of the votes they would have got 123 seats. For obvious reasons their advocacy of proportional representation grew significantly louder.

Disraeli, who went to the House of Lords in 1876 as Lord Beaconsfield, led a Conservative government from 20 February 1874 to 21 April 1880. During this time, as during Gladstone's 1868–74 ministry, pressure for parliamentary reform was muted and little happened. The country, though, wanted more reform, and in a moderate way the issues continued to be raised, especially the issue of county dwellers being relatively disadvantaged. Every year George Trevelyan had brought forward a motion for making the voting qualifications the same in the counties and the boroughs. He had regularly done this in an almost empty House, but after 1873 a number of Liberals took an interest in it. In 1874 Lord Hartington gave it cautious support. This was significant because Gladstone gave up his position as Leader of the Opposition after his 1874 defeat, though remaining an MP and hugely influential. Hartington, the future 8th Duke of Devonshire but then sitting in the Commons, took his place as leader.

For most of its six-year duration Disraeli's government could be counted a success. It achieved a number of creditable social reforms, though many of them were down to Disraeli's ministers. Still, he provided the climate in which it happened. The Congress of Berlin in 1878 was his greatest triumph. He cajoled and threatened Russia into making enough concessions to avoid a war between Britain and Russia. At one point he called for his special train to be prepared so that he could travel home and prepare for war. It worked and his success made him extremely popular. Then, as with the last phase of Gladstone's 1868–74 government, things went wrong, and in particular military campaigns in Afghanistan and Zululand went badly. At the 1880 general election the Liberals won 352 seats, the Conservatives 237 and Irish Home Rulers 63. Disraeli died within a year. He is believed to have been Queen Victoria's favourite prime minister and she asked to call on him when he was dying. Disraeli declined the offer and is reputed to have said that she would have asked him to take a message to Albert, her late husband.

It was not obvious, especially to the queen, that Gladstone would be the next prime minister. Other candidates were Lord Hartington, Liberal Leader in the Commons, and Earl Granville, Liberal Leader in the Lords. The queen sent for Hartington, but he felt unable to accept, so Victoria had no option but to send for Gladstone, who had indicated that he would not serve under anyone else. She did not like him and had recently written to her private secretary, 'She will sooner *abdicate* than send for or have any *communication* with that *half mad firebrand* who would soon ruin everything and be a *Dictator*. Others but herself *may submit* to his democratic rule but *not the Queen*.'[1] So the 70-year-old Gladstone, backed by a healthy majority, started the second of his four ministries.

Gladstone had for some time intended to bring in another reform bill if and when he had the opportunity, so he took office with this very much in mind. However, he intended to do it in the second half of his ministry, and for some very good reasons. Firstly, he had a lot of other things to do, and apart from the Corrupt and Illegal Practices Bill he did not regard reform as pressing. Secondly, it seemed reasonable to suppose that as soon as the franchise was extended he would be strongly pressed to call an election, and that failure to do so would weaken his authority. Furthermore, problems in Ireland made the prospect of an early election undesirable and he feared an unwelcome, to him at least, increase in the number of radical Liberal MPs.[2] So a wait of three or four years seemed sensible.

After the Corrupt and Illegal Practices Act was on the Statute Book, pressure for further reform built up. Proponents included cabinet members Sir George Trevelyan, Sir Charles Dilke and especially Joseph Chamberlain. As told later in this chapter, Dilke was to play a key role in the negotiations about the two bills with the Conservative leader, Lord Salisbury. Chamberlain was the radical President of the Board of Trade and had been a pioneering three times mayor of Birmingham. His name features later in this chapter and elsewhere in the book. He was the father of Neville Chamberlain who became prime minister in 1937, and also of Austen Chamberlain who held a number of cabinet positions and served as leader of the Conservative MPs. A number of large public meetings were held in the autumn of 1883, and in January 1884 a delegation representing 240,000 trade unionists visited Gladstone and urged him to act on further reform.[3] They were pushing at an open door. The great man felt weary at the thought of trying to carry the bill and especially the redistribution of seats measures that would follow, but he was ready.

Not everyone was in favour of extending the franchise in the counties. Some, including some skilled workers, looked down on agricultural labourers and thought that they were not worthy of the vote, or at least not ready for it yet. It was not just agricultural workers. A considerable number of miners lived in pit villages that were located within county constituencies. This in itself was an anomaly that justified attention. A miner living in say Merthyr Tydfil, which was a borough, might have the vote, whereas another miner living in a pit village just a few miles away would not. Lord Randolph Churchill (the father of Winston) had reservations. Speaking in December 1883 he said that, 'If I saw the agricultural labourers in a great state of excitement, holding meetings, tearing down railings – then I would admit that they wanted the vote, had made up their minds to have it, and were therefore fit for it.' Chamberlain responded that such an attitude was a direct incitement to violence and outrage.[4]

Lord Salisbury (then Cranborne) had resigned over the 1867 Act, and he had probably changed his views little or perhaps even not at all, but he recognised the inevitability of extending the franchise in the counties. He was, though, determined that the Conservative Party should not suffer unfairly. It was reasonable to believe that the Liberals would be the likely gainers from the increase in the number of voters in the counties. It was also reasonable to suppose that the Conservatives would be the likely gainers from a fair redistribution of seats.

The Conservatives thought that redistribution of seats was necessary to avoid the new county urban electors swamping the agricultural element. This seemed right to them and coincidentally, or very probably not coincidentally, they thought that failure to redistribute would not be in the interests of the Conservative Party. They thought that existing voters in the counties tended to vote Conservative, and that without redistribution they would be outnumbered by the newly enfranchised agricultural workers, miners and others. These new voters were likely to support the Liberals.

Gladstone accepted the need for redistribution, but his commitment was less than that of many others. Apart from other considerations and having had a parliamentary career that had lasted almost half a century, he recalled many talented men able to enter the Commons via influence in seats with a relatively low number of voters. Palmerston was just one of the many examples. More voters and fair distribution made that less likely.

Some radicals wanted universal manhood suffrage or at least a step towards it; Gladstone, on the other hand, was with the majority who thought that this was dangerous and a big step too far. He, like many others, was wedded to a property-based franchise. He thought that such voters were people with a stake in the country, more likely to be at least basically educated and more likely to use their vote responsibly.

The bill, when introduced, was relatively straightforward. In the counties the 1867 franchise relating to freeholders, copyholders and leaseholders was unchanged, but the borough qualifications were added to them. These were the £10 occupation, the lodger and the household franchises. The £50 rental qualification was abolished. In the boroughs the so-called 'ancient right' franchise was retained – this meant that a number of elderly voters who qualified under franchises that had been abolished in the past did not have their privileges withdrawn. The passage of time had already greatly reduced their number and would continue to do so. There were one or two other minor details. The main effect of the bill was to align the franchise in the counties with the franchise in the boroughs.

The Conservatives were not happy yet accepted the principles and desirability of the bill, but they wanted redistribution of seats to be implemented concurrently with the new franchises. Gladstone planned to do it later. The Conservatives feared that a Parliament elected under the franchises in this bill would control the redistribution of seats, and that they would do so in a way that was not in the interests of the Conservative Party. Sir Michael Hicks-Beach put their worries well when he said,

'You are bound to take some measure to secure that the classes who are the best educated, the most cultivated, who pay the whole of the direct taxation, shall have some means of being heard in Parliament.'[5]

The Conservatives and not a few Liberals, including Hartington, were concerned about the extension of household suffrage to Ireland. As recounted in chapters 10 and 11 the 1867 Act did very little for John Bull's other island. The 1884 Bill redressed the balance and the effect was dramatic. The electorate in the island of Ireland was increased by 240 per cent. Roy Jenkins says that Gladstone and his supporters did this with their eyes open and rather nobly.[6] They knew that it would virtually eliminate their representation in Ireland and the next general election showed that they were correct. The 1885 election figures for Ireland were:

Liberal	0 seats
Irish Conservatives	16 seats
Irish Nationalists	86 seats
	102 seats

These figures do not include the two Conservatives returned for Dublin University, and they do not include the one Irish Nationalist who, remarkably, was returned for a Liverpool constituency. All the sixteen Conservatives were from seats in Ulster. The Irish Nationalists, who were by no means united, were bad news for both the Conservative and Liberal parties. They wanted Home Rule or independence, and in the meantime they wanted better treatment for Ireland. In pursuit of these ends they were prepared to make deals with the Conservatives, the Liberals or both, and they were prepared to obstruct either or both. An amendment to remove the equal treatment of Ireland was defeated by 332 votes to 137.

John Stuart Mill had proposed votes for women as an amendment to the 1867 Act, but this had been decisively rejected. It was proposed again as an amendment in 1884. Its chances were still not good, but this time it was taken much more seriously. It is worth noting that Charles Dilke was among those who had supported it in an 1883 motion. The 'votes for women wagon' was rolling towards the campaign of the suffragettes and the eventual triumphs in 1918 and 1928. One of the compelling arguments in favour of the 1884 amendment was that 30,000 women tenant farmers would not have the vote, but many of the agricultural labourers that they employed would[7]. Women readers of this book should brace themselves to learn that John Bright, the great radical and Liberal statesman, said that he feared the influence that priest and parson would have on female voters. He added his conviction that the alleged grievances of women were either imaginary or exaggerated.[8]

The amendment would have very probably not carried, but its chances, such as they were, died at the hand of Gladstone. He instructed his chief whip to tell his MPs that if the amendment was carried, the bill would be dropped and the government would resign. Gladstone's statement continued, 'This does not imply any judgement on the merits of the proposal, but only on its introduction into the bill. I am myself not strongly opposed to every form and degree of the proposal, but I think that if put into the bill it would give the House of Lords a case for "postponing" it and I know not how to incur such a risk.'[9] The amendment was defeated by 271 votes to 135. Lord Randolph Churchill voted in favour and Sir Charles Dilke, defying Gladstone from within the cabinet, abstained.

An opportunity missed, as most of us see it now and quite a few saw it then, was the failure to end plural voting. This was the situation when a person had more than one vote, and sometimes several votes. It was widespread. Eric J. Evans tells us that the additional qualifications included occupation, lodger, university votes and the once universal forty-shilling freehold, and he reports that it has been estimated that these 'pluralists' represented about 7 per cent of the electorate.[10] Joseph Chamberlain, the radical President of the Board of Trade, had earlier wanted the end of plural voting, despite the fact that he personally enjoyed the privilege of six votes.[11] This was by no means the highest total and a number of citizens had ten votes or more in different constituencies, though whether they could spare the time and expense to use all of them was another matter. Evans also tells us that by the early twentieth century about half a million voters were pluralists.[12] Various amendments to end or limit plural voting were proposed.

The Conservatives, under the leadership in the Commons of Sir Stafford Northcote, did not divide the House. In this they followed the precedent of the Liberals in 1867. They recognised that the bill was very popular in the country and that to oppose it in the elected chamber would be against their interests and futile. So on 26 June the bill passed the Commons and moved to the Lords. Here the Conservative peers had the power to stop the bill. All eyes were on them to see if they would.

It is probably safe to assume that Lord Salisbury and many of his Conservative colleagues were unhappy about the extension of the franchise in the counties and the equal treatment of Ireland, but they did not plan to reject the bill on those grounds. They planned to do so because it did not include the redistribution of seats, which would have been in their favour. If there were going to be more voters, they wanted them to be in the right places. There does seem to be some justice in this view.

Salisbury feared that a separate redistribution bill would only be introduced after a general election fought on the new franchises. It must be admitted that he did have some reason for suspecting this. Gladstone was known to be considering retirement, though of course he did not actually do so. The Grand Old Man would go on to serve two more separate terms as prime minister, and to finally retire at the age of 84, Britain's oldest prime minister. Piloting the forthcoming redistribution bill would be a long and arduous process. This was one of the reasons that Hartington had declined the queen's invitation to form a government.

Gladstone knew that the Conservatives would probably try to have the bill rejected in the Lords, and he tried very hard to rally enough votes to stop it happening. Among his many initiatives, and after consulting the Archbishop of Canterbury, he wrote to twelve bishops seeking their support. This paid off – ten of the twelve, plus one who had not received a letter and the two archbishops, voted in favour. Only the bishops of Gloucester and Bristol voted against.[13] Another initiative was to approach the Poet Laureate, Alfred, Lord Tennyson, whom Gladstone had recently recommended for the Peerage. Tennyson was reluctant, but he did vote in favour. It took two letters to him, one to his wife and one to his son. Gladstone did it again later when it came to a vote on the Irish Home Rule Bill. This time Tennyson responded with a chiding poem, 'Steersman, be not precipitate in thine act'.[14]

It was to no avail; Salisbury's motion of outright rejection was carried by 205 votes to 146. However, quite a few of Salisbury's supporters voted with a heavy heart, and there were grounds for thinking that they would not do it a second time. A constitutional crisis threatened and it was not wanted by Salisbury, Gladstone or most of their supporters. A compromise was in the offing.

Gladstone acted promptly and decisively. He planned to recall Parliament in late October and re-present the bill. He would then promptly follow it up with a Redistribution of Seats bill. This was provided that the two parties could reach an agreement that would give the prospect of reasonable progress. This was eminently sensible and effectively gave Salisbury what he wanted. It was what actually happened. However, there was first a period of mutual invective that was rather unedifying, and also a period of very unhelpful obstruction by the queen.

'Mend them or end them' was a memorable phrase coined by the rising Liberal backbencher John Morley. Predictably, Joseph Chamberlain was often close to the invective. He referred to 'the insolent pretensions of the hereditary caste'.[15] Even more personally he said, 'Lord Salisbury constitutes himself the spokesman of a class – of a class to which he himself belongs, who toil not, neither do they spin.'[16] It was intended as an insult and taken as such, but it is possible to construct it as a compliment. The biblical reference is to Matthew chapter 7, verses 28 (in part) and 29: 'Consider the lilies of the field, how they grow; they toil not, neither do they spin. And yet I say unto you, That even Solomon in all his glory was not arrayed like one of these.' Lord Salisbury might wittily have said that he was honoured to be favourably compared with Solomon in all his glory.

The queen adopted a partisan position, hostile to the bill and, not for the first or last time, hostile to Gladstone personally. She thought that the Lords had the right to reject the bill and that their stance represented the true feelings of the country. She considered refusing Gladstone's request for an autumn session, but did not actually do so. Her preference was for dissolution and a general election. Victoria was cross with various members of the government and Liberal backbenchers as well as with Gladstone, and during the summer she bombarded the unfortunate prime minister with a series of letters complaining about their speeches. Chamberlain and Dilke in particular attracted her displeasure. Gladstone punctiliously and politely responded to each one. On just one occasion he chose a form of words that betrayed his frustration: 'Your Majesty will readily believe that he has neither the time nor the eyesight to make himself acquainted by careful perusal with all the speeches of his colleagues.'[17]

Poor Gladstone did not deserve it, and despite the way that she treated him he behaved correctly to her. Victoria could be vitriolic in private. During this unhappy period and whilst she was at Balmoral, Gladstone made some speeches in Scotland. She wrote to Lord Ponsonby, her private secretary, in the following terms: 'The Queen is *utterly* disgusted with his *stump* oratory so unworthy of his position – almost under her very nose.' Ponsonby wisely kept this to himself and wrote to Gladstone wishing him rest 'after your most successful visit to the North'.[18]

Eventually Gladstone made his case in a paper to the queen. It is worth quoting the key part in full:

> The House of Lords has for a long period been the habitual and vigilant enemy of every Liberal Government …
>
> It cannot be supposed that to any Liberal this is a satisfactory subject of contemplation.
>
> Nevertheless some Liberals, of whom I am one, would rather choose to bear all this for the future as it has been borne in the past, than raise the question of an organic reform of the House of Lords. The interest of the party seems to be in favour of such an alteration: but it should, in my judgement, give way to a higher interest, which is national and imperial: the interest of preserving the hereditary power as it is, if only it will be content to act in such a manner as will render the preservation endurable.
>
> I do not speak of this question as one in which I can have a personal interest or share. Age, and political aversion, alike forbid it. Nevertheless, if the Lords continue to reject the Franchise Bill, it will come …
>
> I wish [an hereditary House of Lords] to continue, for the avoidance of greater evils. These evils are not only long and acrimonious controversy, difficulty in devising any satisfactory mode of reform, and delay in the general business of the country, but other and more permanent mischiefs. I desire the hereditary principle, notwithstanding its defects, to be maintained, for I think it in certain respects an element of good, a barrier against mischief. But it is not strong enough for direct conflict with the representative power, and will only come out of the conflict sorely bruised and maimed. Further; organic change of this kind in the House of Lords may strip and lay bare, and in laying bare may waken, the foundations even of the Throne.

It is not known how much Victoria was influenced by this formidable submission, but shortly after its receipt she moderated her behaviour and the views that she expressed. In fact she went further and urged the parties to compromise. She was pushing at an open door and the negotiators set to work without the weight of royal calumny resting on their shoulders. The negotiations went well, and much of the credit must rest with Dilke, who led for the Liberals. The agreement specified that a Redistribution Bill would be introduced into the Commons as soon as the Lords had passed the Franchise Act. The parties agreed in outline the terms of the forthcoming Redistribution Bill, and they agreed how work would proceed in framing it.

The Third Reform Act (more correctly the Representation of the People Act) received Royal Assent on 6 December 1884. Its provisions differed little from the bill originally introduced into the Commons. There was now a uniform household and lodger franchise – throughout the United Kingdom (including Ireland) and in both the counties and the boroughs. Furthermore, all adult males occupying land or tenements worth at least £10 a year were entitled to vote. Plural voting was retained and so was the ancient rights franchise.

The total electorate was raised from around 3,000,000 to around 5,000,000 or slightly more (estimates vary). About 60 per cent of adult men or slightly more (again, estimates vary) had the vote. The biggest change was in Ireland where the size of the electorate more than tripled.

It is a mistake to overlook the importance of the Redistribution of Seats Act 1885. This perhaps happens because many of us know that there were three great reform acts in the nineteenth century – those of 1832, 1867 and 1884, and the Redistribution Act was not one of them. It was, though, vastly important and it might easily have been made part of the Third Reform Act. It would have been if the Conservatives had had their way. Dilke considered it to be more important than the Reform Act.

Following the compromise and the passage of the Reform Act, three politically neutral boundary commissions were appointed and set to work. There were separate commissions for England and Wales, Scotland and Ireland. Their terms of reference, necessarily simplified and summarised, included the following:

- So far as practicable they were to ensure that each division of a county had a similar population.
- Where there were populous localities of an urban character they were to be included in the same division of a county. This was unless there were particular problems which should override this.
- The divisions were to be as compact as possible.
- The divisions should be based on well known local areas, such as petty sessional divisions or aggregations of parishes.
- Boundaries should be adjusted as appropriate.
- The divisions were to be named after an important town or place within it.

The lengthy Appendix D of this book gives full seat-by-seat details of the redistribution. The principles of it were as follows.

Total Number of Seats and Their Division within the United Kingdom

The total number of seats was set at 670, which was an increase of twelve on the 1867 figure of 658. However, since 1867 three two-member seats had been disenfranchised for corruption, so the Commons previously had 652 members. Then as now it was one of the world's biggest legislatures. The United States population is currently in excess of 316 million, but it gets by with 100 senators and 435 members of the House of Representatives. The number of seats in Scotland increased by twelve to a total of seventy. The number of seats in Ireland was unchanged at 103.

Estimates vary but it is often said that there were about 3 million electors before the Act and about 5 million after the Act. We should always mistrust convenient round numbers, but if they are correct, there was one MP for each 4,681 electors before the Act and one for each 7,462 electors afterwards.

Boroughs with Low Population

All boroughs with a population of less than 15,000 were placed in the county in which they lay and ceased to have separate representation. Eighty-one boroughs in England lost separate representation for this reason, and so too were two boroughs (burghs) in Scotland and twenty-two in Ireland.

Disenfranchised for Corruption

The boroughs of Sandwich and Macclesfield were disenfranchised for corruption. They were placed in the appropriate county divisions.

Other Boroughs Merged into County Divisions

Four boroughs that included significant surrounding countryside were merged into county divisions. They were Aylesbury, Cricklade, East Retford and Shoreham.

Boroughs with a Population Between 15,000 and 50,000

Boroughs with a population between 15,000 and 50,000 lost one of their two members and became single-member constituencies.

Boroughs with a Population in Excess of 50,000

Boroughs with a population in excess of 50,000 continued to be two-member constituencies.

London

Arguably the biggest changes of all were in the capital city, which had been woefully under-represented. Full details are in Appendix D under Middlesex, but the seats, which with one exception had all been returning two members, were divided into a bigger number of seats, each returning one member. Marylebone had been the UK's constituency with the biggest electorate. This two-member seat was divided into eight single-member seats. Tower Hamlets and Finsbury were both changed from single two-member seats to seven single-member seats. The exception was the City of London, so often different in many ways. This four-member constituency was reduced to a two-member constituency. The representation of Middlesex, including London, was raised from eighteen MPs to forty-seven MPs.

Large Provincial Cities

Large cities were divided according to their approximate populations. In some cases some surrounding areas were added to them. As with London the consequences were very significant. Once again full details are given in Appendix D. Liverpool changed from a single three-member seat to nine single-member seats.

Counties

Many more seats were allocated to the counties, which were divided into single-member divisions. The number of seats allocated to counties were made broadly proportionate to their populations. Yorkshire got twenty-six seats and Lancashire got twenty-three. Rutland was one of two counties reduced from two MPs to one. Herefordshire was reduced from a three-member seat to two single-member seats.

Universities

There were no changes affecting the universities.

The increase in the number of single-member seats had the consequence of ending the cosy arrangement where Liberals and Conservatives each entered just one candidate in a two-member constituency. There was a great reduction in the number of uncontested seats – just thirteen at the 1885 general election.

There were two wings to the Liberal Party. One was the Whigs, many of whom came from great families, and the landed gentry. Hartington was a prominent example. He was the heir of the Duke of Devonshire and would succeed to the title in 1891. The radicals were the other wing of the party and the name gives a good indication of their policies. Joseph Chamberlain, whose nickname was 'Radical Joe', and John Bright were prominent radicals. The radicals had been gaining ground at the expense of the Whigs, and the increase in single-member seats speeded up the process. This was because the Liberals had frequently entered a Whig and a radical in two-member seats. When it was a single-member seat the Liberal candidate was more likely to be a radical. Despite this, the advance of the radicals took some time to be reflected at the top of the party. The Whigs dominated for some time.

A consequence of the Second Reform Act had been that after 1867 politics became more organised. Political parties and the way that they were run became more important, and the activities and views of individual MPs and candidates less so. There were more voters and they tended to pay attention to national parties and national leaders. The Third Reform Act added a further 2 million voters and the Redistribution Act moved them round. Constituencies were closer to a uniform size. So not surprisingly this accelerated the trend started in 1867. Many regret this, but it was inevitable. Today the great majority of electors cast their votes on the basis of party policies and competence, and their assessment of the party leaders. Local candidates make only a marginal difference. Indeed, many voters would be hard pressed to name the MP for their constituency. Very few could name the unelected candidates.

The distribution of seats had previously been wrong – the words ludicrous and scandalous are not inappropriate, and the 1867 Act had only made a small difference. The Redistribution of Seats Act 1885 was politically neutral and did the job. It was efficient and fair. An interesting example is the idyllic but relatively sparsely populated county of Cornwall. Prior to 1832 it returned the extraordinary number of forty-four MPs, forty-two representing boroughs and two the county. The 1885 Act gave it seven MPs, one representing a borough and six the county. There have since been further necessary boundary adjustments, but the pattern of seats created in 1885 is still very much recognisable today.

Gladstone had good reason to be pleased with what he and his party had achieved in the course of two years. Three Acts of Parliament had transformed parliamentary elections. The Corrupt and Illegal Practices Act had enormously reduced corruption. The Representation of the People Act had brought justice to the counties and enfranchised something like an extra 2 million voters. The Redistribution of Seats Act was a fair, necessary and massive measure. Sir Edward Hamilton, Gladstone's principal Downing Street secretary, wrote, 'Mr G went off to Hawarden with Herbert. He never quitted London in greater personal triumph. No one could have achieved what he has done, and at the same time kept his party completely in hand.'[19] Herbert was the youngest son of the prime minister, a future home secretary and in 1910 the first Governor General of the Union of South Africa. William Gladstone, on the other hand, was not quite so pleased. According to Roy Jenkins[20] he never took particular pride in the Seats Bill, regarding it as little more than a key to unlock the door to franchise enlargement.

The no-longer weary Gladstone did not retire, but at the age of nearly 76 led his party in the general election held from 24 November to 18 December 1885. He was not rewarded for his contribution to parliamentary reform, though other issues were probably in the minds of the electors. In particular he was blamed for the delay in sending a relief force to rescue the greatly admired General Gordon who, whilst acting against the wishes of the government, had been besieged in Khartoum for nearly a year. The rescuers arrived two days after the city had fallen and Gordon had been killed. Gladstone was sometimes known affectionately as the 'GOM' (Grand Old Man); some people reversed the order of the letters and made it 'MOG' (Murderer of Gordon). The queen had been furious with her prime minister. She sent him an angry telegram of rebuke and did not use the customary cypher. It was handed to him by the station master of Carnforth Railway Station.

Gladstone had enjoyed a substantial majority in the House of Commons, but after the 1885 election and after a brief interval he headed a minority government dependent on the support of the Irish Nationalists. What he and many others had feared came to pass. The full distribution of seats was as follows:

Liberal	319 seats
Conservative	247 seats
Irish Parliamentary	86 seats
Independent Liberal	11 seats
Independent Liberal and Crofters Party	4 seats
Independent Conservative	2 seats
Lib–Lab	1 seat

Gladstone's biggest clash with the House of Lords was not far off. What happened is told in Chapter 15.

NOTES

1.   Roy Jenkins, *Gladstone*, p.435.
2.   Charles Seymour, *Electoral Reform in England and Wales*, p.459.
3.   Ibid., p.460.
4.   Ibid., p.462.
5.   Ibid., p.468.
6.   Roy Jenkins, *Gladstone*, p.488.
7.   Charles Seymour, *Electoral Reform in England and Wales*, p.477.
8.   Ibid., p.476.
9.   Roy Jenkins, *Gladstone*, p.492.
10. Eric J. Evans, *Parliamentary Reform c.1770–1918*, p.70.
11. Ibid., p.71.
12. Ibid., p.72.
13. Roy Jenkins, *Gladstone*, p.493.
14. Ibid., p.493.
15. Ibid., p.496.
16. John W. Derry, *Parliamentary Reform*, p.51.
17. Roy Jenkins, *Gladstone*, p.495.
18. Ibid., p.495.
19. Ibid., p.499.
20. Ibid., p.499.

Enter Mr Bradlaugh: The Oaths Act 1888

At one time elected representatives were required to take three oaths before taking their seat in the House of Commons. Peers had to do the same before taking their seat in the House of Lords. For many years religious restrictions effectively barred persons of certain faiths who were unwilling to take a Christian oath, in particular Jews and Quakers, though no doubt some members were willing to compromise their beliefs by taking an oath that did not conform with their convictions. In practice the House of Commons had sometimes been willing to turn a blind eye provided that the prospective member behaved in a decorous way. Among those so accommodated were the Quaker MP Joseph Pease who was allowed to affirm, and the Jewish MPs Baron Lionel de Rothschild and David Salomons, who took the oath omitting the words 'on the true faith of a Christian'. This tolerance was not extended to prospective MPs with no faith at all, namely atheists.

Enter the atheist Charles Bradlaugh, who was elected for Northampton at the 1880 general election. For the next few years the matter of his right to take his seat took up a lot of parliamentary time, weakened Gladstone's government and made the House of Commons look exceedingly silly. He did eventually take his seat and in 1888 was instrumental in the passage of the Oaths Act. This allowed prospective members to affirm, which is a non-religious statement, as an alternative to taking the oath, and established the right of successful candidates of all faiths or none to take their seats. Bradlaugh was a remarkable man. His story and his ultimately successful campaign deserve to be recounted in some detail.

Charles Bradlaugh was born in 1833. He left school at the age of 11 and became a teenage Sunday School teacher at his local Anglican church. When 16 he became worried about some doctrinal problems concerning the Thirty-Nine Articles, the doctrines of the Church of England, and discussed his concerns with the vicar. This man, perhaps reasonably, suspended him as a Sunday School teacher and as a consequence his father required him to leave home. He became a convinced atheist and at 17 published a pamphlet and started giving lectures. He was rapidly recognised as an exceptionally compelling speaker.

At 25 he became the President of the London Secular Society and at 27 he was editor of the secularist newspaper *The National Reformer*. At 33 he was the co-founder of the National Secular Society. In 1877 he was the co-publisher of a pamphlet advocating birth control. This resulted in his being prosecuted for publishing an obscene libel. He was convicted and given a heavy fine and six months' imprisonment, but the conviction was overturned on a legal technicality.

Among the many causes that he advocated were trade unionism, republicanism, women's suffrage and Irish Home Rule. He was a Liberal and opposed socialism, a stance that baffled many of his allies. Bradlaugh was a very effective campaigner who courted controversy. His meetings were sometimes banned and he periodically used great ingenuity to circumnavigate the restrictions. On one occasion his planned meeting in a seaside town was banned, but the area affected by the ban stopped at the point on the beach where the sea started. He hired a boat, moved it a few yards offshore and addressed his supporters through a loudhailer. It is tempting, but of course frivolous, to suggest that his actions might a century later have inspired Radio Caroline, the pirate radio station that broadcast from an offshore position.

Bradlaugh contested the 1874 general election in Northampton and was not successful. When the results of the poll were read out his supporters suspected a fix and demanded a recount. The demand was denied and this resulted in a riot in the town square. The mayor read the Riot Act, which did not have the desired effect. Troops were called and the crowd only dispersed when shots were fired over the heads of the rioters. These events became known as the Bradlaugh Riots.

He contested the 1880 general election, again for Northampton, and this time he was elected. Bradlaugh asked to affirm instead of taking the Oath of Allegiance, and quoted the Evidence Further Amendment Act 1869 which he contended made this permissible. Speaker Brand was unsure and referred the matter to the House for a decision. As a result a select committee was set up.

The committee, which had sixteen members, split on party lines. Eight Liberals sided with Bradlaugh. Seven Conservatives and one Liberal opposed him. The chairman, who was a Conservative, used his casting vote to deny him the right to affirm. Bradlaugh responded by notifying the Speaker that he would attend the House in order to take the oath. Prior to doing this he wrote an open letter to *The Times* newspaper. In it he said that it would have been hypocritical to voluntarily take the oath 'including words of idle and meaningless character' without protest, but that he would now do so and 'regard myself as bound not by the letter of the words, but by the spirit which the affirmation would have conveyed had I been permitted to use it'.

Bradlaugh's opponents were offended by the letter and the Conservative MP Sir Henry Drummond Wolff rose to object to the administration of the oath. The prime minister, William Gladstone, then moved that a second Select Committee be set up to consider the matter further, and this was done.

Bradlaugh appeared before the Select Committee and said that if it decided that he did not have the right to affirm, he would take the oath and regard it as binding on his conscience. The Committee's report stated that in its opinion 'the House ought to prevent Bradlaugh taking the Oath'. It went on to recommend that if Bradlaugh sought to affirm he should be allowed to do so, in order that a legal action could be taken to clarify the law.

After two days of debate the House decided that Bradlaugh should not be allowed to take the oath and should not be allowed to affirm. This was carried by 275 votes to 230. In favour were 210 Conservatives, 34 Liberals and 31 Irish Home Rulers. Against were 218 Liberals, 10 Irish Home Rulers and 2 Conservatives. Bradlaugh was then permitted to address the House from behind the bar, which was technically outside the Chamber. He made a very good speech from a very difficult position, but the decision had been taken and it made no difference.

Bradlaugh was then told by the Speaker to withdraw, which he did not do. He said that he 'respectfully refused to obey an order which was against the law'. A motion was then passed that Bradlaugh be taken into custody, and he was briefly imprisoned in a small cell under Big Ben.

The Northampton seat was declared vacant and four successive by-elections ensued, all of them won by Bradlaugh. He had the distinction of winning elections for the same seat five times in the course of a single Parliament. The whole thing was a farce, though of course a farce with very serious implications. On one occasion he affirmed, took his place on the Liberal benches and participated in a vote. He was then unseated. Another time he marched up to the table, took a paper from his pocket and administered the oath to himself. At one time four legal actions were in progress.[1] He sued the deputy sergeant-at-arms for the alleged assault during what he contended was his illegal arrest. He was being prosecuted for blasphemy. There was an action to impose bankruptcy penalties on him in connection with his illegal vote, and finally his supporters were challenging the right of the House to exclude him.

Bradlaugh was re-elected for Northampton at the 1885 general election. This time the new speaker, Arthur Wellesley Peel, refused to hear any objections and swore him in as an MP. On this occasion he did not seek to affirm. This ended the whole ridiculous saga. For much of it he had enjoyed the support of most of the Liberal Party and probably the country at large. Against him had been the Archbishop of Canterbury, many senior Anglican and Roman Catholic churchmen and most of the Conservative Party. A notable exception was Lord Beaconsfield (Disraeli), who correctly warned that Bradlaugh would be turned into a martyr.

In the opinion of Roy Jenkins,[2] 'The House of Commons then proceeded to coat its previous prejudice and hysteria with a sentimental surface which made its overall performance no more attractive.' Ramsay Macdonald, writing in *The Dictionary of National Biography*, said of Bradlaugh that 'he became very popular with the House of Commons'. He had a special interest in Indian affairs and was generally accepted as an able and effective MP. In 1888 he secured the passage of a new Oaths Act. This put beyond doubt the right of members of the Commons and the Lords to affirm. It also clarified and extended the law concerning witnesses in civil and criminal cases.

Bradlaugh died in 1891 at the early age of 57. His funeral was attended by 3,000 mourners, including the 21-year-old Mohandas Gandhi, later known by the honorific title Mahatma, and as one might expect he was buried in unconsecrated ground. He was a colourful character and his small but significant contribution to parliamentary reform justifies his name appearing in the heading of this chapter.

NOTES

1.   Roy Jenkins, *Gladstone*, p.451.
2.   Ibid., p.452.

15

The 1911 Parliament Act and What Came Before

The main purpose of this chapter is to give details of the Parliament Act 1911, which placed a legislative curb on the powers of the House of Lords. In addition, an account is given of the tumultuous events that took place between the Liberal landslide in the January/February 1906 general election and the passage of the Act. However, before this it is helpful to set the scene and explain what happened in the nineteenth century.

As explained in the first chapter of this book, for many centuries the House of Lords ranked at least equally with the House of Commons, and it can be argued that it ranked more highly. Some figures support this conclusion. Sir Robert Walpole took office in 1721 and is generally acknowledged to have been the first prime minister. He held office continuously for the next twenty-one years, still the longest tenure of any of them. Earl Grey took the position in 1830 and was in office when the First Reform Act was passed. He sat in the Lords and was the twenty-third prime minister. Eight of the first twenty-three sat in the Commons, fourteen in the Lords and Pitt the Elder moved from one to the other as the Earl of Chatham. The nine prime ministers after Grey covered the period from 1834 to 1902 when Lord Salisbury retired. Four sat in the Commons and three in the Lords. Disraeli and Lord John Russell spent time in each.

In the nineteenth century it was common for at least half the cabinet to sit in the Lords. In 1874 six out of Disraeli's cabinet of twelve sat in that place, and in Gladstone's 1880 cabinet it was seven out of twelve. At this time Britannia ruled the waves and a great deal of the atlas was coloured pink. How did Disraeli and Gladstone manage with just twelve cabinet ministers? David Cameron needed something like twice as many, and with a further half-dozen or so able to attend cabinet meetings. Perhaps we have something to learn from our nineteenth century forebears. What is the explanation? It is of course partly that modern prime ministers have large cabinets for party and political reasons. Perhaps we should reflect on W.S. Gilbert's words in *The Gondoliers*, 'When everyone is somebody, then no one's anybody.'

Britain had and has an unwritten constitution, and the potentially explosive relationship between the two Houses of Parliament generally worked because of conventions and understandings. In the nineteenth century the Lords would warn, cajole, advise, delay, amend and perhaps reject once, but it would ultimately accept the will of the elected House if it had the support of the people. The Lords claimed, though, the right to block constitutional changes. The convention was that the Lords would not deny 'supply' to the government of the day. This meant that money bills would not be blocked. What constituted 'supply' could be a contentious question, and it was a key issue in the bitterness leading up to the 1911 Parliament Act. The views of Lord Salisbury are instructive. He was Conservative prime minister three times and was a key figure when the Lords rejected Gladstone's two Home Rule Bills. He said the following when recommending that the Lords reject the 1872 Ballot Act:

> I am rejecting the Bill on the second reading for this reason. It appears to me of vital necessity that our acceptance of bills to which we are opposed should be regulated on some principle. If we listen to the Liberals we should accept all important bills which had passed the House of Commons by a large majority. But that would in effect be to efface the House of Lords. Another principle – which is, so far as I can gather, what commends itself to Derby – is to watch newspapers, public meetings and so forth, and only to reject when 'public opinion' thus ascertained, growls very loud. This plan gives a premium to bluster and will bring the House into contempt. The plan which I prefer is frankly to acknowledge that the nation is our master, though the House of Commons is not, and to yield to our own opinion only when the judgement of the nation has been challenged at the polls and decidedly expressed.[1]

In the nineteenth century the House of Lords had a permanent Tory, then Conservative majority, something that was made even more pronounced by the defection of the Liberal Unionist peers over the issue of Home Rule for Ireland. The Conservative Party eventually became the Conservative and Unionist Party. There were two reasons for the Conservative preponderance before this. Prior to Earl Grey's ministry in 1830 there had been for sixty years an almost continuous succession of Tory governments. This naturally led to the creation of many Tory peers. The second reason was that rich, landed aristocrats, sitting in the House of Lords and with vested interests to defend, tended to lean towards conservatives with a small c and a large c – meaning both conservatives and the Conservative Party.

It was only a problem when there was a Liberal government. In the event of a Conservative government the various parts of it agreed with each other, or if they did not the problems were resolved internally. There was then no constitutional issue. In 1894 Lord Rosebery, who succeeded Gladstone as prime minister, wrote to the queen, 'When the Conservative Party is in power, there is practically no House of Lords, but the moment a Liberal government is formed, this harmless body assumes an active life and its activity is entirely exercised in opposition to the government.'[2]

If a compromise was not possible and if neither House was willing to concede, the only way out for the Commons was the creation of new peers. This was threatened in the crises of 1830/32 and 1909/11. In both cases the threat and the monarch's promise were sufficient, and new peers were not actually created.

Monarchs hated the idea of large-scale creation of peers, but William IV and George V very reluctantly gave undertakings that if all else failed they would do it. The reality of large-scale creation would devalue the House of Lords and pose a threat to the hereditary principle, and of course the monarchy depends on the hereditary principle. If it could be done in one place, it might be considered in another place. Leading Whigs and Liberals also did not like the prospect, though a few radicals might have. Gladstone did not ask the queen to create more peers in 1884, but she would undoubtedly have reacted with horror. An objection that is seldom mentioned is the question of whether it might be necessary more than once. Suppose that a large number of Liberal peers were created to allow the passage of a blocked Liberal bill, then suppose that a Liberal majority in the Lords blocked a bill from a future Conservative government. Would more Conservative peers be created? The House of Lords could potentially grow and grow. It is growing and growing in the twenty-first century, but for different reasons.

Chapter 13 concluded by stating that in 1885 a further clash with the Lords was not far off. It came when the Lords overwhelmingly defeated Gladstone's second Home Rule Bill in 1893. The result of the 1885 election was that the Liberals had the most seats, but that the Irish held the balance of power. Gladstone had lost authority and the queen sent for Lord Salisbury, who on 23 June 1885 commenced the first of his three ministries. It was to be very short.

Gladstone had come to the conclusion that Ireland had to have Home Rule, a view that was not shared by many members of his party. He hoped that in the national interest, as he saw it, the Conservatives might move in this direction, but they did not do so. The issue caused the new Conservative government to fall at the first hurdle. It happened immediately after the opening of the new session of Parliament, and the cause was an amendment concerning approval of the government's programme as set out in the Queen's Speech. The amendment regretted the omission from the speech of any measures benefitting the rural labourer, and it became known as the 'three acres and a cow amendment'. Despite the wording it was well understood that the real issue was whether or not Gladstone should form a Home Rule government. Some Liberals voted against, and Hartington the former party leader was one of them. Seventy-six Liberals were absent or abstained, but the amendment was carried by seventy-nine votes. Salisbury was out and the Liberals were split.

Gladstone's third ministry commenced on 1 February 1886 and it finished on 20 July in the same year, just 170 days later. Its end followed the failure of his first Home Rule Bill to get past the Commons. The voting was 341 to 311 against. Chamberlain, Hartington and Bright were among the Liberals who opposed it. In a House containing 670 members, only 18 failed to vote. The split in the Liberal Party saw a sizeable minority, including Chamberlain and Hartington, break away to form the Liberal Unionists. They were joined by a number of Liberal peers. The Conservatives won the resulting election and with the support of the Liberal Unionists stayed in power for all but three of the following nineteen years. The Liberal Unionists were eventually subsumed into what was named the Conservative and Unionist Party.

Gladstone returned to Downing Street following the 1892 election. The Liberals had 313 seats and the Irish 81. Taken together they had a majority of forty-one over the combined Conservatives and Unionists. There were four other MPs. At the age of 82 it was Gladstone's last hurrah, and in his election address Lord Randolph Churchill had called him an old man in a hurry.[3] The remark was spot on. He was in a hurry and it was to get Home Rule for Ireland. The Unionists had already left the Liberals and part of Gladstone's cabinet was not enthusiastic, but a second Home Rule Bill was introduced into the Commons. It aroused considerable passion over eighty-two sittings and the shocking spectacle of about forty members fighting just before the final vote was taken on 1 September 1893.[4] The government majority was thirty-four, with three Liberals voting against and two abstaining. Unlike its predecessor the bill had passed the Commons, but Gladstone must have known that its chances of passing the Lords were very remote.

The bill then went straight to the Lords. Roy Jenkins perceptively and with his customary elegant turn of phrase says that, 'the House of Lords indulged in one of the seismic actions of its history. Yet it was an earthquake almost without noise or excitement, if that is a possible concept.'[5] They spent only four days on the bill, compared with eighty-two days spent by the Commons, and it came to a vote on 8 September. The case for frustrating the wish of the elected House was well put by Hartington, now sitting as the Duke of Devonshire and leader of the Unionists in the Lords. He said:

> You know that not being a Representative Assembly, and not backed by the strength which a representative character gives to a Legislative Body, and not sharing altogether the democratic principles which are making progress in this as in other countries, it would be unwise, impolite, and unpatriotic to insist upon your personal political convictions by enforcing them in opposition to what is believed to be the decided view of the country.

He went on to say that the country did not support this particular bill.

The strength of feeling in the Lords against Home Rule can be gauged by the fact that although dismissal of the bill was a foregone conclusion, no fewer than 460 peers took part in the vote. At the time 560 peers had the right to do so. The backwoodsmen came to London and did their duty as they saw it. Rejection was by the crushing vote of 419 to 41. Not a single bishop voted in favour, and seventeen of them and both archbishops voted against. Twenty-two dukes voted against and none were in favour.

This time there was no talk of creating peers to secure the will of the Commons. The Lords vote was absolutely decisive and Home Rule was out of the question for some time to come. The demand had not gone away though, and it almost came to a civil war in the run-up to the 1914–18 conflict. What happened showed the continuing power and willingness of the Lords to override the wishes of the Commons. It is perhaps fair to acknowledge that the will of the Commons was faltering, though as has often been said a majority of one is enough. It is also fair to say that the Lords did perhaps reflect the will of the people outside Ireland.

Gladstone resigned as prime minister six months after the Lords vote. The reason was that in a cabinet decision on the naval estimates he was in a minority of one. He was very deaf and losing his sight. At the time of his resignation he was 84 years and 63 days old, which made him Britain's oldest ever prime minister (Palmerston was 80 years and 364 days and Churchill was 80 years and 127 days). The great man continued as an MP until the 1895 election but did not attend Parliament. He was permanently paired with Charles Villiers, a Liberal Unionist aged 91 and also permanently absent. Villiers was still an MP when he died at the age of 95.

Gladstone wrote that his resignation meeting with the queen was 'long and courteous, but of little meaning'. She had a final snub for what was probably her least favourite prime minister. She asked his foreign secretary, Lord Rosebery, to form the next government, and did so without asking Gladstone's advice. According to Roy Jenkins the resigning prime minister was rather hurt and, if asked, would have recommended Earl Spencer, the First Lord of the Admiralty.[6]

Rosebery served as prime minister for a rather ineffectual fifteen months, and then it was ten years of Conservative government under Lord Salisbury followed by his nephew Arthur Balfour. The issue of the role of the House of Lords lay dormant, but it then returned to sour the political landscape.

Arthur Balfour's Conservative government was weakened by internal dissention over free trade and he ended it with his resignation on 4 December 1905. Henry Campbell-Bannerman led the Liberals into power with a minority government, and immediately called a general election for January/February 1906. The result was humiliation for the disunited Conservatives and Unionists, and a landslide victory for the Liberals. The results were:

Liberal	397 seats
Conservative	131 seats
Liberal Unionist	25 seats
Labour	29 seats
Irish Parliamentary	82 seats
Other	6 seats

The Liberals had a majority of 241 over the Conservatives and Unionists, and 104 over all the other parties combined. It left a recently elected Liberal government, with a radical programme and an enormous majority, facing a Conservative-dominated House of Lords. In 1906 a total of 602 peers were entitled to vote in the House of Lords. Of these 355 of them described themselves as Conservatives, 124 as Liberal Unionists and 88 as Liberal.[7] It was not hard to foresee trouble ahead. It was also not hard to foresee that the usual Lords reason for blocking a bill would not be valid. This was that the government did not have a recent mandate and that the country did not support it.

Balfour made his position clear at an early stage. In an election speech on 15 January 1906 he said that, 'the Great Unionist Party should still control, whether in power or in opposition, the destinies of this great Empire'. In opposition and with the support of the Conservative peers under their leader, Lord Lansdowne, he put his words into practice. During the next three years no measures that did not have Balfour's approval reached the Statute Book without being drastically amended. Money Bills were the only exception. In a later speech Lloyd George said that, 'the House of Lords is not the watchdog of the constitution. It is Mr Balfour's poodle.' It was an apt and memorable phrase and *Mr Balfour's Poodle* is the title of one of Roy Jenkins' earlier and best books.

A very clear and early example was the fate of the Education Bill, which was the first major bill introduced by the new government. It was intended to remedy some of the grievances felt by Nonconformists following the previous government's 1902 Education Act. As well as upsetting the Conservatives, it was opposed by both the Anglican and Roman Catholic churches. It was put forward by a government that a few months previously had won one of the biggest general election victories in history. The opposition in the Commons harried it unmercifully and forced the government into extensive use of the guillotine. It spent twenty days in committee and was eventually given a third reading by 369 votes to 177. In the Commons Balfour had said:

> The real discussion of this question is not now in this House and has not been for some time; the real discussion must be elsewhere; and everybody is perfectly reconciled to the fact that another place is going to deal with large tracts of the Bill which we have not found time to even touch upon … it is in the highest degree improbable that the Bill will come back in the shape in which it leaves us. The honourable Gentleman who has just sat down controverted a prophecy of mine that the Bill will never pass. Does he think that the Bill will ever pass? I do not think that he or anybody else does.

It was an extraordinary performance by the leader of a party that had just been slaughtered in a general election. It was, though, a prophecy that came to pass. The Lords made so many fundamental amendments that the bill came back to the Commons badly mangled. In fact so severe were the changes that it arguably strengthened the 1902 Act that it was intended to ameliorate. The Commons then voted by 416 votes to 107 to reject the Lords' amendments en bloc. The Upper House swiftly responded by approving the motion 'that this House do insist on its amendments to which the Commons have disagreed'.

It was an impasse and the government withdrew the bill. The angry prime minister said:

It is plainly intolerable that a Second Chamber should, while one party in the State is in power, be its willing servant, and when that party has received an unmistakable and emphatic condemnation by the country, the House of Lords should then be able to neutralise, thwart, and distort the policy which the electors have approved ... But, Sir, the resources of the British Constitution are not wholly exhausted, the resources of the House of Commons are not exhausted, and I say with conviction that a way must be found, a way will be found, by which the will of the people expressed through their elected representatives in this House will be made to prevail.

At this point the government missed a trick. It could have requested a dissolution and asked the people for a specific mandate to Reform the House of Lords and reduce its powers. This would almost certainly have been given by a large majority. The king, faced with such a mandate, would surely but reluctantly have agreed to the creation of peers if necessary. When the issue came to a head in 1909/11 the government was less popular and its mandate was less recent. Not asking for dissolution was a mistake.

The Lords followed this up a few months later by refusing passage of the Plural Voting Bill. This was an attempt to end the anachronism of one man having the right to exercise several votes. There were no fewer than seventeen franchises in force, though the right to exercise some of them was held by tiny numbers. It is reasonable to think that a man legitimately casting several votes was more likely than not to be both relatively rich and a Conservative.

The third session of the 1906 Parliament saw the Lords reject a further Education Bill and also the Licensing Bill. This provided for a compulsory reduction in the number of public houses in relation to the population of the area that they served. Compensation for licences terminated would last for fourteen years and would be funded by a levy on the liquor trade. The temperance movement liked it, but the furious liquor trade was a traditional supporter of the Conservative Party.

Lord Salisbury, the former prime minister, observed that he felt no more inclined to sleepiness at his home in Hatfield, where there were more than fifty bedrooms, than at a seaside villa with perhaps a dozen.[8] It is an interesting analogy and has relevance to the introduction of 24-hour drinking in the twenty-first century. Has it now led to an increase in drunkenness and bad behaviour? Many would say that it has. Be that as it may, the Lords rejected the Licensing Bill by 272 votes to 96.

There was a change of prime minister during this rather humiliating period. Following a short illness Campbell-Bannerman resigned on 3 April 1908, and died just nineteen days later whilst still in Downing Street. His successor was Herbert Henry Asquith, sometimes known as Herbert Asquith, sometimes as Henry Asquith and sometimes as H.H. Asquith. In this book he is referred to as just Asquith. He held the office of prime minister until 5 December 1916, which was the longest continuous term between the premierships of Lord Liverpool (1812 to 1827) and Margaret Thatcher (1979–90). This was the man who would preside over the Liberal government during the volatile period culminating in the passage of the 1911 Parliament Act.

The turbulence started with a vengeance with the presentation of Lloyd George's budget in April 1909. Like so many chancellors before and since he needed more money. One of the reasons was that the country was engaged in an arms race with Germany, and each country was building expensive battleships. Another was the cost of the recently introduced old-age pensions, which were at that time funded by taxation and not by national insurance contributions. They still are to a considerable extent, and it continues to cause problems: problems that due to an ageing population will intensify. The increased naval expenditure was resented by many Liberals. It was politically expedient that the extra revenue be raised by taxing the rich and the privileged – the sort of people who sat in the House of Lords, together with their relatives, friends and supporters, and others too of course. To be fair to the peers, many of them genuinely considered that some of the budget proposals were unfair, vindictive, divisive, dangerous, likely to harm the country and verging on the unconstitutional.

The need for extra revenue was likely to continue, and indeed to increase. Once again this is a state of affairs familiar to modern chancellors. With this in mind Lloyd George's proposals included the following (the sums are expressed in pre-decimal currency). As readers of this book undoubtedly know, there were 12 pennies in a shilling and 20 shillings in a pound.

Income Tax
The rate remained at 9d in the pound for incomes under £2,000, but there was a new rate of 1s 2d for incomes over £2,000. There was a new £10 children's allowance for incomes under £500.

Super Tax
This was a new tax to be levied at the rate of 6d in the pound on the amount by which all incomes of £5,000 or more exceeded £3,000.

Death Duties
Death duties, and the associated legacy, succession and settled estate duties were raised. Estates over £1 million pounds were to pay a total duty of approximately 25 per cent.

Land Taxes
These were new and there were three of them:

1. There was to be a tax of 20 per cent on the unearned income increment in land values. It was to be paid on death or when the land was sold.
2. There was to be a capital tax of ½d in the pound on the value of undeveloped land and minerals.
3. There was to be a 10 per cent reversion duty on any benefit which came to a lessor at the end of a lease.

Concessions on the first two of these were made at the committee stage.

Other

There was a reduction of £3 million pounds in the sinking fund payment.

Taxes on alcohol and tobacco were to be increased.

There were to be taxes on car and motorcycle licences, and a tax on petrol.

The new super tax would raise the most revenue, and the death duties the second most. It was, though, the new land taxes that provoked the most outrage. Landowners, the aristocracy, the rich and the Conservatives did not like them one bit, and neither did some Liberals. They correctly saw that the budget was intended to be redistributive, and not just designed to adjust the government's revenue.

The Conservatives were vastly outnumbered in the Commons, but they put up an unprecedented fight on the Finance Bill. They had no chance of succeeding with amendments that the government was not willing to concede, but they forced no fewer than 554 divisions. It took seventy parliamentary days to get the bill through the Commons, and this interfered with other business. The House regularly sat very late and on several occasions it sat all night. Procedural devices to delay business were used. The end result, though, was not in doubt and the bill was approved by the Commons on the very late date of 4 November.

Opinion is divided about whether or not Lloyd George and the government intended to provoke the Lords into rejecting the budget, and thus bring about the constitutional crisis that would lead to the reduction of their powers. The majority view is that it was not their intention. It was, though, what happened. Government ministers campaigned to get public opinion on their side, and Lloyd George in particular made a number of provocative speeches. The most famous was at Limehouse on 30 July where he used excoriating language to lambast the opponents of his budget. His remarks included 'a fully-equipped duke costs as much to keep up as two dreadnoughts [battleships] but they are much less easy to scrap'. This caused great offence and the king sent a letter of rebuke to the prime minister.

The constitutional convention, but not the law, was that the Lords could amend a money bill, but would ultimately accept the will of the Commons. They had not rejected a money bill for 250 years. This time they said that it was not entirely a money bill, and most peers thought that they would be within their rights if they denied it passage. This is exactly what happened: by 350 votes to 75 on 30 November. The decision made some Conservatives uneasy and fearful of the consequences. Lord Knollys, the king's private secretary, told the clerk to the privy council that he thought the Lords mad.[9]

The inevitable result of the Lords' vote was immediate dissolution followed by an election. On 2 December Asquith moved that 'the action of the House of Lords in refusing to pass into law the financial provision made by this House for the service of the year is a breach of the constitution and a usurpation of the rights of the Commons'. The election was held in January 1910, and the Conservatives did not enter it in a mood of despondency. The government had become unpopular and had lost a string of by-elections. The Conservatives were confident that at the very least they would regain many of the seats lost in the 1906 landslide, and that they would get close to the Liberals. Some even thought that they would get more seats than the Liberals. Their confidence was justified and in conjunction with the Liberal Unionists they got within two seats of the Liberals. The distribution of seats was as follows:

Liberal	274 seats
Conservative	240 seats
Liberal Unionists	32 seats
Various Irish	82 seats
Labour	40 seats
Other	2 seats

Lord Longford called it a draw,[10] but the reality was that a draw was not enough. The Liberals had the support of the Labour MPs, and also the support of the Irish. The latter promised their backing because of a promise to move towards Home Rule. They could hardly look to a grouping that called itself Unionist, and they would only get Home Rule if the Lords veto was removed. During the tense period that followed the election the Lords accepted the inevitable and on 29 April 1910 the Finance Bill received Royal Assent, one year to the day after Lloyd George had presented what had become known as the 'People's Budget'.

The power of the House of Lords and the continuation of free trade had been the main issues at the election. The Liberal victory had secured free trade and the people now expected action to reduce the power of the Lords. Asquith made a faltering start, perhaps occasioned by weariness after such a demanding period. It was not clear whether the government intended to try and reform the Lords, end its veto or perhaps both. This lack of clarity alarmed some of its supporters and especially the Irish, on whose support the government depended. To get Home Rule they needed an end to the veto. Nothing else would do.

Faced with the demands for an end of the veto Asquith firmed up his position and moved in that direction. He had asked the king for an undertaking that he would, if necessary, create enough new peers to enable the will of the Commons to prevail. The question was put in confidence and the answer, which was also given in confidence, was no. Four hundred or more creations could be required, which would irrevocably alter the character of the hereditary chamber. Like William IV eighty years previously Edward recoiled from the prospect; he said that he would only do it if a second election had clearly shown that the end of the Lords veto was the will of the people.

Placing resolutions on the paper of the House of Commons was a step prior to the introduction of a bill. This was done on 21 March and the resolutions indicated the following:

- The Lords could not reject or amend a money bill. The Speaker of the House of Commons would, according to a set of rules, determine what was and what was not a money bill.
- The Lords could delay other bills for up to two years and one month.
- A bill sent to the Lords in three successive sessions would become law without the assent of the Upper House. This would happen if it had not been passed within twenty-eight days without amendments by the Lords, except for amendments agreed by both Houses. The three sessions could be spread over more than one Parliament.
- The maximum duration of a Parliament would be reduced from seven years to five years.

After eleven Parliamentary days of debate and extensive use of the guillotine, the resolutions were approved. During this period Asquith made the government's intentions clear with the following words:

> If the Lords fail to accept our policy, or to decline to consider it as it is formally presented to the House, we shall feel it our duty immediately to tender advice to the Crown as to the steps which will have to be taken if that policy is to receive statutory effect in this Parliament. What the precise terms of that advice will be, it would of course not be right for me to say now; but if we do not find ourselves in a position to ensure that statutory effect shall be given to that policy in this Parliament, we shall then either resign our offices or recommend the dissolution of Parliament. Let me add this, that in no case will we recommend a dissolution except under such conditions as will secure that in the new Parliament the judgment of the people as expressed at the elections will be carried into law.

This amounted to a statement that the government would, if necessary, ask the king to create a sufficient number of new peers.

Shortly afterwards the cruel hand of fate intervened. On 6 May King Edward died suddenly at the relatively early age of 68. His successor, George V, was relatively inexperienced. George's personality was less outgoing than that of his popular father, but he was conscientious, took his duty very seriously and was anxious to do the right thing. It is sometimes said that his sympathies were more instinctively Unionist than Edward's had been, but if they were (and many would say that they were not) it did not stop him striving to perform his duties impartially. He came to the throne at a very difficult time and his reign started with a baptism of fire.

There was much sympathy for the new king and many of the protagonists did not want to make things difficult for him. Perhaps too they did not want to be seen making things difficult for him, which is not quite the same thing. At an early audience Asquith told George that in order to avoid another election he would try to reach an understanding with the opposition.[11] This developed into an invitation to set up a two-party constitutional conference. The offer was accepted and it was agreed that the proceedings would be free-ranging and confidential. The government's members were Asquith, Lloyd George, Lord Crewe and Augustine Birrell. From the opposition it was Balfour, Lansdowne, Austen Chamberlain and Lord Cawdor. The setting up of the conference was not universally welcomed. Labour MPs were worried and the Irish were suspicious. A conference hinted at a compromise, and a compromise was not wanted by many on both sides.

To a greater or lesser extent the participants did try to reach an agreement, and Balfour and Asquith worked to achieve this. Concessions were made and ideas were floated. Realistic schemes, fanciful schemes and ridiculous schemes were all discussed. Ideas floated included joint sessions and referenda. Despite his previous belligerence Lloyd George tried to get an agreement and put forward many constructive ideas. He even suggested a coalition government with an agreed programme. He saw Asquith as prime minister sitting in the Lords, and Balfour as Leader in the Commons. This was surely a non-starter, but the idea was given serious consideration.

The issues were so stark that the chances of an agreed compromise must have been negligible. Apart from anything else the looming issue of Irish Home Rule was a major stumbling block. The Irish held the balance of power in the Commons and they would not support the government without a Home Rule commitment. The Liberals, with varying degrees of enthusiasm, wanted it too. The right to block Home Rule was something that the Unionists would not concede. Even if the eight participants had reached a compromise agreement, could they have sold its terms to their supporters? There must be grave doubts.

The conference broke down on 10 November and the government quickly asked the king for a dissolution and an election to be held before Christmas. This was accompanied by a request that, 'in the event of the policy of the government being approved by an adequate majority in the new House of Commons, His Majesty will be ready to exercise his constitutional powers (which may involve the prerogative of creating peers), if needed to secure that effect should be given to the decision of the country'. Asquith had previously told the king that the threat of mass creation would be sufficient and that it would not have to be carried out. This turned out to be correct.

An agonised George did not want to give what were known as 'guarantees', and he received directly conflicting advice from his two private secretaries. Sir Arthur Bigge rashly told him that he should not give guarantees, and Lord Knollys told him that he should; very reluctantly George took the advice of Knollys and, in confidence, made the requested promise.

Roy Jenkins says that, 'the almost impossible position into which the Tory Party had manoeuvred itself was making many converts of convenience to reform'.[12] The Lords discussed various concessions and proposals that had been put forward at the constitutional conference. Many of them were not in favour of holding out for no changes at all.

The election was rather a dull affair and the number voting indicated that the electors did not appreciate being troubled twice within a year. In fact the number voting dropped by more than 20 per cent. The future of the House of Lords was not the only issue: Home Rule and free trade also achieved some prominence. The result for all the parties was almost exactly the same as in the January election. The Liberal majority over the Conservatives and Unionists reduced from two (274 to 272) to one (272 to 271). It was short of a ringing endorsement but the Liberals had won three general elections in a row, the first time that this had happened since 1832. It was the mandate that they wanted.

When I was a boy I sometimes played cowboys and indians with my friends (I am sorry that this is not politically correct) and one boy would never admit to being shot. We used to complain that, 'he's dead but he won't lie down'. It is a tortured analogy but it sums up the attitude of the opposition peers in the Lords. Some diehards wanted to hold out for no change, but most favoured varied reforms of their own. They were, though, not of one mind on what the reforms should be. The Duke of Bedford wanted a wholly elected Senate, others favoured referenda and joint sittings, and there were many other ideas. Roy Jenkins refers to 'a babel of Tory tongues, each proclaiming a different plan for the composition of the new Second Chamber'.[13] Perhaps a reference to headless chickens would not be misplaced.

Whilst all this was going on the government's Parliament Bill made its way through the Commons. The third reading was on 23 May and it went through by 362 votes to 241. The Lords did not reject the bill, but they might as well have done. It was sent back to the Commons with a series of amendments that substituted their views of what it should contain. The bill was changed out of all recognition and made completely unacceptable to the government.

It was now time for the government to play its trump card, namely the king's confidential undertaking to create more peers if required. On 14 July the cabinet wrote to him and the communication included, 'Hence, in the contingency contemplated, it will be the duty of Ministers to advise the Crown to exercise its Prerogative so as to get rid of the deadlock and secure the passing of the bill. In such circumstances Ministers cannot entertain any doubt that the Sovereign would feel it to be his Constitutional duty to accept their advice.' A few days later and at the king's suggestion, Asquith sent the following letter to both Balfour and Lord Lansdowne, the Tory leader in the Lords:

Dear

I think it courteous and right, before any public decisions are announced, to let you know how we regard the political situation.

When the Parliament Bill in the form which it has now assumed returns to the House of Commons, we shall be compelled to ask the House to disagree with the Lords' amendments.

In the circumstances, should the necessity arise, the Government will advise the King to exercise his Prerogative to secure the passing into Law of the Bill in substantially the same form in which it left the House of Commons, and His

Majesty has been pleased to signify that he will consider it his duty to accept and act on that advice.

Yours sincerely
H.H. Asquith

Balfour had long strongly suspected that the king had given guarantees, so it did not come as a surprise to him. Lansdowne, on the other hand, had been much less sure. Many Conservative and Unionist peers had not believed the rumours and thought that the implied threat was a bluff. They all now had to face the reality that the government was going to get its bill, and furthermore that their beloved House of Lords could be swamped by the creation of between 400 and 500 new peers, a prospect that they found repugnant.

They divided into two groups that became known as the 'hedgers' and the 'ditchers'. The hedgers, who included Lansdowne, favoured abstaining and thus letting the bill through. This was the course ultimately adopted by the Duke of Wellington in 1832, when faced with the prospect of mass creation to secure passage of the Reform Act. The ditchers wanted to fight in the last ditch, vote against and face the consequences. The hedgers were in the majority, but they faced a problem. Such was the enormous Tory majority in the Lords, that with the hedgers abstaining, the still determined ditchers might summon up enough votes to defeat the bill.

The end was almost at hand, but still to come was a disgraceful scene in the House of Commons. It involved the shouting down of Asquith, who was about to outline the government's intentions on the motion to consider the Lord's amendments. As he rose to speak he was greeted by roars of abuse. The terms used varied but they included the appallingly insulting, 'Who killed the king?' It was organised, not spontaneous, and it lasted for the half hour or so that he tried to commence his statement. It stopped him speaking and eventually he had to sit down. Balfour sat impassively through the uproar. He did not participate, but neither did he try to stop it.

F.E. Smith and Lord Hugh Cecil were among the instigators of the mayhem. Shortly afterwards Smith tried to speak but, not surprisingly, was given a hard time by the government supporters. The Speaker then belatedly suspended the sitting because grave disorder had arisen. It was the first time since 1893 that a sitting had been suspended for that reason. The horrible events were a discredit to the participants, and neither Balfour nor the Speaker emerged with credit. Winston Churchill, then home secretary, reported to the king that, 'the ugliest feature was the absence of any real passion or spontaneous feeling. It was a squalid, frigid, organised attempt to insult the Prime Minister.'[14] Afterwards several Tories, though not the participants, wrote letters of apology to Asquith. One of them was Lord Halsbury, the 87-year-old former lord chancellor and a leading ditcher. Perhaps it would be fair to say that he was the leading ditcher.

The Unionists in the Lords were bitterly divided. Lansdowne and the other hedgers tried to persuade the ditchers to abstain, but they were well organised and most of them were adamant. The cabinet made a concession by deciding that they would not advise the king to create new peers before the final crucial vote in the Lords was taken. As passage in the Lords was by no means assured, this ran the risk that the bill would have to be started again. Both sides were busy calculating their likely support, which was not easy. A number of 'backwoodsmen', who had previously not taken their seats and qualified to vote, did so now. It seemed probable that they would tend to support the ditchers. Lord Morley, the government leader in the Lords, calculated that he would probably need forty Unionists to vote for the bill.

The proceedings in the Lords opened on 9 August, which was at the time the hottest day on record. The temperature at Greenwich Observatory reached 100 degrees Fahrenheit (37.8 centigrade). Until the vote was taken no one knew what the result would be, and it was felt that the speeches would be particularly important. In the event the bill was passed by 131 votes to 114, a government majority of 17. It was seen that eighty-one Liberals and thirty-seven Unionists had voted in favour. The other thirteen votes had come from bishops and archbishops. Most of the Unionists abstained.

The vote caused much bitterness in the Unionist ranks. One manifestation of it was the organised hissing in the Carlton Club of some of the thirty-seven Unionists who had voted in favour of the bill. But the long-running matter was settled. The Parliament Act 1911 passed into law. A summary of the Act's provisions is as follows.

Preamble

This included the words, 'It is intended to substitute for the House of Lords as it at present exists a Second Chamber constituted on a popular instead of hereditary basis, but such substitution cannot be immediately brought into operation.' This was an aspiration rather than a requirement, and in practice it turned out to be almost meaningless. More than a century later we are still wrestling with the reform of the House of Lords.

Money Bills

The Lords could only delay money bills for a period of a month. The Speaker of the House of Commons would certify what was a money bill.

Other Bills

The Lords could only delay other bills for a period up to two years. An exception was made for a bill that extended the life of a parliament beyond five years. This meant that a bill sent to the Lords more than three years into the life of a parliament could be delayed until after an election.

Life of a Parliament

The maximum life of a parliament was reduced from seven years to five years.

Payment of MPs

MPs who were not ministers were to be paid a salary of £400 per year. Ministers were already paid.

NOTES

1. Lord Longford, *A History of the House of Lords*, p.116.
2. Ibid., p.117.
3. Roy Jenkins, *Gladstone*, p.564.
4. Ibid., p.604.
5. Ibid., p.606.
6. Ibid., p.609.
7. Lord Longford, *A History of the House of Lords*, p.138.
8. Roy Jenkins, *Mr Balfour's Poodle*, p.60.
9. Ibid., p.105.
10. Lord Longford, *A History of the House of Lords*, p.146.
11. Roy Jenkins, *Mr Balfour's Poodle*, p.147.
12. Ibid., p.184.
13. Ibid., p.198.
14. Ibid., p.232.

16

Votes for Women

Until the latter part of the nineteenth century the position of women was greatly inferior to that of men, and this extended to the total absence of voting rights for women. An unmarried woman, technically a *femme sole*, owned property and other possessions in her own right, but prior to the Married Women's Property Acts of 1870 and 1882 married women did not. On marriage a woman's property was vested in her husband. This applied to property owned at the time of the marriage, and also to property acquired after the marriage. This included property or money acquired by means of wages, investments, gifts or inheritance. A married man's will could dispose as he saw fit of property brought to the marriage by his wife. The universities and nearly all the professions were denied to women.

There were many other inequalities. Until 1884 husbands were permitted to confine wives who refused to have sex with them. In the early nineteenth century husbands were allowed, within limits, to physically chastise their wives. Under the 1867 Divorce Act men could divorce their wives on the grounds of adultery, but women could not divorce their husbands for the same reason. Women had to prove bigamy, bestiality, rape, sodomy, cruelty or long-term desertion. Before moving on it is worth making the point that in practice the great majority of men did not take advantage of their wives in the ways described in these first two paragraphs. Just because they could, it did not mean that they did.

Campaigners for votes for women thought that it was simple justice that women should vote on the same basis as men, and it should be remembered that until 1884 much fewer than half of men had the vote. It was 1918 before all men did. They thought that women deserved the vote, even though women's education and opportunities were generally inferior. They also thought that votes for women, who comprised more than half the population, would be a major step towards removing the injustices that beset women at the time.

There were early and ineffective stirrings in 1832 when Mary Smith had a women's suffrage petition presented to Parliament. In the same year Henry Hunt moved an amendment to the Reform Bill to secure votes for women on the same terms as men. This was a gesture and it obtained only a derisory number of votes. Later in the 1830s the early Chartists had considered putting votes for women as a seventh point in their Charter, but they decided that it was a step too far and did not do so.

Though there was no chance of it succeeding, the cause did better at the time of the Second Reform Act in 1867. John Stuart Mill's amendment to enfranchise women was defeated by 196 votes to 73.

The country was still not ready to allow women the vote, or at least the politicians were not ready, but an amendment giving votes for women did considerably better at the time of the Third Reform Act in 1884. Gladstone was personally ambivalent, but he believed that its inclusion would cause great delay and perhaps result in the Lords rejecting the bill. He therefore instructed his chief whip to tell his MPs that if the amendment was carried, the bill would be dropped and the government would resign. The amendment probably would not have been carried, but this killed its chances, such as they were. The amendment was defeated by 271 votes to 135. The leading Liberal, Sir Charles Dilke, was in favour, and despite Gladstone's disapproval abstained from within the cabinet. The Lords would very probably have rejected it anyway. Nevertheless, despite the obstacles there were 135 votes in favour; it showed that opinion was shifting, though there was still a long way to go.

The final drive for women to vote on the same basis as men occurred in the years 1903 to 1928, and most of the rest of this chapter is devoted to this period. However, it is first of all instructive to look at developments from the early 1860s. There were no women's suffrage societies in 1860, but in 1914 there were fifty-six of them, with a combined membership of 300,000.[1] There were several in the mid-1860s and in 1868 many of them amalgamated to form the National Society for Women's Suffrage. As is the way with many political groups, there were divisions in the society and it split. However, it later reunited.

Disunity and splits were a common feature of several of the societies. It is not just men and men's groups that are prone to this. A frequent cause of disunity was different ideas about aims. Some members and societies wanted the aim to be exclusively votes for women. Others wanted this linked with other causes, such as women's property rights. The societies attracted many prominent, well-connected and upper class women. One example was Catherine Osler, who was the sister-in-law of the leading cabinet minister Joseph Chamberlain.

During the late nineteenth and early twentieth centuries women did not have the vote in parliamentary elections, but they increasingly did in other spheres. Furthermore, they were more often occupying positions outside the home. The fact that they generally used these votes responsibly and held the positions successfully was held to be an argument that they were ready for the vote in parliamentary elections. One very prominent woman did not see it that way. Queen Victoria, the head of state and figurehead of the world's greatest empire, referred to, 'this mad, wicked folly of women's rights'.[2]

Women ratepayers had had the right to vote for poor law guardians since 1834, and from 1875 they served as poor law guardians. In 1869 the Municipal Franchise Act gave women the right to vote in local elections, though three years later a legal judgment restricted this to unmarried women and widows. It seems bizarre that a woman acquired the right to vote in local elections because her husband had died.

County councils were created in 1888 and women were allowed to vote on the same terms as men. From 1907 women were allowed to stand as councillors in municipal and county council elections.

The year of 1903 was a significant one because it marked the founding by Emmeline Pankhurst of the Women's Social and Political Union (WSPU). She was an extraordinary woman, as will become apparent later in this chapter. She came from a political family and had recently been widowed. Her husband, Richard Pankhurst, was twenty-four years her senior and a barrister. He had twice stood for Parliament and had supported a very wide range of progressive (some would say outrageous) causes. They included free speech, universal free secular education, republicanism, Irish Home Rule, independence for India and the abolition of the House of Lords. He supported women's suffrage and had drafted a parliamentary bill to try and get it on to the Statute Book. It was quite a list and not one likely to endear him to Queen Victoria or, it has to be said, her government or most of her subjects. He was one of the early pioneers of the Independent Labour Party (ILP).

With Emmeline he was the father of three daughters, Christabel, Sylvia and Adela. Emmeline had been involved in some of her husband's causes, especially his campaign for women's suffrage. When she started the WSPU her daughters joined her in the movement.

The WSPU was criticised because it was not run on democratic lines, which was ironic because it was campaigning for democracy. The organisation was largely run by Emmeline, her daughters, other members of her family and her friends. The leaders, and above all Emmeline and Christabel, made the decisions and announced them to the members. In this it had a lot in common with the National Viewers' and Listeners' Association. This was founded in 1965 by Mary Whitehouse, and campaigned against what she saw as offensive and degrading broadcasting, especially by the BBC. It gained vast publicity and achieved some success, despite attracting quite a bit of derision. There was no democracy within the association. It was run by Mary Whitehouse with people that she chose.

There were many splits during the life of the WSPU, something that seemed endemic in many societies campaigning for women's suffrage. It was noted by men who did not approve. It was a women-only society, and even sympathetic men were not allowed to join. Emmeline, Christabel and the WSPU had quite a lot of success with middle class and upper class women. A prominent example was Constance Lytton, who was a Conservative. Her father had been a viceroy of India, and her mother had been a lady-in-waiting to Queen Victoria.[3]

Emmeline and Christabel had an interesting disagreement about the Independent Labour Party (ILP). Emmeline was on the ILP's organising committee and assumed that the ILP and the WSPU would work together. Christabel thought that the ILP was male-dominated and would turn out to be as unhelpful as the other political parties. One incident seemed to prove Christabel right. Women were barred from attending an ILP meeting in Manchester. The supreme irony was that the hall in which the meeting was held was named after Emmeline's late husband, a friend of

Kier Hardy, a man who supported women's suffrage and a man who had done so much for the party.[4] Ramsay MacDonald, the future Labour prime minister, referred to the WSPU as 'tomfoolery'.[5]

The National Union of Women's Suffrage (NUWS) was a powerful movement that by 1914 had 50,000 members.[6] It used peaceful and legal means to pursue its ends. The WSPU initially used just legal and peaceful means, but in 1905 its leaders decided that militant action and breaking the law was justified, initially in a mild way, but over time more purposefully and sometimes violently. At an early stage the *Daily Mail* dubbed its members 'suffragettes'. From 1903 both movements used a variety of legal methods, some of them very imaginative. In the case of the WSPU this was in addition to illegal methods.

Numerous demonstrations and meetings to publicise the cause were held. Some of them were very large. The Free Trade Hall in Manchester was twice filled and large meetings were held at the Royal Albert Hall in London. Newspapers were published and cycle rides displaying the movement's colours were held. At the 1908 FA Cup Final a kite with 'Votes for Women' written on it was flown over the pitch, and leaflets were distributed to the spectators and at the railway station. A launch displaying 'Votes for Women' banners took to the Thames at the time of the Boat Race, and suffragists in a boat with a loudhailer harangued MPs taking tea on the terrace at Westminster.[7]

Before describing the actions of the suffragettes it is worth examining the balance of opinion in Parliament. The Liberals were in government and women's suffrage had majority support within the cabinet and among Liberal MPs generally. Enthusiasm for the cause varied, but within the cabinet supporters included Lloyd George, Grey, Haldane, Churchill (after initial opposition), Birrell, Walter Runciman and Reginald McKenna. Against were Sir William Harcourt, John Burns and Herbert Samuel. The crucial figure of Asquith, who was prime minister from 1908, was also against. He did not like it, could not see what the fuss was about and was outraged by the behaviour of the suffragettes. He thought that women who conducted themselves in that way did not deserve the vote and could not be trusted to use it responsibly. On the other side of the House Balfour was in favour, but the majority of his colleagues were against.[8] The House of Lords was very probably against, but after the 1911 Parliament Act they no longer had a long-term veto.

As is the way with politicians, both those for and against were agitated by what it would mean for them and their parties. It was very hard to know, or even to estimate. Giving women the vote on the same basis as men would more than double the size of the electorate. Doing this would perhaps help the Liberals and the Labour Party. A very restricted women's franchise might favour the Conservatives. Rather than votes for women it would be votes for ladies, and probably Tory ladies.

The adoption of illegal methods by the suffragettes started in October 1905 when Christabel Pankhurst and Annie Kenney disrupted a meeting being addressed by the Liberal politicians Sir Edward Grey and Winston Churchill. The women refused to pay a fine and each spent a week in prison. Following this, non-violent but illegal activities included the refusal to pay taxes and non-cooperation with the 1911 census.

Developing and escalating law breaking included suffragettes chaining themselves to railings, using acid to write slogans on golf course greens and the attacking of paintings. This was done several times, the most famous target being a painting by Velasquez hung in the National Gallery. There was a spate of window smashing, which was appallingly unfair to shopkeepers and others who had to have their windows replaced. In the famous words of Dale Carnegie, it was hardly likely to 'win friends and influence people'. Windows smashed included some at 10 Downing Street, which seemed unlikely to convert Mr Asquith to the cause. Even worse was arson attacks on property, and fire was used to damage or destroy post in letter boxes.

Lloyd George was attacked in his car and a home-made bomb exploded in his house. The prime minister was harried and slogans were continually shouted at him. On more than one occasion he was physically attacked. Women tried to rip his clothes off and were only restrained by the intervention of his daughter. He was repeatedly hit over the head with a dog whip, but fortunately a top hat provided a lot of protection. The Irish leader John Redmond was wounded in the ear by a hatchet when sharing a railway carriage with the prime minister in Dublin. Not all the intimidation was perpetrated by the suffragettes, and they were sometimes on the receiving end of rough treatment by men. Emmeline Pankhurst was roughly handled by some ruffians who put her in a barrel and attempted to roll her down a hill, and the police did not always behave in a sympathetic way.

The most famous and the most tragic event took place during the running of the Epsom Derby on 4 June 1913. Emily Wilding Davison positioned herself next to the track at Tattenham Corner, then ran into the pack of horses as they went by. Her intentions are not absolutely clear, but she was probably trying to drape a Votes for Women scarf or banner over the king's horse Anmer. The horse fell and she was trampled by its hooves. The horse then ran off dragging its unconscious jockey whose foot was trapped in a stirrup. The jockey recovered but Emily died four days later. It is generally believed that her actions were not an attempt to kill herself, but she did and she placed in danger the lives of the jockeys and horses.

Emily had a record of violent protest, including an attack on a man that she mistakenly thought was the Chancellor of the Exchequer. She had been jailed nine times and force-fed forty-nine times. Some of her activities, including the Derby protest, were carried out without the prior knowledge of the WSPU. The organisation declared her to be the 'suffragette martyr' and organised a grand funeral that attracted massive crowds.

The suffragettes adopted a policy of very extensive hunger strikes, which caused difficulties for the government. The obvious suffering and, if continued, the risk of death tends to attract sympathy. At first the women were released as soon as their health was at risk, but then a policy of force-feeding was introduced. During the campaign over a thousand women were force-fed,[9] and it was done in a brutal way. The medical magazine *The Lancet* printed the following:

Prisoners were held down by force, flung on the floor, tied to chairs and iron bedsteads ... while the tube was forced up the nostrils. After each feeding the nasal pain gets worse. The wardress endeavoured to make the prisoner open her mouth by sawing the edge of the cup along the gums ... the broken edge caused laceration and severe pain. Food into the lung of one unresisting prisoner immediately caused severe choking, vomiting ... persistent coughing. She was hurriedly released next day suffering from pneumonia and pleurisy. We cannot believe that any of our colleagues will agree that this form of prison treatment is justly described in Mr McKenna's [the home secretary] words as necessary medical treatment.

On 25 April 1913 the Prisoners' Temporary Discharge for Ill-Health Act became law, and it was rapidly dubbed the Cat and Mouse Act. It allowed women to be temporarily released from prison when their health was at risk, then returned when their health had recovered. Emmeline Pankhurst was released and returned to prison a number of times. It led a journalist to calculate that at that rate it would be 1930 before she had finished the sentence. Sylvia Pankhurst was released and then returned to prison no fewer than thirteen times.

The country went to war with Germany in August 1914, and the women of Britain made a big contribution to winning it. They already had a very strong case for having the vote, but Parliament recognised that this made it conclusive. Emmeline and Christabel Pankhurst were very patriotic and very anti-German. Shortly after war was declared the WSPU called off its campaign, and most of the other suffrage societies did the same. Emmeline said that there was no point in continuing to fight for the vote when there might be no country to vote in.[10] Emmeline and Christabel threw themselves into co-operating with the government in recruiting women for war work. This involved working with Lloyd George, their former target, who had been made Minister of Munitions. Among other things they advocated the conscription of women for war work, the interment of conscientious objectors and the banning of trade unions.

During the war the number of women employed in domestic service reduced from 1,658,000 to 1,258,000. Women employed in transport services increased from 18,000 to 117,000 and they took over men's jobs in a wide variety of occupations. They served in the Land Army and in many areas as volunteers. The biggest contribution was in the munitions factories. Woolwich Arsenal employed 125 women in 1914, but by 1917 it was 25,000. It was dangerous work and more than a third of them suffered ill health as a result of TNT poisoning.

It is a tortuous analogy, but a popular song published in 1919 in America included the words 'How ya gonna keep 'em down on the farm, after they've seen Paree?' Translated this is, 'How are you going to keep them down on the farm after they have seen Paris?' It made the serious point that American farm boys would not be content with their old life when they returned from the war in Europe. It could be said to be applicable to British women too. They would want changes after their splendid war work.

During the course of the war MPs came to the conclusion that many issues had to be addressed and that a new reform act was needed. Problems included the fact that vast numbers of men who were fighting for their country did not have the vote, and that fighting men who did have the vote were losing it because they no longer satisfied the residence qualification. It was widely accepted that this time something should be done for the women. This was partly in recognition of their valuable war work and partly because acceptance of the justice of their case was now widespread. It helped that in 1916 Lloyd George, who favoured votes for women, had replaced Asquith, who did not. However, by the latter stages of the war Asquith had rather grudgingly changed his mind.

A Speaker's Conference was set up to examine the issues and make recommendations. Its membership, apart from the Speaker of the House of Commons, comprised thirteen Liberals, thirteen Conservatives, four Irish Home Rulers and four representatives of the Labour Party. The conference recommended that the vote be given to women over the age of 30 or 35. It declined to say which. This was provided that the woman was a householder or married to a householder, or had a university degree. This favoured married women and excluded most of the workers in the munitions factories who had attracted so much admiration. They were mainly young and working class, so even the older ones were less likely to be householders or married to householders.

The Speaker's Conference led on to the Representation of the People Act, which received Royal Assent on 6 February 1918. This is the subject of Chapter 17 and only its effect on women are included here. The Act followed the recommendations of the conference, making the eligible age 30 rather than 35. Women aged 30 or over were given the vote if they were either entitled to be entered on the Local Government Register or married to a man who was entitled to be entered on it, a property owner, or a graduate voting in a university constituency.

This was a big step forward, but it was a long way short of equality with men, who were given votes for all at the age of 21 by the same Act. The electorate was increased to about 21,000,000 and about 40 per cent of it was female. About 22 per cent of women aged 30 or over and all women aged under 30 were left without the vote.

Shortly afterwards the Parliament (Qualification of Women) Act 1918 was enacted. This permitted women aged 21 or over to stand as candidates and, if elected, to serve as MPs. It was curious that a woman aged under 30 could be an MP but could not vote. At the December 1918 general election just one woman was elected. This was Countess Constance Markievicz, who was elected for Dublin St Patrick's. She was the Sinn Fein candidate and was in prison at the time. The lady had a chequered history, which included being sentenced to death for her part in the 1916 Easter Uprising. She had been reprieved. She refused to take her seat because it meant taking an oath of allegiance. The first woman MP to take her seat was Nancy Astor on 1 December 1919. She represented the Coalition Conservatives and won by a by-election in Plymouth Sutton.

Hardly anyone thought that the 1918 Act was the final step on the journey to achieve votes for women. They saw that it was a halfway house. The country would get used to 'respectable' women voting, and then go the rest of the way. Various societies carried on lobbying in a restrained way, but not the WSPU. With very little opposition Stanley Baldwin's Conservative government gave them the Representation of the People (Equal Franchise) Act 1928. This gave women the vote on exactly the same terms as men. The struggle was over.

Much of the public has the perception that votes for women were achieved in 1918, and that the reason was a combination of the agitation by suffragettes and recognition of the work done by women during the war. The bit about war work is correct, but the other two points should perhaps be challenged. Votes for women were only partially achieved in 1918; it was a good start, but votes were still denied to all women under 30 and 22 per cent of women aged 30 or over. Full votes for women came in 1928, ten years later.

Some, but by no means all, take the view that the suffragettes did not speed up the achievement of votes for women, and that they may even have delayed it. The suffragists had an almost unanswerable case, and many of them put it in a legal, reasonable and persuasive way. They were making good progress, and men of goodwill were listening and some of them were being persuaded. The suffragettes were a thundering nuisance (they would have taken that as a compliment) and antagonised the men who would make the decisions.

Not everything that the suffragettes did is mentioned in this chapter, but their activities included wrecking political meetings, chaining themselves to railings, smashing windows, setting fire to pillar boxes, vandalising golf courses, flooding the organ at the Royal Albert Hall, burning down major buildings, letting off a bomb in the Chancellor of the Exchequer's house, attacking politicians, insulting the king and spoiling the world's greatest horse race. Even men of goodwill who supported their cause were liable to be annoyed, and to think that a group of people capable of such behaviour did not deserve the vote and could not be trusted to use it responsibly.

The counter-argument is that the unanswerable case had been put responsibly for a long time, and that justice had not been obtained. People without basic rights, it is claimed, are entitled to use passive resistance and to break the law in order to pursue their just ends. The citizens of former colonies did it to get independence and it generally worked, but violence was also used in many cases. The only person who died was Emily Wilding Davison, though a few hunger strikers badly damaged their health. Thousands of suffragettes suffered, and the campaign successfully kept the issue in front of the politicians and the public. It must surely have had an effect.

Just before the First World War there was a sad and fundamental estrangement in the Pankhurst family, and it led to considerable bitterness. Sylvia and Adela remained true to their socialist heritage. Sylvia opposed the war and was for a time a member of the Communist Party. The views of Emmeline and Christabel, on the other hand, moved sharply to the right. Among many other things they campaigned against Bolshevism.

Christabel became an evangelical Christian and in 1936 she was made a Dame Commander of the British Empire. This was despite her record of being the chief organiser of the pre-war suffragette lawlessness. The British have a long record of bringing former rebels into the establishment. In 1928 Emmeline was adopted as a Conservative Party parliamentary candidate, but she died before fighting an election. Her death was on the very day, 14 June 1928, that the House of Lords voted to give votes to all women.

NOTES

1. Paula Bartley, *Votes for Women 1860–1928*, p.30.
2. L.E. Snellgrove, *Suffragettes and Votes for Women*, p.20.
3. Paula Bartley, *Votes for Women 1860–1928*, p.38.
4. David Downing, *Emmeline Pankhurst*, p.22.
5. Ibid., p.22.
6. Eric J. Evans, *Parliamentary Reform c.1770–1918*, p.75.
7. Paula Bartley, *Votes for Women 1860–1928*, p.51.
8. Roy Jenkins, *Asquith*, p.248.
9. Paula Bartley, *Votes for Women 1860–1928*, p.75.
10. Ibid., p.98.

17

Representation of the People Act 1918

The long journey to universal suffrage started with the Great Reform Act of 1832, and the further Reform Acts of 1867 and 1884 took it to the position where just over 60 per cent of men had the vote. The franchise was property based, there was plural voting and women were totally disenfranchised. Back in 1832 a very small number of radicals had advocated universal manhood suffrage, and an even smaller number, Henry Hunt being one, had advocated votes for women as well. Each step towards these ends had been welcomed by its proponents and left them looking for more. By the second decade of the twentieth century many felt that it was time for a further advance. Then the Great War made the pressure irresistible.

A significant proportion of the men who marched off to fight for king and country did not have the vote. The percentage that did was less than the 60 per cent figure for all men; this was because they tended to be young and therefore less likely to satisfy the property-based qualification. There was a strong feeling that this was wrong, and that if a man was good enough to fight for his country and in all too many cases to die for his country, he was good enough to vote in it. Almost none of Wellington's troops had the vote when they triumphed at Waterloo, but that was not good enough for Earl Haig's men when they were losing their lives on the Western Front.

An anomaly badly needed correction. There was a residence requirement of a year to qualify for the vote, and many of the fighting men had lost it because they had been away from home for longer than that. In addition it was widely accepted that women, or some of them at least, should have the vote. Apart from other considerations, their war work had shown that they deserved it. One more point: the times were turbulent and when the decisions were made Russia was on the brink of revolution. The British do not do that sort of thing, but it was felt that an extension of the franchise would make it even less likely.

The looming need for a general election presented problems. There was a legal requirement that one be held by January 1916, five years after the last one, but it was very difficult in wartime conditions. A 1915 Act extended the life of the parliament by a year, and it was subsequently extended further. A 1916 Act required a new electoral register to be drawn up. The next general election was actually held in December 1918, just five weeks after the end of the war and eight years after the previous election. By then votes for most women and what is sometimes called the Fourth Reform Act were in place.

The various issues were referred to a Speaker's Conference that was set up in 1916. This was charged with making recommendations on franchise reform and associated matters. The conference was an inter-party one and its deliberations were conducted entirely behind closed doors. The Speaker was the greatly experienced James Lowther. He had been Deputy Speaker from 1895 to 1905, and was Speaker for sixteen years from 1905 to 1921. Lowther was a Conservative and had previously opposed allowing women to vote, but it was known that his views on this had mellowed. Apart from the Speaker there were thirty-four members – thirteen of them were Conservatives (eleven MPs and two peers), thirteen were Liberals (ten MPs and three peers), and there were four from the Labour Party and four Irish Home Rulers.

The conference started work on 12 October 1916 and it presented its report on 26 January 1917. During this period it met twenty-six times, which indicates that it must have approached its task with a considerable degree of urgency. The whole job took 106 days, including Christmas and weekends. Its main recommendations were universal male suffrage and votes for some women.

The conference voted by fifteen votes to six in favour of allowing votes for some women, but by twelve votes to ten against treating women the same as men. Universal suffrage, with women voting on the same basis as men, would have meant that 53 per cent of the electorate was female. The all-male conference felt that this was a step too far, though they must surely have realised that it would happen eventually. Given the importance of the decisions, it is surprising that so many members did not vote. The recommendation was that women aged either 30 or more or 35 or more should be given the vote, provided that either they or their husbands were on the local government electors register. The five years between 30 and 35 is a long period of time, so it is puzzling that they did not express a view, instead leaving it to Parliament.

The Conservatives had been instrumental in the setting up of the conference, but some sections of the party were distinctly unhappy when draft legislation based on its recommendations was produced.[1] They thought that the large increase in the electorate would not be in the interests of their party, and that many of the new voters would be inclined to vote Liberal or Labour. The results of the next general election would show that these fears were largely misplaced. Nevertheless, the party accepted the principle of universal male suffrage and votes for many women, but successfully worked to get some of the details of the legislation changed.[2]

There was to be a redistribution of seats and the details were amended in ways that helped the Conservatives. There were more suburban seats, especially in the south-east of England, and these tended to elect Conservative MPs. Redistribution within Ireland was amended to favour the Protestant and Unionist parts of the island. It is believed that the net effect of the redistribution was a benefit of about thirty seats for the Conservatives.[3]

There had been around half a million people with more than one vote, the so-called plural voters. The conference wanted their number reduced to about 159,000 who qualified for business premises and about 68,000 who qualified as graduates. Plural voters tended to be prosperous and tended to vote Conservative. The Conservatives went along with the reduction in the number of plural voters, but got a concession on business premises that worked in their favour.[4]

The Labour Party and the franchise societies wanted votes for all women, but decided to accept the bill provided that the minimum voting age for women was set at 30 and not 35. This was done. They took the view that half a loaf (or perhaps two thirds of a loaf) was better than no loaf, and that universal female suffrage would come later, which of course it did. They did not want to risk losing the bill.

The bill had cross-party support in the Commons and on the third reading it passed by 385 votes to 55. There was some concern that it would have trouble in the Lords, especially over the enfranchisement of women, but the fears turned out to be unfounded. Lord Curzon was President of the National League for Opposing Women's Suffrage, and it was thought that he would lead the opposition. However, he decided to abstain and many peers followed his lead. The bill passed the Lords by 134 votes to 71.

The Representation of the People Act received Royal Assent on 6 February 1918. It was a time of great peril for the nation. The Germans were transferring troops away from the Russian front and preparing for their last great offensive in the west, but Britain and her allies did prevail. The Armistice was signed on 11 November and the Act governed the general election, which was held on 14 December. The main provisions of the Act were as follows.

Male Franchise

The vote was given to all men aged 21 or over. It was on the basis of residence and the residence qualification was reduced from one year to six months. The previous property-based qualifications were discontinued and it was universal male suffrage.

Servicemen

The vote was given to all men who had served in the armed forces during the First World War from the age of 19.

Women

Women aged 30 years or over were given the vote if they were entitled to be entered on the Local Government Register or married to a man entitled to be entered on the Local Government Register in respect of property worth £5 per year rental value, or they occupied a dwelling house on the same basis as men who had been entitled to enfranchisement under the 1884 Reform Act. They also had the vote if they were a graduate voting in a university constituency.

Plural Voting

Plural voting was limited to a maximum of two votes per person. This was residence, plus either on the basis of business premises or as a graduate.

Redistribution of Seats

There was to be a redistribution of seats in accordance with the need for constituencies to have a roughly equivalent number of voters.

Electoral Register

There was to be an annual electoral register.

Election Expenses

Candidates were no longer required to pay the expenses of the returning officer.

Voting to Be on a Fixed Day

Voting in general elections was to be on a single day instead of over a period as previously.

The Representation of the People Act roughly trebled the size of the electorate. It went from approximately 7,700,000 to approximately 21,400,000. Three quarters of the people who voted in the 1918 election were doing so for the first time. There were roughly 8,400,000 women entitled to vote and they made up 43 per cent of the electorate.

Previous chapters in this book made the point that the increases in the size of the electorate in 1867 and 1884 increased the importance of organisation and of parties. The 1918 increase was by far the biggest of all and it had the same consequence. There were three times as many people for the parties to appeal to and keep in touch with. Some Conservatives had feared that the Act would damage their prospects, but they did very well in the 1918 election. They were in coalition with Lloyd George's faction of the Liberal Party, with Lloyd George being prime minister. The Coalition Conservatives obtained 332 seats and the Coalition Liberals got 127. Other Conservatives obtained forty-seven seats and Asquith's faction of the Liberals got thirty-seven. The Irish Sinn Fein Party got seventy-three, but its candidates did not take their seats. Asquith lost his seat, as did the Labour leaders Ramsay MacDonald and Arthur Henderson.

Asquith had been a long time opponent of votes for women, but he had rather reluctantly accepted its inclusion in the 1918 Act. However, his true views may be gauged from the following, which was included in a private letter that he wrote later: 'There are about fifteen thousand women on the Register – a dim, impenetrable lot, for the most part hopelessly ignorant of politics, credulous to the last degree, and flickering with gusts of sentiment like a candle in the wind.'[5]

NOTES

1. Eric J. Evans, *Parliamentary Reform c.1770–1918*, p.87.
2. Ibid., p.88.
3. Ibid., p.88.
4. Ibid., p.89.
5. Paula Bartley, *Votes for Women 1860–1928*, p.98.

18

Developments Since 1918

This concluding chapter reviews events in the long period since the 1918 Representation of the People Act. One major development though, probably the biggest of all, is the granting of the vote to women under the age of 30. This happened in 1928 and it is covered in chapters 16 and 17.

THE CONSTITUENT PARTS OF THE UNITED KINGDOM

Ireland

The twin Acts of Union were passed in 1800, and the United Kingdom of Great Britain and Ireland came into being on 1 January 1801. Despite the name, Great Britain and 'John Bull's Other Island' seemed for much of the time far from united. Previous chapters of this book have mentioned the Irish campaign for Home Rule and Gladstone's two doomed Home Rule Bills. Shortly before the First World War Ireland almost reached a state of civil war, with Unionist Ulster vowing to resist being part of an Ireland that had been given Home Rule. In the period leading up to the war Asquith's Liberal government dealt with the constitutional crisis over the powers of the House of Lords, faced massive industrial unrest, was harried by the suffragettes and faced possible civil war in Ireland.

The Government of Ireland Act received Royal Assent on 18 September 1914, but its implementation was delayed until after the war. This would have given Home Rule to Ireland, but turbulent events meant that it never was implemented. Instead the Irish Free State came into being on 6 December 1922. The six counties of Ulster had the option of not being part of it and, very predictably, on 7 December decided to stay with Great Britain in what became the United Kingdom of Great Britain and Northern Ireland. The remaining twenty-six counties became an independent Dominion of the British Commonwealth, rather like Canada. In 1937 it became an independent country outside of the Commonwealth.

Northern Ireland

From 7 June 1921 until 30 March 1972 the devolved legislature for Northern Ireland was the Parliament of Northern Ireland. After a period of suspension this was abolished in 1973 under the Northern Ireland Constitution Act. It was replaced by the Northern Ireland Assembly, but this was abolished in 1974. Another Assembly was set up in 1982, but this was abolished in 1986.

The present Assembly was set up in 1998. It has legislative powers and responsibility for electing the Northern Ireland Executive. The Assembly has the authority to legislate on a wide range of 'transferred matters'. Members are elected under the single transferable vote system of proportional representation. The Assembly elects most of its ministers using the principle of power sharing between the Unionist and Nationalist communities.

Scotland

The proposal to set up a Scottish Assembly was put to the people of Scotland in a referendum in 1979. It was a requirement that as well as a majority of those voting, the proposal should obtain the support of 40 per cent of the eligible voting population. Of the votes, 51.6 per cent were cast in favour, but this amounted to only 32.9 per cent of the eligible voting population. The proposal therefore failed. In a referendum held in 1997 the people of Scotland voted in favour of devolution and the setting up of a Scottish Parliament. Power was transferred on 1 July 1999.

The Scottish Parliament is single-chamber, and operates with four-year terms. All matters not reserved for the Parliament of the United Kingdom are matters for the Scottish Parliament. The Parliament of the United Kingdom has the power to vary the matters that are reserved for it. Devolved matters include health, education, justice and agriculture, and the Scottish Parliament has limited tax-varying capacity.

The Scottish Parliament has 129 members. Seventy-three of them represent individual constituencies and are elected on the first past the post system. The other fifty-six members are from eight regions, each electing seven members. They are elected by an additional members system, which seeks to make the overall results more proportional.

A referendum held in Scotland in September 2014 posed the question: 'Should Scotland be an independent country?' Of those that voted, 55.3 per cent answered no. The turnout was 84.6 per cent, which is the highest recorded for any general election or referendum held in the United Kingdom since the introduction of universal suffrage. Shortly before the referendum the leaders of the three main parties in the UK Parliament promised that, in the event of a 'no' vote, extensive additional powers would be devolved to the Scottish Parliament.

Wales

The proposed setting up of a Welsh Assembly was put to the people of Wales in a referendum in 1979. They rejected it by the overwhelming majority of four to one. The question was put again in a 1997 referendum, and this time the voting was 50.3 per cent in favour. The Assembly was created by the Government of Wales Act in 1998. The Government of Wales Act 2006 gave the Assembly limited primary legislative powers in areas that were devolved. Following a further referendum in 2011 the Assembly was given direct law-making powers in devolved matters, without the requirement to consult Westminster. An example of the use of these powers is the abolition of charges for NHS prescriptions in Wales. The Welsh Assembly has more limited powers than the Scottish Parliament and the Northern Ireland Assembly.

The Welsh Assembly has sixty members who are each elected for four-year terms. The voting system is the same as in Scotland, namely the additional member system. Forty members are elected from individual constituencies using the first past the post system of voting, and twenty are elected from five electoral regions using proportional representation.

England

Scotland has its own Parliament, and Northern Ireland and Wales have their own Assemblies. Different powers are devolved to each of them, and in particular the powers devolved to the Scottish Parliament are extensive and likely to be increased. In September 2014 a referendum in Scotland rejected the proposal that the country be fully independent. However, shortly before the vote opinion polls had indicated that the result was too close to call, and that there was a definite possibility that there would be a 'yes' vote. Whether or not in response to this – but let's be realistic and say that it was in response to this – the leaders of the three main parties at Westminster said that if there was a 'no' vote, extensive additional powers would be devolved to the Scottish Parliament.

So where does this leave England? Of the UK's population, 84 per cent live in England, and MPs representing seats in Scotland, Northern Ireland and Wales sit in the Parliament of the United Kingdom. They participate in debates on matters affecting just England, and they vote on matters that affect just England. There are fifty-nine seats in Scotland (in 2010 forty-one of them returned Labour MPs), forty in Wales (in 2010 twenty-six of them returned Labour MPs) and eighteen in Northern Ireland. Many people in England and elsewhere think that this is unfair. What to do about the anomaly has been dubbed the 'West Lothian Question'. The term was first used by Enoch Powell in 1977 after Tam Dalyell, who was the Labour MP for the Scottish constituency of that name, repeatedly raised the matter. He continued to do so for many years and never got a satisfactory answer. His persistence in repeatedly asking the same questions was legendary. He drove Mrs Thatcher and others to distraction with his questions about the sinking of the ship the *General Belgrano* during the Falklands War.

Following the 'no' vote in the Scottish independence referendum the prime minister, David Cameron, said that 'the question of English votes for English laws – the so-called West Lothian Question – requires a decisive answer'. He announced a commission to develop proposals for constitutional reform to be included in a bill to be published in January 2015. Suggestions have included the following:

- Create a separate English Parliament, similar to the Scottish Parliament. This would leave the Parliament of the United Kingdom with responsibility for things such as foreign policy, defence and monetary policy.

- Continue as before, but not permit MPs who do not represent an English constituency to participate in matters affecting just England.
- Do nothing and let the anomaly continue. This is on the grounds that any change would have unfortunate consequences. As Hilaire Belloc just might have humorously summed up the situation:
And always keep a–hold of Nurse
For fear of finding something worse.

Any change, or indeed no change at all, will create questions and difficulties. It is not always clear what business applies exclusively to just England. What would be the position of the House of Lords, where peers do not represent geographical constituencies?

THE HOUSE OF LORDS

As detailed in Chapter 15 the terms of the 1911 Parliament Act left the Lords able to hold up money bills by up to a month, and to hold up other bills by up to two years. The right to sit in the House of Lords continued to be based on the hereditary principle, and as with the Commons it was men only. New peers were appointed by the sovereign on the advice of the prime minister. The preamble to the 1911 Parliament Act included the words, 'It is intended to substitute for the House of Lords as it at present exists a Second Chamber constituted on a popular instead of hereditary basis, but such substitution cannot be immediately brought into operation.' This amounted to an aspiration rather than a plan, and changes were very slow coming. Reform of the House of Lords is still a long way from being complete, and is a contentious matter.

The appointment of new peers by the sovereign on the advice of the prime minister has at times, to say the least, been controversial; it has been noticed that appointments are sometimes made following substantial donations to party funds. Notorious early examples occurred in Lloyd George's premiership after the First World War. These resulted in the Honours (Prevention of Abuses) Act 1925. To this day there are criticisms that some of the appointments are to friends, to repay favours, to reward long service and for reasons of party advantage. Of course some appointments, including some in the categories mentioned, are of good and suitable people. At the time of writing the House of Lords has 789 members, not including those who are on leave of absence or are disqualified from sitting. Not all peers attend regularly, and some do not attend at all.

The first significant change was the Parliament Act 1949. This reduced the delaying power of the House of Lords from two years to one.

A major change was brought about by the Life Peerages Act 1958. As the title implies it enables peers to be created for life, but their title and position dies with them and is not inherited. The creation of hereditary peers is still possible, but since

1958 almost all creations have been of life peers. The Life Peerages Act allowed women to sit in the House of Lords for the first time.

The Peerage Act 1963 allows hereditary peerages to be disclaimed. A person wishing to disclaim a peerage must do so within a year of succeeding to it, or if under the age of 21 on succeeding, before the peer's 22nd birthday. If at the time of succession the peer is a member of the House of Commons, the disclaimer must be made within one month of succession, and until it is disclaimed the peer may not sit or vote in the Commons.

When the Peerage Act came into force, sitting peers had one year to renounce their titles if they wished to do so. Lord Home (Sir Alec Douglas Home) and Lord Hailsham (Quintin Hogg) did this, and Sir Alec became prime minister in 1964. Both men subsequently returned to the Lords as life peers.

The House of Lords Act 1999 was originally intended to remove the right to sit in the House of Lords of all peers who inherited their seats. However, an amendment to the bill left ninety-two hereditary peers sitting with all the life peers. This was to be an interim measure, which would remain in place until a final solution was found. A further ten hereditary peers were created life peers, enabling them to continue to sit in the Lords.

The ninety-two peers included the Earl Marshall and the Lord Great Chamberlain. The other ninety were elected according to the standing orders of the House. These elections were conducted according to the principles of preferential voting, not first past the post. Whenever there is a vacancy it is filled by a by-election. Hereditary peers are permitted to sit in the House of Commons, so long as they are not members of the House of Lords.

The Labour government introduced the Constitutional Reform and Governance Bill in 2009. Among other measures this would have stopped the by-elections, so that in time the number of hereditary peers in the Lords would have dropped to zero. However, this clause was dropped before the passage of the Act.

There are still ninety-two hereditary peers, sitting with what seems to be an ever increasing number of life peers. The 1999 interim measure is still in place. There is no consensus of opinion on future reform; some favour a fully elected House, and some a fully appointed House. Others favour a mixture of the two, part elected and part appointed. There are many other suggestions.

An indication of the declining prestige of the House of Lords is that in July 2014 the reshuffled cabinet did not include the Leader of the House of Lords.

PROPORTIONAL REPRESENTATION

Most European countries use some form of proportional representation in elections for their parliaments. It frequently results in a coalition government, and sometimes to a delay in forming a government. There are many systems and it is now used in many elections within the United Kingdom. These include (in part at least) elections to the Scottish Parliament, and to the Northern Ireland and Welsh Assemblies. It is used, as required by EU law, in elections for the European Parliament, and Police and Crime Commissioners are elected in this way. It is not, though, used in elections for the House of Commons.

The 2010 coalition agreement between the Conservative and Liberal Democrat parties included provision for a referendum on the introduction of the alternative vote system of voting for parliamentary elections. The referendum was held in May 2011 and the question was:

> At present the UK uses the 'first past the post' system to elect MPs to the House of Commons. Should the 'alternative vote' system be used instead?

On a turnout of 42.2 per cent, 32.1 per cent voted yes and 67.9 per cent voted no. The demand for proportional representation has not gone away and, as might be expected, it is strongly favoured by parties whose proportion of MPs is less than their proportion of votes. The Liberals and then the Liberal Democrats have long been in that position. Cynics might note that the Liberals did not do anything about it many years ago when they formed the government. The people decisively rejected it in the referendum, and it seems that first past the post will remain for a considerable time.

UNIVERSITY SEATS AND OTHER PLURAL VOTING

Qualifying graduates of universities had a vote in their university seat and another vote in the constituency in which they were a resident. The single transferable vote was introduced for university constituencies in 1918. The university seats and all forms of plural voting were abolished in 1948.

MINIMUM VOTING AGE AND MINIMUM AGE TO BE A CANDIDATE

The minimum voting age for parliamentary elections was lowered from 21 to 18 in 1969. There have been suggestions that it be further lowered to 16, but there is no consensus on the matter and it seems unlikely to happen in the foreseeable future. The minimum voting age in the 2014 Scottish independence referendum was set at 16, but this does not apply in parliamentary elections.

The minimum age at which it is possible to be a candidate in a parliamentary election was lowered from 21 to 18 in 2006.

POSTAL VOTING

After the First World War postal voting was temporarily introduced for servicemen and others prevented 'by reason of the nature of their occupation from voting in a poll'. At the same time permanent arrangements were made for proxy voting by servicemen. Temporary arrangements for postal voting by servicemen were again made in 1945. In 1948 postal voting was made available to servicemen and, in strictly defined circumstances, to civilians.

The circumstances in which an absent vote (postal or proxy) could be obtained were extended in 1985; however, owing to the fear of fraud, this did not apply in Northern Ireland. Postal voting on demand was introduced in 2001.

The turnout in the 1950 general election, when postal voting was not generally available, was 83.9 per cent. In 2001 when postal voting was available on demand, it was 59.4 per cent. The figures are evidence of the reduced interest of the people. In the 2010 election turnout had moved up to 65.1 per cent.

FIXED-TERM PARLIAMENTS

Prior to 2011 Parliament was dissolved by the monarch at any time, but normally on the advice of and at the request of the prime minister. The maximum period of a Parliament was five years. This was changed by the Fixed-term Parliament Act 2011.

Parliaments now have a fixed term of five years. Polling day must be the first Thursday in May on the fifth year following the previous general election. The prime minister has the power by order made by Statutory Instrument to provide that the polling day is to be held up to two months later than this date. Such a Statutory Instrument must be approved by each House of Parliament. The Act provides two circumstances in which an early general election will be called:

- If the House of Commons resolves 'That this House has no confidence in Her Majesty's Government', and does not within the subsequent fourteen days pass the resolution 'That this House has confidence in Her Majesty's Government'.
- If the House of Commons with the support of two-thirds of its total membership resolves 'That there shall be an early parliamentary general election'. Total membership includes vacant seats and members who choose not to vote.

The Act provides that 'Parliament cannot otherwise be dissolved'. This removes the royal prerogative to dissolve Parliament.

The ability of the prime minister to call a general election at a time of his or her choosing has been a great advantage to his or her party. This privilege has now been removed.

There could be times where the inability to call an election could cause problems. There have been several occasions where early elections have been desirable in the national interest, not just for party advantage. There were two general elections in 1910, two within eight months in 1974, two within nineteen months in 1964–66, two within twenty months in 1950–51 and three within two years in 1922–24. There is also the factor that there may be times when not much is being done in a dead period before an election.

RECALL OF MPS

The Recall of MPs Bill was introduced into Parliament in late 2014. At the time of writing it has not reached the Statute Book.

The bill provides for a recall petition if an MP is sentenced to a prison term or is suspended from the Commons for at least twenty-one sitting days. A petition would be open for signing for a period of eight weeks. If during that time at least 10 per cent of the eligible electors signed, the seat would be declared vacant and a by-election called. The recalled member would be permitted to stand in the election.

List of Parliamentary Constituencies at the Time of the 1830 General Election

England – Boroughs

	Members		Members
Abingdon	1	Bridgnorth	2
Aldborough	2	Bridgwater	2
Aldeburgh	2	Bridport	2
Amersham	2	Bristol	2
Andover	2	Buckingham	2
Appleby	2	Bury St Edmunds	2
Arundel	2	Callington	2
Ashburton	2	Calne	2
Aylesbury	2	Cambridge	2
Banbury	1	Camelford	2
Barnstaple	2	Canterbury	2
Bassetlaw	2	Carlisle	2
Bath	2	Castle Rising	2
Bedford	2	Chester	2
Bere Alston	2	Chichester	2
Berwick-upon-Tweed	2	Chippenham	2
Beverley	2	Christchurch	2
Bewdley	1	Cirencester	2
Bishop's Castle	2	Clitheroe	2
Blechingley	2	Cockermouth	2
Bodmin	2	Colchester	2
Boroughbridge	2	Corfe Castle	2
Bossinney	2	Coventry	2
Boston	2	Cricklade	2
Brackley	2	Dartmouth	2
Bramber	2	Derby	2

	Members		Members
Devizes	2	Leominster	2
Dorchester	2	Lewes	2
Downton	2	Lichfield	2
Droitwich	2	Lincoln	2
Dunwich	2	Liskeard	2
Durham City	2	Liverpool	2
East Grinstead	2	London	4
East Looe	2	Lostwithiel	2
East Retford	2	Ludgershall	2
Evesham	2	Ludlow	2
Exeter	2	Lyme Regis	2
Eye	2	Lymington	2
Fowey	2	Maidstone	2
Gatton	2	Maldon	2
Gloucester	2	Malmesbury	2
Grantham	2	Malton	2
Great Bedwyn	2	Marlborough	2
Great Grimsby	2	Midhurst	2
Great Marlow	2	Milborne Port	2
Great Wenlock	2	Minehead	2
Guildford	2	Mitchell	2
Harwich	2	Monmouth Boroughs	1
Haslemere	2	Morpeth	2
Hedon	2	Newark	2
Helston	2	Newcastle-under-Lyme	2
Hereford	2	Newcastle-upon-Tyne	2
Hertford	2	Newport (Cornwall)	2
Heytesbury	2	Newport (Isle of Wight)	2
Higham Ferrers	1	Newton-le-Willows	2
Hindon	2	Newton	2
Honiton	2	Newtown	2
Horsham	2	Northallerton	2
Huntingdon	2	Northampton	2
Ilchester	2	Norwich	2
Ipswich	2	Nottingham	2
King's Lynn	2	Okehampton	2
Kingston-upon-Hull	2	Old Sarum	2
Knaresborough	2	Orford	2
Lancaster	2	Oxford	2
Launceston	2	Penryn	2
Leicester	2	Peterborough	2

	Members		Members
Petersfield	2	Tewkesbury	2
Plymouth	2	Thetford	2
Plympton Erle	2	Thirsk	2
Pontefract	2	Tiverton	2
Poole	2	Totnes	2
Portsmouth	2	Tregony	2
Preston	2	Truro	2
Queenborough	2	Wallingford	2
Reading	2	Wareham	2
Reigate	2	Warwick	2
Richmond	2	Wells	2
Ripon	2	Wendover	2
Rochester	2	Wenlock	2
St Albans	2	West Looe	2
St Germans	2	Westbury	2
Salisbury	2	Westminster	2
Saltash	2	Weymouth and Melcombe	
Scarborough	2	Regis	4
Shaftesbury	2	Whitchurch	2
Shrewsbury	2	Wigan	2
Southampton	2	Wilton	2
Southwark	2	Winchester	2
Stafford	2	Windsor	2
Stamford	2	Woodstock	2
Steyning	2	Wootton Bassett	2
Stockbridge	2	Worcester	2
Sudbury	2	Wycombe	2
Tamworth	2	Yarmouth (Norfolk)	2
Taunton	2	Yarmouth (Isle of Wight)	2
Tavistock	2	York	2

Cinque Ports

	Members		Members
Dover	2	Rye	2
Hastings	2	Sandwich	2
Hythe	2	Seaford	2
Romney	2	Winchelsea	2

England – Counties

	Members		Members
Bedfordshire	2	Lincolnshire	2
Berkshire	2	Middlesex	2
Buckinghamshire	2	Monmouthshire	2
Cambridgeshire	2	Norfolk	2
Cheshire	2	Northamptonshire	2
Cornwall	2	Northumberland	2
Cumberland	2	Nottinghamshire	2
Derbyshire	2	Oxfordshire	2
Devon	2	Rutland	2
Dorset	2	Shropshire	2
Durham	2	Somerset	2
Essex	2	Staffordshire	2
Gloucestershire	2	Suffolk	2
Hampshire	2	Surrey	2
Herefordshire	2	Sussex	2
Hertfordshire	2	Warwickshire	2
Huntingdonshire	2	Westmorland	2
Kent	2	Wiltshire	2
Lancashire	2	Worcestershire	2
Leicestershire	2	Yorkshire	4

Wales – Boroughs

	Members		Members
Beaumaris	1	Denbigh Boroughs	1
Brecon	1	Flint Boroughs	1
Caernarvon Boroughs	1	Haverfordwest	1
Cardiff Boroughs	1	Montgomery	1
Cardigan Boroughs	1	New Radnor Boroughs	1
Carmarthen	1	Pembroke Boroughs	1

Wales – Counties

	Members		Members
Anglesey	1	Flintshire	1
Breconshire	1	Glamorganshire	1
Cardiganshire	1	Merionethshire	1
Caernarvonshire	1	Montgomeryshire	1
Carmarthenshire	1	Pembrokeshire	1
Denbighshire	1	Radnorshire	1

Scotland – Boroughs (Burghs)

	Members		Members
Aberdeen Burghs	I	Haddington Burghs	I
Anstruther Easter Burghs	I	Inverness Burghs	I
Ayr Burghs	I	Linlithgow Burghs	I
Dumfries Burghs	I	Perth Burghs	I
Dysart Burghs	I	Stirling Burghs	I
Edinburgh	I	Tain (Northern) Burghs	I
Elgin Burghs	I	Wigtown Burghs	I
Glasgow Burghs	I		

Scotland – Counties

	Members		Members
Aberdeenshire	I	Elginshire	I
Argyllshire	I	Fifeshire	I
Ayrshire	I	Forfarshire	I
Banffshire	I	Haddingtonshire	I
Berwickshire	I	Inverness-shire	I
Buteshire and		Kincardineshire	I
Caithness-shire	I	Kirkcudbright-Stewartry	I
(each county elected a member		Lanarkshire	I
in alternate parliaments)		Linlithgowshire	I
Clackmannanshire and		Midlothian	I
Kinross-shire	I	Orkney and Shetland	I
(each county elected a member		Peeblesshire	I
in alternate parliaments)		Perthshire	I
Cromarty and		Renfrewshire	I
Nairnshire	I	Ross-shire	I
(each county elected a member		Roxburghshire	I
in alternate parliaments)		Selkirkshire	I
Dumfriesshire	I	Stirlingshire	I
Dunbartonshire	I	Sutherlandshire	I
Edinburghshire	I	Wigtownshire	I

Ireland – Boroughs

	Members		Members
Athlone	I	Cashel	I
Bandon	I	Clonmel	I
Belfast	I	Coleraine	I
Carlow	I	Cork	I
Carrickfergus	I	Downpatrick	I

	Members		Members
Drogheda	1	Lisburn	1
Dublin	2	Londonderry City	1
Dundalk	1	Mallow	1
Dungannon	1	New Ross	1
Dungarvan	1	Newry	1
Ennis	1	Portarlington	1
Eniskillen	1	Sligo	1
Galway	1	Tralee	1
Kilkenny	1	Waterford City	1
Kinsale	1	Wexford	1
Limerick City	1	Youghal	1

Ireland – Counties

	Members		Members
Antrim	2	Limerick	2
Armagh	2	Londonderry	2
Carlow	2	Longford	2
Cavan	2	Louth	2
Clare	2	Mayo	2
Cork	2	Meath	2
Donegal	2	Monaghan	2
Down	2	Queen's County	2
Dublin	2	Roscommon	2
Fermanagh	2	Sligo	2
Galway	2	Tipperary	2
Kerry	2	Tyrone	2
Kildare	2	Waterford	2
Kilkenny	2	West Meath	2
King's County	2	County Wexford	2
Leitrim	2	Wicklow	2

Universities

	Members		
Cambridge	2	Oxford	2
Dublin	2		

NOTES

1. Monmouth and Monmouthshire are included in England
2. Some of the constituencies had alternative names or alternative spellings

Appendix B

List of Parliamentary Constituencies Immediately after the 1832 Reform Act

England Boroughs

	Members		Members
Abingdon	1	Caine	1
Andover	2	Cambridge	2
Arundel	1	Canterbury	2
Ashburton	1	Carlisle	2
Ashton-under-Lyne	1	Chatham	1
Aylesbury	2	Cheltenham	1
Banbury	1	Chester	2
Barnstaple	2	Chichester	2
Bath	2	Chippenham	2
Bedford	2	Christchurch	1
Berwick-upon-Tweed	2	Cirencester	2
Beverley	2	Clitheroe	1
Bewdley	1	Cockermouth	2
Birmingham	2	Colchester	2
Blackburn	2	Coventry	2
Bodmin	2	Cricklade	2
Bolton	2	Dartmouth	1
Boston	2	Derby	2
Bradford	2	Devizes	2
Bridgnorth	2	Devonport	2
Bridgwater	2	Dorchester	2
Bridport	2	Dover	2
Brighton	2	Droitwich	1
Bristol	2	Dudley	1
Buckingham	2	Durham City	2
Bury	1	East Retford	2
Bury St Edmunds	2	Evesham	2

	Members		Members
Exeter	2	Lymington	2
Eye	2	Macclesfield	2
Finsbury	2	Maidstone	2
Frome	1	Maldon	2
Gateshead	1	Malmesbury	1
Gloucester	2	Malton	2
Grantham	2	Manchester	2
Great Grimsby	1	Marlborough	2
Great Marlow	2	Marylebone	2
Great Yarmouth	2	Midhurst	1
Greenwich	2	Morpeth	1
Guildford	2	Newark-on-Trent	2
Halifax	2	Newcastle-under-Lyme	2
Harwich	2	Newcastle-upon-Tyne	2
Hastings	2	Newport	2
Helston	1	New Shoreham	2
Hereford	2	Northallerton	1
Hertford	2	Northampton	2
Honiton	2	Norwich	2
Horsham	1	Nottingham	2
Huddersfield	1	Oldham	2
Huntingdon	2	Oxford	2
Hythe	1	Penryn and Falmouth	2
Ipswich	2	Peterborough	2
Kendal	1	Petersfield	1
Kidderminster	1	Plymouth	2
King's Lynn	2	Pontefract	2
Kingston Upon Hull	2	Poole	2
Knaresborough	2	Portsmouth	2
Lambeth	2	Preston	2
Lancaster	2	Reading	2
Launceston	1	Reigate	1
Leeds	2	Richmond	2
Leicester	2	Ripon	2
Leominster	2	Rochdale	1
Lewes	2	Rochester	2
Lichfield	2	Rye	1
Lincoln	2	St Albans	2
Liskeard	1	St Ives	1
Liverpool	2	Salford	1
City of London	4	Salisbury	2
Ludlow	2	Sandwich	2
Lyme Regis	1	Scarborough	2

	Members		Members
Shaftesbury	1	North Shields	1
Sheffield	2	Wakefield	1
Shrewsbury	2	Wallingford	1
Southampton	2	Walsall	1
South Shields	1	Wareham	1
Southwark	2	Warrington	1
Stafford	2	Warwick	2
Stamford	2	Wells	2
Stockport	2	Wenlock	2
Stoke-upon-Trent	2	Westbury	1
Stroud	2	Westminster	2
Sudbury	2	Weymouth and	
Sunderland	2	Melcombe Regis	2
Tamworth	2	Whitby	1
Taunton	2	Whitehaven	1
Tavistock	2	Wigan	2
Tewkesbury	2	Wilton	1
Thetford	2	Winchester	2
Thirsk	1	Windsor	2
Tiverton	2	Wolverhampton	2
Totnes	2	Woodstock	1
Tower Hamlets	2	Worcester	2
Truro	2	Wycombe	2
Tynemouth and		York	2

England – Counties

	Members		Members
Bedfordshire	2	Dorset	3
Berkshire	3	Durham Northern	2
Buckinghamshire	3	Durham Southern	2
Cambridgeshire	3	Essex Northern	2
Cheshire Northern	2	Essex Southern	2
Cheshire Southern	2	Gloucestershire Eastern	2
Cornwall Eastern	2	Gloucestershire Western	2
Cornwall Western	2	Hampshire Northern	2
Cumberland Eastern	2	Hampshire Southern	2
Cumberland Western	2	Herefordshire	3
Derbyshire Northern	2	Hertfordshire	3
Derbyshire Southern	2	Huntingdonshire	2
Devon Northern	2	Isle of Wight	1
Devon Southern	2	Kent Eastern	2

	Members		Members
Kent Western	2	Somerset Eastern	2
Lancashire Northern	2	Somerset Western	2
Lancashire Southern	2	Staffordshire Northern	2
Leicestershire Northern	2	Staffordshire Southern	2
Leicestershire Southern	2	Suffolk Eastern	2
Lincolnshire Northern	2	Suffolk Western	2
Lincolnshire Southern	2	Surrey Eastern	2
Middlesex	2	Surrey Western	2
Norfolk Eastern	2	Sussex Eastern	2
Norfolk Western	2	Sussex Western	2
Northamptonshire Northern	2	Warwickshire Northern	2
Northamptonshire Southern	2	Warwickshire Southern	2
Northumberland Northern	2	Westmorland	2
Northumberland Southern	2	Wiltshire Northern	2
Nottinghamshire Northern	2	Wiltshire Southern	2
Nottinghamshire Southern	2	Worcestershire Eastern	2
Oxfordshire	3	Worcestershire Western	2
Rutland	2	East Riding of Yorkshire	2
Shropshire Northern	2	North Riding of Yorkshire	2
Shropshire Southern	2	West Riding of Yorkshire	2

Wales – Boroughs

	Members		Members
Brecon	1	Merthyr Tydfil	1

Wales – Counties

	Members		Members
Anglesey	1	Glamorganshire	2
Breconshire	1	Merionethshire	1
Caernarvonshire	1	Monmouthshire	2
Cardiganshire	1	Montgomeryshire	1
Carmarthenshire	2	Pembrokeshire	1
Denbighshire	2	Radnorshire	1
Flintshire	1		

Wales – District

	Members		Members
Beaumaris	1	Cardiff District	1
Caernarvon Boroughs	1	Cardigan District	1

	Members		Members
Carmarthen Boroughs	1	Montgomery Boroughs	1
Denbigh Boroughs	1	Pembroke Boroughs	1
Flint Boroughs	1	Radnor Boroughs	1
Haverfordwest	1	Swansea District	1
Monmouth Boroughs	1		

Scotland – Boroughs (Burghs)

	Members		Members
Aberdeen	1	Greenock	1
Dundee	1	Paisley	1
Edinburgh	2	Perth	1
Glasgow	2		

Scotland – Counties

	Members		Members
Aberdeenshire	1	Renfrewshire	1
Argyllshire	1	Ross and Cromarty	1
Ayrshire	1	Roxburghshire	1
Banffshire	1	Selkirkshire	1
Berwickshire	1	Stirlingshire	1
Buteshire	1	Sutherland	1
Caithness	1	Wigtownshire	1
Clackmannans and Kinross	1		
Dumfriesshire	1	**Scotland – District**	
Dunbartonshire	1	Ayr Burghs	1
Elginshire and Nairnshire	1	Dumfries Burghs	1
Fife	1	Elgin Burghs	1
Forfarshire	1	Falkirk Burghs	1
Haddingtonshire	1	Haddington Burghs	1
Inverness-shire	1	Inverness Burghs	1
Kincardineshire	1	Kilmarnock Burghs	1
Kirkcudbright Stewartry	1	Kirkaldy Burghs	1
Lanarkshire	1	Leith Burghs	1
Linlithgowshire	1	Montrose Burghs	1
Midlothian		St Andrews Burghs	1
(aka Edinburghshire)	1	Stirling Burghs	1
Orkney and Shetland	1	Wick Burghs	1
Peeblesshire	1	Wigtown Burghs	1
Perthshire	1		

Ireland – Boroughs

	Members		Members
Armagh	1	Enniskillen	1
Athlone	1	Galway Borough	2
Bandon	1	Kilkenny City	1
Belfast	2	Kinsale	1
Carlow	1	Limerick City	2
Carrickfergus	1	Lisburn	1
Cashel	1	Londonderry City	1
Clonmel	1	Mallow	1
Coleraine	1	New Ross	1
Cork City	2	Newry	1
Downpatrick	1	Portarlington	1
Drogheda	1	Sligo	1
Dublin	2	Tralee	1
Dundalk	1	Waterford City	2
Dungannon	1	Wexford	1
Dungarvan	1	Youghal	1
Ennis	1		

Ireland – Counties

	Members		Members
Antrim	2	County Limerick	2
County Armagh	2	County Londonderry	2
County Carlow	2	County Longford	2
Cavan	2	County Louth	2
Clare	2	Mayo	2
County Cork	2	Meath	2
Donegal	2	Monaghan	2
Down		Queen's County	2
County Dublin	2	Roscommon	2
Fermanagh	2	County Sligo	2
County Galway	2	Tipperary	2
Kerry	2	Tyrone	2
Kildare	2	County Waterford	2
County Kilkenny	2	Westmeath	2
King's County	2	County Wexford	2
Leitrim	2	Wicklow	2

Universities

	Members		Members
Cambridge University	2	Oxford University	2
Dublin University	2		

Redistribution of Seats Provided by the Reform Act (England And Wales) 1867 and the Reform Act (Scotland) 1868

Disenfranchised English boroughs

Arundel	(lost 1 member)
Ashburton	(lost 1 member)
Dartmouth	(lost 1 member)
Great Yarmouth	(lost 2 members)
Honiton	(lost 2 members)
Lancaster	(lost 2 members)
Lyme Regis	(lost 1 member)
Reigate	(lost 1 member)
Thetford	(lost 2 members)
Totnes	(lost 2 members)
Wells	(lost 2 members)

Great Yarmouth, Lancaster and Reigate were disenfranchised for corruption but are included in this appendix.

English boroughs that lost one of their two members

Andover
Bodmin
Bridgnorth
Bridport
Buckingham
Chichester
Chippenham
Cirencester
Cockermouth
Devizes

Dorchester
Evesham
Guildford
Harwich
Hertford
Huntingdon
Knaresborough
Leominster
Lewes
Lichfield
Ludlow
Lymington
Maldon
Marlow
Malton
Marlborough
Newport, Isle of Wight
Poole
Richmond
Ripon
Stamford
Tavistock
Tewkesbury
Windsor
Wycombe

English boroughs newly enfranchised

Burnley	(1 member)
Chelsea	(2 members)
Darlington	(1 member)
Dewsbury	(1 member)
Gravesend	(1 member)
Hackney	(2 members)
Hartlepool	(1 member)
Middlesborough	(1 member)
Stalybridge	(1 member)
Stockton	(1 member)
Wednesbury	(1 member)

English boroughs with increased representation

Birmingham	(3 members instead of 2)
Leeds	(3 members instead of 2)
Liverpool	(3 members instead of 2)

Manchester	(3 members instead of 2)
Merthyr Tydfil	(2 members instead of 1)
Salford	(2 members instead of 1)

Increased representation in English counties

The following counties were divided into three districts instead of two, with each district returning two members:

Cheshire
Derbyshire
Devonshire
Essex
Kent
Lincolnshire
Norfolk
Somerset
Staffordshire
Surrey

Lancashire was divided into four two-member districts instead of a three-member district and a two-member district.

The West Riding of Yorkshire was divided into three districts each returning two members.

English universities

University of London was given one seat. It joined Oxford and Cambridge universities which already had two seats each.

Scotland

Glasgow and Dundee were each given an extra seat making three each in total.

Aberdeenshire, Ayrshire and Lanarkshire were each given an extra seat, but were each divided into two single-member constituencies.

Hawick District was created with one member.

Peebles and Selkirk were united with one member.

Two university seats were created, each with one member.

* Edinburgh and St Andrews
* Glasgow and Aberdeen

Appendix D

Full Details of the Provisions of the Redistribution of Seats Act 1885

ENGLAND

Bedfordshire (Representation decreased from 4 to 3 MPs)

BOROUGHS		
Before 1885	**After 1885**	
Bedford (two MPs)	Bedford (one MP)	Representation reduced to one MP.
COUNTY DIVISIONS		
Before 1885	**After 1885**	
Bedfordshire (undivided) (two MPs)	Northern or Biggleswade Division (one MP)	Split into two divisions.
	Southern or Luton Division (one MP)	

Berkshire (Representation decreased from 8 to 5 MPs)

BOROUGHS		
Before 1885	**After 1885**	
Abingdon (one MP)		Abolished. Gave its name to a county division.
Reading (two MPs)	Reading (one MP)	Boundaries widened, representation reduced to one MP.
Wallingford (one MP)		Abolished.
Windsor (one MP)	Windsor (one MP)	No change.
COUNTY DIVISIONS		
Before 1885	**After 1885**	
Berkshire (undivided) (three MPs)	Northern or Abingdon Division (one MP)	Split into three divisions. The abolished boroughs of Abingdon and Wallingford were included in the Abingdon Division.
	Southern or Newbury Division (one MP)	
	Eastern or Wokingham Division (one MP)	

Buckinghamshire (Representation decreased from 8 to 3 MPs)

BOROUGHS		
Before 1885	**After 1885**	
Aylesbury (two MPs)		Abolished. Gave its name to a county division.
Buckingham (one MP)		Abolished. Gave its name to a county division.
Chipping Wycombe (one MP)		Abolished. Gave its name ("Wycombe") to a county division.
Great Marlow (one MP)		Abolished.
COUNTY DIVISIONS		
Before 1885	**After 1885**	
Buckinghamshire (undivided) (3 MPs)	Mid or Aylesbury Division (one MP)	Split into three divisions. The Aylesbury Division absorbed the abolished boroughs of Aylesbury and Great Marlow. The Buckingham Division absorbed Buckingham and the Wycombe Division absorbed Chipping Wycombe.
	Northern or Buckingham Division (one MP)	
	Southern or Wycombe Division (one MP)	

Cambridgeshire (Representation decreased from 5 to 4 MPs)

BOROUGHS		
Before 1885	**After 1885**	
Cambridge (two MPs)	Cambridge (one MP)	Representation reduced to one MP.
COUNTY DIVISIONS		
Before 1885	**After 1885**	
Cambridgeshire (undivided) (three MPs)	Western or Chesterton Division (one MP)	Split into three divisions.
	Eastern or Newmarket Division (one MP)	
	Northern or Wisbech Division (one MP)	

Cheshire (Representation increased from 12 to 13 MPs)

BOROUGHS		
Before 1885	**After 1885**	
Birkenhead (one MP)	Birkenhead (one MP)	No change.
Chester (two MPs)	Chester (one MP)	Representation reduced to one MP.
Macclesfield (one MP)		Disenfranchised for corruption. Gave name to county division.
Stalybridge (one MP)	Stalybridge (one MP)	Boundaries extended.
Stockport (two MPs)	Stockport (two MPs)	No change.

COUNTY DIVISIONS		
Before 1885	**After 1885**	
East Division (two MPs)	Altrincham Division (one MP)	Divided into 8 divisions:
	Crewe Division (one MP)	• The East Division formed the basis of the new Macclesfield Division.
	Eddisbury Division (one MP)	• The Mid Division was divided into the new Altrincham, Hyde and Knutsford Divisions (with parts going to the Crewe, Macclesfield and Northwich Divisions).
Mid Division (two MPs)	Hyde Division (one MP)	
	Knutsford Division (one MP)	
	Macclesfield Division (one MP)	• The South Division was divided into the new Eddisbury and Wirral Divisions (with parts going to the Crewe Division and the Northwich Division).
West Division (two MPs)	Northwich Division (one MP)	
	Wirral Division (one MP)	

Cornwall (Representation decreased from 12 to 7 MPs)

BOROUGHS		
Before 1885	**After 1885**	
Bodmin (one MP)		Abolished. Gave its name to a county division.
Helston (one MP)		Abolished.
Launceston (one MP)		Abolished.
Liskeard (one MP)		Abolished.
Penryn and Falmouth (two MPs)	Penryn and Falmouth (one MP)	Representation reduced to one MP.
St Ives (one MP)		Abolished. Gave its name to a county division.
Truro (two MPs)		Abolished. Gave its name to a county division.

COUNTY DIVISIONS		
Before 1885	**After 1885**	
Eastern Division (two MPs)	Mid or St Austell Division (one MP)	Divided into 6 Divisions:
	North-Eastern or Launceston Division (one MP)	• The Eastern Division was divided into the new North-Eastern and South-Eastern Divisions (with part going to the Mid Division).
	North-Western or Camborne Division (one MP)	
	South-Eastern or Bodmin Division (one MP)	• The Western Division was divided into the new North-Western, Truro and Western Divisions (with part going to the Mid Division).
Western Division (two MPs)	Truro Division (one MP)	
	Western or St Ives Division (one MP)	

Cumberland (Representation decreased from 8 to 6 MPs)

BOROUGHS		
Before 1885	**After 1885**	
Carlisle (two MPs)	Carlisle (one MP)	Representation reduced to one MP.
Cockermouth (one MP)		Abolished. Gave its name to a county division.
Whitehaven (one MP)	Whitehaven (one MP)	No change.
COUNTY DIVISIONS		
Before 1885	**After 1885**	
Eastern Division (two MPs) Western Division (two MPs)	Cockermouth Division (one MP)	Reorganised into four divisions, absorbed abolished Borough of Cockermouth.
	Egremont (or Western) Division (one MP)	
	Eskdale (or Northern) Division (one MP)	
	Penrith (or Mid) Division (one MP)	

Derbyshire (Representation increased from 8 to 9 MPs)

BOROUGHS		
Before 1885	**After 1885**	
Derby (two MPs)	Derby (two MPs)	Boundaries extended.
COUNTY DIVISIONS		
Before 1885	**After 1885**	
East Division (two MPs) North Division (two MPs) South Division (two MPs)	Chesterfield Division (one MP)	Reorganised into seven divisions.
	Mid Division (one MP)	
	North-Eastern Division (one MP)	
	Southern Division (one MP)	
	Western Division (one MP	
	High Peak Division (one MP)	
	Ilkeston Division (one MP)	

Devon (Representation decreased from 17 to 13 MPs)

BOROUGHS		
Before 1885	**After 1885**	
Barnstaple (two MPs)		Abolished. Gave its name to a county division.
Devonport (two MPs)	Devonport (two MPs)	No change.
Exeter (two MPs)	Exeter (one MP)	Representation reduced to one MP.
Plymouth (two MPs)	Plymouth (two MPs)	No change.

| Tavistock (one MP) | | Abolished. Gave its name to a county division. |
| Tiverton (two MPs) | | Abolished. Gave its name to a county division. |

COUNTY DIVISIONS		
Before 1885	**After 1885**	
East Division (two MPs)	Eastern or Honiton Division (one MP)	Reorganised into eight divisions, absorbed abolished boroughs of Barnstaple, Tavistock and Tiverton.
	Mid or Ashburton Division (one MP)	
	Northern or South Molton Division (one MP)	
North Division (two MPs)	North-Eastern or Tiverton Division (one MP)	
	North-Western or Barnstaple Division (one MP)	
South Division (two MPs)	Torquay Division (one MP)	
	Southern or Totnes Division (one MP)	
	Western or Tavistock Division (one MP)	

Dorset (Representation decreased from 10 to 4 MPs)

BOROUGHS		
Before 1885	**After 1885**	
Bridport (one MP)		Abolished..
Dorchester (one MP)		Abolished.
Poole (one MP)		Abolished.
Shaftesbury (one MP)		Abolished.
Wareham (one MP)		Abolished.
Weymouth and Melcombe Regis (two MPs)		Abolished.
COUNTY DIVISIONS		
Before 1885	**After 1885**	
Dorset (undivided) (three MPs)	Eastern Division (one MP)	Split into four divisions, absorbing the six abolished boroughs.
	Northern Division (one MP)	
	Southern Division (one MP)	
	Western Division (one MP)	

Durham (Representation increased from 13 to 16 MPs)

BOROUGHS		
Before 1885	**After 1885**	
Darlington (one MP)	Darlington (one MP)	Boundaries widened.
Durham City (two MPs)	Durham City (one MP)	Representation reduced to one MP.
Gateshead (one MP)	Gateshead (one MP)	No change.

Hartlepool (one MP)	Hartlepool (one MP)	No change.
South Shields (one MP)	South Shields (one MP)	No change.
Stockton (one MP)	Stockton (one MP)	No change.
Sunderland (two MPs)	Sunderland (two MPs)	No change.

COUNTY DIVISIONS		
Before 1885	**After 1885**	
Northern Division (two MPs Southern Division (two MPs)	Barnard Castle Division (one MP)	Reorganised into eight divisions.
	Bishop Auckland Division (one MP)	
	Chester Le Street (one MP)	
	Houghton Le Spring Division (one MP)	
	Jarrow Division (one MP)	
	Mid Division (one MP)	
	North-Western Division (one MP)	
	South-Eastern Division (one MP)	

Essex (Representation increased from 9 to 11 MPs)

BOROUGHS		
Before 1885	**After 1885**	
Colchester (two MPs)	Colchester (one MP)	Representation reduced to one MP.
Harwich (one MP)		Abolished. Gave its name to a county division.
Maldon (one MP)		Abolished. Gave its name to a county division.
Formed part of South Division of County	West Ham, North Division (one MP)	New parliamentary borough of West Ham, divided into two single-member divisions.
	West Ham, South Division (one MP)	

COUNTY DIVISIONS		
Before 1885	**After 1885**	
East Division (two MPs) South Division (two MPs) West Division (two MPs)	Eastern or Maldon Division (one MP)	Reorganised into eight divisions. Part of former South Division constituted as parliamentary Borough of West Ham.
	Mid or Chelmsford Division (one MP)	
	Northern or Saffron Walden Division (one MP)	
	North-Eastern or Harwich Division (one MP)	
	Southern or Romford Division (one MP)	
	South-Eastern Division (one MP)	
	South-Western or Walthamstow Division (one MP)	
	Western or Epping Division (one MP)	

Gloucestershire (Representation decreased from 13 to 11 MPs)

BOROUGHS		
Before 1885	**After 1885**	
Bristol (two MPs)	Bristol, East Division (one MP)	Boundaries of parliamentary borough extended to include St George, Horfield, and Stapleton, and part of Bedminster. Divided into four single-member divisions.
	Bristol, North Division (one MP)	
	Bristol, South Division (one MP)	
	Bristol, West Division (one MP)	
Cheltenham (one MP)	Cheltenham (one MP)	Boundaries extended to include Charlton Kings.
Cirencester (one MP)		Abolished. Gave its name to a county division.
Gloucester (two MPs)	Gloucester (one MP)	Representation reduced to one MP.
Stroud (two MPs)		Abolished. Gave its name to a county division.
Tewkesbury (one MP)		Abolished. Gave its name to a county division.
COUNTY DIVISIONS		
Before 1885	**After 1885**	
Eastern Division (two MPs)	Eastern or Cirencester Division (one MP)	Reorganised into five divisions, absorbing boroughs of Stroud and Tewkesbury.
	Forest of Dean Division (one MP)	
	Mid or Stroud Division (one MP)	
Western Division (two MPs)	Northern or Tewkesbury Division (one MP)	Part of former Western Division included in parliamentary borough of Bristol.
	Southern or Thornbury Division (one MP)	

Hampshire and Isle of Wight (Representation decreased from 16 to 12 MPs)

BOROUGHS		
Before 1885	**After 1885**	
Andover (one MP)		Abolished. Gave its name to a county division.
Christchurch (one MP)	Christchurch (one MP)	No change.
Lymington (one MP)		Abolished. Gave its name to a county division.
Newport (Isle of Wight) (one MP)		Abolished. Area included in Isle of Wight division.
Petersfield (one MP)		Abolished. Gave its name to a county division.
Portsmouth (two MPs)	Portsmouth (two MPs)	No change.
Southampton (two MPs)	Southampton (two MPs)	Boundaries widened to include Millbrook, Bitterne and St Mary Extra areas.
Winchester (two MPs)	Winchester (one MP)	Representation reduced to one MP.

COUNTY DIVISIONS		
Before 1885	After 1885	
Northern Division (two MPs)	Eastern or Petersfield Division (one MP)	Reorganised into five single-member divisions, absorbing parliamentary boroughs of Andover, Lymington and Petersfield.
	New Forest Division (one MP)	
	Northern or Basingstoke Division (one MP)	
Southern Division (two MPs)	Southern or Fareham Division (one MP)	
	Western or Andover Division (one MP)	
Isle of Wight Division (one MP)	Isle of Wight Division (one MP)	Absorbed the parliamentary borough of Newport.

Herefordshire (Representation decreased from 6 to 3 MPs)

BOROUGHS		
Before 1885	After 1885	
Hereford (two MPs)	Hereford (one MP)	Representation reduced to one MP.
Leominster (one MP)		Abolished. Gave its name to a county division.
COUNTY DIVISIONS		
Before 1885	After 1885	
Herefordshire (undivided) (three MPs)	Leominster or Northern Division (one MP)	Split into two divisions, absorbed parliamentary borough of Leominster.
	Ross or Southern Division (one MP)	

Hertfordshire (Representation remained at 4 MPs)

BOROUGHS		
Before 1885	After 1885	
Hertford (one MP)		Abolished. Gave its name to a county division.
COUNTY DIVISIONS		
Before 1885	After 1885	
Hertfordshire (undivided) (three MPs)	Eastern or Hertford Division	Split into four divisions, absorbed parliamentary borough of Hertford.
	Mid or St Albans Division	
	Northern or Hitchin Division	
	Western or Watford Division	

Huntingdonshire (Representation decreased from 3 to 2 MPs)

BOROUGHS		
Before 1885	**After 1885**	
Huntingdon (one MP)		Abolished. Gave its name to a county division.
COUNTY DIVISIONS		
Before 1885	**After 1885**	
Huntingdon (undivided) (two MPs)	Northern or Ramsey Division	Split into two divisions, absorbed parliamentary borough of Huntingdon.
	Southern or Huntingdon Division	

Kent (Representation decreased from 21 to 19 MPs)

BOROUGHS		
Before 1885	**After 1885**	
Canterbury (two MPs)	Canterbury (one MP)	Representation reduced to one MP.
Chatham (one MP)	Chatham (one MP)	No change.
Dover (two MPs)	Dover (one MP)	Representation reduced to one MP.
Gravesend (one MP)	Gravesend (one MP)	No change.
Greenwich (two MPs)	Greenwich (one MP)	Boundaries altered, with areas transferred to create new boroughs of Deptford and Woolwich, each represented by one MP.
	Deptford (one MP)	
	Woolwich (one MP)	
Hythe (one MP)	Hythe (one MP)	No change.
Formed part of West Division of county	Lewisham (one MP)	New parliamentary borough.
Maidstone (two MPs)	Maidstone (one MP)	Boundaries altered. Representation reduced to one MP.
Rochester (two MPs)	Rochester (one MP)	Representation reduced to one MP.
Sandwich (two MPs)		Disenfranchised for corruption.

COUNTY DIVISIONS		
Before 1885	**After 1885**	
Eastern Division (two MPs)	Southern or Ashford Division (one MP)	Reorganised into eight single-member divisions, absorbing parliamentary borough of Sandwich.
	North-Western or Dartford Division (one MP)	
Mid Kent (two MPs)	North-Eastern or Faversham Division (one MP)	
	Isle of Thanet Division (one MP)	
	Mid or Medway Division (one MP)	
	Eastern or St Augustine's Division (one MP)	
Kent West (two MPs)	Western or Sevenoaks Division (one MP)	
	South Western or Tunbridge Division (one MP)	

Lancashire (Representation increased from 30 to 57 MPs)

BOROUGHS		
Before 1885	**After 1885**	
Ashton-under-Lyne (one MP)	Ashton-under-Lyne (one MP)	Boundaries extended to include the local government district of Hurst.
Formed part of North Division of county	Barrow-in-Furness (one (MP)	New parliamentary borough.
Blackburn (two MPs)	Blackburn (two MPs)	Boundaries extended to include entire municipal borough.
Bolton (two MPs)	Bolton (two MPs)	Boundaries extended to include entire municipal borough.
Burnley (one MP)	Burnley (one MP)	No change.
Bury (one MP)	Bury (one MP)	Boundaries extended to include entire municipal borough.
Clitheroe (one MP)		Abolished. Gave its name to a county division.
Liverpool (3 MPs)	Abercromby Division (one MP)	Boundaries of parliamentary borough extended to include entirety of Toxteth Park and parts of Walton-on-the-Hill, Wavertree, and West Derby. Divided into nine single-member divisions
	East Toxteth Division (one MP)	
	Everton Division (one MP)	
	Exchange Division (one MP)	
	Kirkdale Division (one MP)	
	Scotland Division (one MP	
	Walton Division (one MP)	
	West Derby Division (one MP)	
	West Toxteth Division (one MP)	

Manchester (3 MPs)	East Division (one MP)	Boundaries of parliamentary borough extended to include the local government districts of Moss Side and Rusholme and a detached part of the parish of Gorton. Divided into six single-member divisions.
	North Division (one MP)	
	North East Division (one MP)	
	North West Division (one MP)	
	South Division (one MP)	
	South West (one MP)	
Oldham (two MPs)	Oldham (two MPs)	Boundaries extended to include entire municipal borough.
Preston (two MPs)	Preston (two MPs)	Boundaries changed to comprise entire municipal borough of Preston, (with extended boundaries due to come into effect on 1 June 1889), and the local government district of Fulwood.
Rochdale (one MP)	Rochdale (one MP)	No change.
Formed from part of South West Division of county	St Helens (one MP)	New parliamentary borough.
Salford (two MPs)	North Division (one MP)	Divided into three single-member divisions.
	South Division (one MP)	
	West Division (one MP)	
Warrington (one MP)	Warrington (one MP)	No change.
Wigan (two MPs)	Wigan (one MP)	Representation reduced to one MP.

COUNTY DIVISIONS

Before 1885	After 1885	
North Division (two MPs)	Blackpool Division (one MP)	Divided into four single-member divisions, part constituted as new parliamentary borough of Barrow-in-Furness.
	Chorley Division (one MP)	
	Lancaster Division (one MP)	
	North Lonsdale Division (one MP)	
North-East Division (two MPs)	Accrington Division (one MP)	Absorbed former parliamentary borough of Clitheroe, divided into four single-member divisions.
	Clitheroe Division (one MP)	
	Darwen Division (one MP)	
	Rossendale Division (one MP)	
South-East Division (two MPs)	Eccles Division (one MP)	Divided into eight single-member divisions.
	Gorton Division (one MP)	
	Heywood Division (one MP)	
	Middleton Division (one MP)	
	Prestwich Division (one MP)	
	Radcliffe cum Farnworth Division (one MP)	
	Stretford Division (one MP)	
	Westhoughton Division (one MP)	

South-West Division (two MPs)	Bootle Division (one MP)	Divided into seven single-member divisions, part constituted as new parliamentary borough of St Helens.
	Ince Division (one MP)	
	Leigh Division (one MP)	
	Newton Division (one MP)	
	Ormskirk Division (one MP)	
	Southport Division (one MP)	
	Widnes Division (one MP)	

Leicestershire (Representation remained at 6 MPs)

BOROUGHS		
Before 1885	**After 1885**	
Leicester (two MPs)	Leicester (two MPs	No change.
COUNTY DIVISIONS		
Before 1885	**After 1885**	
Northern Division (two MPs)	Eastern (or Melton) Division (one MP)	Divided into four single-member divisions.
	Mid (or Loughborough) Division (one MP)	
Southern Division (two MPs)	Southern (or Harborough) Division (one MP)	
	Western (or Bosworth) Division (one MP)	

Lincolnshire (Representation decreased from 13 to 11 MPs)

BOROUGHS		
Before 1885	**After 1885**	
Boston (two MPs)	Boston (one MP)	Representation reduced to one MP. Boundaries simplified.
Grantham (two MPs)	Grantham (one MP)	Representation reduced to one MP.
Great Grimsby (one MP)	Great Grimsby (one MP)	No change.
Lincoln (two MPs)	Lincoln (one MP)	Representation reduced to one MP. Boundaries extended to include Bracebridge.
Stamford (one MP)		Abolished. Gave its name to a county division.

COUNTY DIVISIONS		
Before 1885	After 1885	
Lincolnshire Mid (two MPs)	North Lindsey (or Brigg) Division (one MP)	Divided into seven single-member divisions.
	West Lindsey (or Gainsborough) Division (one MP)	
Lincolnshire North (two MPs)	South Lindsey (or Horncastle) Division (one MP)	
	East Lindsey (or Louth) Division (one MP)	
Lincolnshire South (two MPs)	North Kesteven (or Sleaford) Division (one MP)	
	Holland (or Spalding) Division (one MP)	
	South Kesteven (or Stamford) Division (one MP)	

Middlesex (Representation increased from 18 to 47 MPs)

BOROUGHS		
Before 1885	After 1885	
Chelsea (two MPs)	Chelsea (one MP)	Divided into four parliamentary boroughs, three of which returned one MP each, and one (Kensington) was itself divided into two single-member divisions.
	Fulham (one MP)	
	Hammersmith (one MP)	
	Kensington, North Division (one MP)	
	Kensington, South Division (one MP)	
City of London (four MPs)	City of London (two MPs)	Representation reduced to two MPs.
Finsbury (two MPs)	Finsbury, Central Division (one MP)	Divided into two parliamentary boroughs: Finsbury, consisting of 3 single-member divisions; and Islington divided into 4 single-member divisions.
	Finsbury, East Division (one MP)	
	Finsbury, Holborn Division (one MP)	
	Islington, East Division (one MP)	
	Islington, North Division (one MP)	
	Islington, South Division (one MP)	
	Islington, West Division (one MP)	

Hackney (two MPs)	Bethnal Green, North East Division (one MP)	Divided into three parliamentary boroughs: Bethnal Green (divided into 2 one-member divisions), Hackney (divided into 3 one-member divisions) and Shoreditch (divided into 2 one-member divisions).
	Bethnal Green, South West Division (one MP)	
	Hackney, Central Division (one MP)	
	Hackney, North Division (one MP)	
	Hackney, South Division (one MP)	
	Shoreditch, Haggerston Division (one MP)	
	Shoreditch, Hoxton Division (one MP)	
Created from part of parliamentary county	Hampstead (one MP)	New parliamentary borough of Hampstead.
Marylebone (two MPs)	Marylebone, East Division (one MP)	Divided into three parliamentary boroughs: Marylebone (divided into 2 divisions), Paddington (2 divisions) and St Pancras (4 divisions).
	Marylebone, West Division (one MP)	
	Paddington, North Division (one MP)	
	Paddington, South Division (one MP)	
	St Pancras, East Division (one MP)	
	St Pancras, North Division (one MP)	
	St Pancras, South Division (one MP)	
	St Pancras, West Division (one MP)	
Tower Hamlets (two MPs)	Bow and Bromley (one MP)	Divided into 7 single-member divisions.
	Limehouse Division (one MP)	
	Mile End Division (one MP)	
	Poplar Division (one MP)	
	St George Division (one MP)	
	Stepney Division (one MP)	
	Whitechapel Division (one MP)	
Westminster (two MPs)	Westminster (one MP)	Divided into three parliamentary boroughs, each returning one MP.
	St George, Hanover Square (one MP)	
	Strand (one MP)	

COUNTY DIVISIONS		
Before 1885	**After 1885**	
Middlesex (undivided) two MPs)	Brentford Division (one MP)	Divided into seven single-member divisions, part constituted as new parliamentary borough of Hampstead.
	Ealing Division (one MP)	
	Enfield Division (one MP)	
	Harrow Division (one MP)	
	Hornsey Division (one MP)	
	Tottenham Division (one MP)	
	Uxbridge Division (one MP)	

Norfolk (Representation unchanged (10 MPs))

BOROUGHS		
Before 1885	**After 1885**	
King's Lynn (two MPs)	King's Lynn (one MP)	Representation reduced to one MP. Boundaries extended to include entire municipal borough.
Norwich (two MPs)	Norwich (two MPs)	No change.
Formed from part of North Division of the county	Great Yarmouth (one MP)	New parliamentary borough of Great Yarmouth.
COUNTY DIVISIONS		
Before 1885	**After 1885**	
North Division (two MPs)	Eastern Division (one MP)	Reorganised into six single-member divisions, part constituted as new parliamentary borough of Great Yarmouth.
	Mid Division (one MP)	
South Division (two MPs)	North Division (one MP)	
	North West Division (one MP)	
	South Division (one MP)	
West Division (two MPs)	South West Division (one MP)	

Northamptonshire (Representation decreased from 8 to 7 MPs)

BOROUGHS		
Before 1885	**After 1885**	
Peterborough (two MPs)	Peterborough (one MP)	Representation reduced to one MP.
Northampton (two MPs)	Northampton (two MPs)	No change.
COUNTY DIVISIONS		
Before 1885	**After 1885**	
Northern Division (two MPs)	Eastern Division (one MP)	Reorganised into four single-member divisions.
	Mid Division (one MP)	
Southern Division (two MPs)	Northern Division (one MP)	
	Southern Division (one MP)	

Northumberland (Representation decreased from 10 to 8 MPs)

BOROUGHS		
Before 1885	**After 1885**	
Berwick-upon-Tweed (two MPs)		Abolished. Gave its name to a county division.
Morpeth (one MP)	Morpeth (one MP)	No change.
Newcastle-upon-Tyne (two MPs)	Newcastle-upon-Tyne (two MPs)	No change.
Tynemouth and North Shields (one MP)	Tynemouth (one MP)	Renamed.
COUNTY DIVISIONS		
Before 1885	**After 1885**	
Northern Division (two MPs)	Berwick-upon-Tweed Division (one MP)	Reorganised into four single-member divisions.
	Hexham Division (one MP)	
Southern Division (two MPs)	Tyneside Division (one MP)	
	Wansbeck Division (one MP)	

Nottinghamshire (Representation decreased from 10 to 7 MPs)

BOROUGHS		
Before 1885	**After 1885**	
East Retford (two MPs)		Abolished.
Newark (two MPs)		Abolished. Gave its name to a county division.
Nottingham (two MPs)	East Division (one MP)	Boundaries extended to include entire municipal borough. Divided into three single-member divisions.
	South Division (one MP)	
	West Division (one MP)	
COUNTY DIVISIONS		
Before 1885	**After 1885**	
Northern Division (two MPs)	Bassetlaw Division (one MP)	Reorganised into four single-member divisions, absorbed parliamentary boroughs of East Retford and Newark.
	Mansfield Division (one MP)	
Southern Division (two MPs)	Newark Division (one MP)	
	Rushcliffe Division (one MP)	

Oxfordshire (Representation decreased from 6 to 4 MPs)

BOROUGHS		
Before 1885	**After 1885**	
Banbury (one MP)		Abolished. Gave its name to a county division.
Oxford (two MPs)	Oxford (one MP)	Representation reduced to one MP.

Woodstock (one MP)		Abolished. Gave its name to a county division.

COUNTY DIVISIONS		
Before 1885	After 1885	
Oxfordshire (undivided) (three MPs)	Northern or Banbury Division (one MP)	Divided into three single-member divisions, absorbing parliamentary boroughs of Banbury and Woodstock.
	Mid or Woodstock Division (one MP)	
	Southern or Henley Division (one MP)	

Rutland (Representation reduced from 2 MPs to 1)

PARLIAMENTARY COUNTY		
Before 1885	After 1885	
Rutland (undivided) (two MPs)	Rutland (one MP)	Representation reduced to one MP.

Shropshire (Representation decreased from 10 to 5 MPs)

BOROUGHS		
Before 1885	After 1885	
Bridgnorth (one MP)		Abolished.
Ludlow (one MP)		Abolished. Gave its name to a county division.
Shrewsbury (two MPs)	Shrewsbury (one MP)	Representation reduced to one MP.
Wenlock (two MPs)		Abolished.

COUNTY DIVISIONS		
Before 1885	After 1885	
Northern Division (two MPs)	Mid or Wellington Division (one MP)	Reorganised as four single-member divisions, absorbing abolished parliamentary boroughs of Bridgnorth, Ludlow and Wenlock.
	Northern or Newport Division (one MP)	
Southern Division (two MPs)	Southern or Ludlow Division (one MP)	
	Western or Oswestry Division (one MP)	

Somerset (Representation decreased from 12 to 10 MPs)

BOROUGHS		
Before 1885	**After 1885**	
Bath (two MPs)	Bath (two MPs)	No change.
Frome (two MPs)		Abolished. Gave its name to a county division.
Taunton (two MPs)	Taunton (one MP)	Representation reduced to one MP.
COUNTY DIVISIONS		
Before 1885	**After 1885**	
East Division (two MPs)	Bridgwater Division (one MP)	Reorganised as seven single-member divisions.
	Eastern Division (one MP)	
Mid Division (two MPs)	Frome Division (one MP)	
	Northern Division (one MP)	
	Southern Division (one MP)	
	Wells Division (one MP)	
Western Division (two MPs)	Western or Wellington Division (one MP)	

Staffordshire (Representation decreased from 20 to 17 MPs)

BOROUGHS		
Before 1885	**After 1885**	
Lichfield (one MP)		Abolished. Gave its name to a county division.
Newcastle-under-Lyme (two MPs)	Newcastle-under-Lyme (one MP)	Representation reduced to one MP. Boundaries extended to include entire municipal borough, Tunstall local government district and part of the parish of Wolstanton.
Stafford (two MPs)	Stafford (one MP)	Representation reduced to one MP. Boundaries extended to include entire municipal borough.
Stoke-upon-Trent (two MPs)	Stoke-upon-Trent (one MP)	Divided into two new parliamentary boroughs.
	Hanley (one MP)	
Tamworth (two MPs)		Abolished. Gave its name to a county division of Warwickshire.
Walsall (one MP)	Walsall (one MP)	No change.
Wednesbury (one MP)	Wednesbury (one MP)	Divided into two new parliamentary boroughs.
	West Bromwich (one MP)	
Wolverhampton (two MPs)	East Division (one MP)	Divided into three single-member divisions.
	South Division (one MP)	
	West Division (one MP)	

COUNTY DIVISIONS		
Before 1885	**After 1885**	
East Division (two MPs)	Burton Division (one MP)	Reorganised into seven singe-member divisions.
	Handsworth Division (one MP)	
	Kingswinford Division (one MP)	
North Division (two MPs)	Leek Division (one MP)	
	Lichfield Division (one MP)	
	North-Western Division (one MP)	
West Division (two MPs)	Western Division (one MP)	

Suffolk (Representation decreased from 9 to 8 MPs)

BOROUGHS		
Before 1885	**After 1885**	
Bury St Edmunds (two MPs)	Bury St Edmunds (one MP)	Representation reduced to one MP.
Eye (one MP)		Abolished. Gave its name to a county division.
Ipswich (two MPs)	Ipswich (two MPs)	No change.
COUNTY DIVISIONS		
Before 1885	**After 1885**	
Eastern Division (two MPs)	Northern or Lowestoft Division (one MP)	Reorganised into five single-member divisions, absorbing parliamentary borough of Eye.
	North-Eastern or Eye Division (one MP)	
	North-Western or Stowmarket Division (one MP)	
Western Division (two MPs)	South or Sudbury Division (one MP)	
	South-Eastern or Woodbridge Division (one MP)	

Surrey (Representation increased from 11 to 22 MPs)

BOROUGHS		
Before 1885	**After 1885**	
Created from parts of the Eastern and Mid Division of parliamentary county	Battersea and Clapham, Battersea Division (one MP)	New parliamentary borough of Battersea and Clapham formed from the parish of Battersea from Mid Division and the parish of Clapham from Eastern Division. Divided into two single-member divisions.
	Battersea and Clapham, Clapham Division (one MP)	

Created from part of Eastern Division of parliamentary county	Croydon (one MP)	New parliamentary borough of Croydon.
Guildford (one MP)		Abolished. Gave its name to a county division.
Lambeth (two MPs)	Camberwell, Dulwich Division (one MP)	Reconstituted as three new parliamentary boroughs: Camberwell (incorporating Dulwich from the Eastern Division of county), Lambeth and Newington. The three boroughs were divided into nine single-member divisions.
	Camberwell, North Division (one MP)	
	Camberwell, Peckham Division (one MP)	
	Lambeth, Brixton Division (one MP)	
	Lambeth, Kennington Division (one MP)	
	Lambeth, North Division (one MP)	
	Lambeth, Norwood Division (one MP)	
	Newington, Walworth Division (one MP)	
	Newington, West Division (one MP)	
Southwark (two MPs)	Southwark, Bermondsey Division (one MP)	Representation increased to three members; divided into three single-member divisions.
	Southwark, Rotherhithe Division (one MP)	
	Southwark, West Division (one MP)	
Created from parts of the Eastern and Mid Divisions of parliamentary county	Wandsworth (one MP)	New parliamentary borough of Wandsworth.

COUNTY DIVISIONS		
Before 1885	**After 1885**	
Eastern Division (two MPs)	Kingston Division (one MP)	Reorganised into six single-member divisions.
	Mid or Epsom Division (one MP)	
	North-Eastern or Wimbledon Division (one MP)	
Mid Division (two MPs)	North-Western or Chertsey Division (one MP)	
	South Eastern or Reigate Division (one MP)	
Western Division (two MPs)	South-Western or Guildford Division (one MP)	

Sussex (Representation decreased from 15 to 9 MPs)

BOROUGHS		
Before 1885	**After 1885**	
Brighton (two MPs)	Brighton (two MPs)	No change.
Chichester (one MP)		Abolished. Gave its name to a county division.
Hastings (two MPs)	Hastings (one MP)	Boundaries altered. Representation reduced to one MP.
Horsham (one MP)		Abolished. Gave its name to a county division.

Lewes (one MP)		Abolished. Gave its name to a county division.
Midhurst (one MP)		Abolished.
New Shoreham (two MPs)		Abolished.
Rye (one MP)		Abolished. Gave its name to a county division.

COUNTY DIVISIONS		
Before 1885	**After 1885**	
Eastern Division (two MPs)	Eastern or Rye Division (one MP)	Absorbed abolished parliamentary boroughs of Chichester, Horsham, Lewes, Midhurst, New Shoreham and Rye. Reorganised into six single-member divisions.
	Mid or Lewes Division (one MP)	
	Northern or East Grinstead Division (one MP)	
	North-Western or Horsham Division (one MP)	
Western Division (two MPs)	Southern or Eastbourne Division (one MP)	
	South-Western or Chichester Division (one MP)	

Warwickshire (Representation increased from 11 to 14 MPs)

BOROUGHS		
Before 1885	**After 1885**	
Created from part of Northern Division of parliamentary county	Aston Manor (one MP)	New parliamentary borough of Aston Manor
Birmingham (three MPs)	Birmingham, Bordesley Division (one MP)	Boundaries of parliamentary borough extended to include local government districts of Balsall Heath, Harborne, and Saltley, and the hamlet of Little Bromwich. Representation increased to seven MPs, divided into seven single-member divisions.
	Birmingham, Central Division (one MP)	
	Birmingham, East Division (one MP)	
	Birmingham, Edgbaston Division (one MP)	
	Birmingham, North Division (one MP)	
	Birmingham, South Division (one MP)	
	Birmingham, West Division (one MP)	
Coventry (two MPs)	Coventry (one MP)	Representation reduced to one MP.
Warwick (two MPs)	Warwick and Leamington (one MP)	Parliamentary borough of Warwick extended to include the municipal borough of Royal Leamington Spa and the local government districts of Milverton and Lillington. Representation reduced to one MP.

COUNTY DIVISIONS		
Before 1885	**After 1885**	
Northern Division (two MPs)	Northern or Tamworth Division (one MP)	Reorganised into four single-member divisions.
	North-Eastern or Nuneaton Division (one MP)	
Southern Division (two MPs)	South-Eastern or Rugby Division (one MP)	
	South Western or Stratford on Avon Division (one MP)	

Westmorland (Representation decreased from 3 to 2 MPs)

BOROUGHS		
Before 1885	**After 1885**	
Kendal (one MP)		Abolished. Gave its name to a county division.
COUNTY DIVISIONS		
Before 1885	**After 1885**	
Westmorland (undivided) (two MPs)	Northern or Appleby Division (one MP)	Reorganised into two single-member divisions, absorbing abolished parliamentary borough of Kendal.
	Southern or Kendal Division (one MP)	

Wiltshire (Representation decreased from 15 to 6 MPs)

BOROUGHS		
Before 1885	**After 1885**	
Calne (one MP)		Abolished.
Chippenham (one MP)		Abolished. Gave its name to a county division.
Cricklade (two MPs)		Abolished. Gave its name to a county division.
Devizes (one MP)		Abolished. Gave its name to a county division.
Malmesbury (one MP)		Abolished.
Marlborough (one MP)		Abolished.
Salisbury (two MPs)	Salisbury (one MP)	Boundaries extended to include entire parish of Fisherton Anger, part of the parish of Milford. Representation reduced to one MP.
Westbury (one MP)		Abolished. Gave its name to a county division.
Wilton (one MP)		Abolished. Gave its name to a county division.

COUNTY DIVISIONS		
Before 1885	After 1885	
Northern Division (two MPs)	Eastern or Devizes Division (one MP)	Reorganised as five single-member divisions, absorbing the abolished parliamentary boroughs of Calne, Chippenham, Cricklade, Devizes, Malmesbury, Marlborough, Westbury and Wilton.
	Northern or Cricklade Division (one MP)	
	North-Western or Chippenham Division (one MP)	
Southern Division (two MPs)	Southern or Wilton Division (one MP)	
	Western or Westbury Division (one MP)	

Worcestershire (Representation decreased from 11 to 8 MPs)

BOROUGHS		
Before 1885	After 1885	
Bewdley (one MP)		Abolished. Gave its name to a county division.
Droitwich (one MP)		Abolished. Gave its name to a county division.
Dudley (one MP)	Dudley (one MP)	No change.
Evesham (one MP)		Abolished. Gave its name to a county division.
Kidderminster (one MP)	Kidderminster (one MP)	No change.
Worcester (two MPs)	Worcester (one MP)	Representation reduced to one MP.
COUNTY DIVISIONS		
Before 1885	After 1885	
Eastern Division (two MPs)	Eastern Division (one MP)	Reorganised as five single-member divisions, absorbing the abolished parliamentary boroughs of Bewdley, Droitwich and Evesham.
	Mid or Droitwich Division (one MP)	
	Northern Division (one MP)	
Western Division (two MPs)	Southern or Evesham Division (one MP)	
	Western or Bewdley Division (one MP)	

Yorkshire (Representation increased from 38 to 52 MPs)

BOROUGHS		
Before 1885	After 1885	
Bradford (two MPs)	Bradford, Central Division (one MP)	Boundaries widened to include entire municipal borough. Representation increased to three MPs, divided into three single-member divisions.
	Bradford, East Division (one MP)	
	Bradford, West Division (one MP)	
Dewsbury (one MP)	Dewsbury (one MP)	No change.

Halifax (two MPs)	Halifax (two MPs)	No change.
Huddersfield (one MP)	Huddersfield (one MP)	No change.
Kingston-upon-Hull (two MPs)	Kingston-upon-Hull, Central Division (one MP)	Boundaries extended to include entire municipal borough. Representation increased to three MPs, divided into three single-member divisions.
	Kingston-upon-Hull, East Division (one MP)	
	Kingston-upon-Hull, West Division (one MP)	
Knaresborough (one MP)		Abolished.
Leeds (three MPs)	Leeds, Central Division (one MP)	Representation increased to five MPs, divided into five single-member divisions.
	Leeds, East Division (one MP)	
	Leeds, North Division (one MP)	
	Leeds, South Division (one MP)	
	Leeds, West Division (one MP)	
Malton (one MP)		Abolished. Gave its name (with Thirsk) to a county division.
Middlesborough (one MP)	Middlesborough (one MP)	Boundaries extended to include entire municipal borough.
Northallerton (one MP)		Abolished.
Pontefract (two MPs)	Pontefract (one MP)	Representation reduced to one member.
Richmond (one MP)		Abolished. Gave its name to a county division.
Ripon (one MP)		Abolished. Gave its name to a county division.
Scarborough (two MPs)	Scarborough (one MP)	Representation reduced to one member.
Sheffield (two MPs)	Sheffield, Attercliffe Division (one MP)	Representation increased to five members. Divided into five single-member divisions.
	Sheffield, Brightside Division (one MP)	
	Sheffield, Central Division (one MP)	
	Sheffield, Ecclesall Division (one MP)	
	Sheffield, Hallam Division (one MP)	
Thirsk (one MP)		Abolished. Gave its name (with Malton) to a county division.
Wakefield (one MP)	Wakefield (one MP)	Boundaries extended to include the Belle Vue area of the parish of Sandal Magna.
Whitby (one MP)		Abolished. Gave its name to a county division.
York (two MPs)	York (two MPs)	Boundaries extended to include entire municipal borough.

COUNTY DIVISIONS		
Before 1885	**After 1885**	
East Riding Division (two MPs)	Buckrose Division (one MP)	Divided into three single-member divisions.
	Holderness Division (one MP)	
	Howdenshire Division (one MP)	
North Riding Division (two MPs)	Cleveland Division (one MP)	Divided into four single-member divisions, absorbing abolished parliamentary boroughs of Malton, Northallerton, Richmond, Thirsk and Whitby.
	Richmond Division (one MP)	
	Thirsk and Malton Division (one MP)	
	Whitby Division (one MP)	
Eastern Division of the West Riding (two MPs)	Barkston Ash Division (one MP)	Divided into six single-member divisions, absorbing the abolished parliamentary boroughs of Knaresborough and Ripon.
	Osgoldcross Division (one MP)	
	Otley Division (one MP)	
	Pudsey Division (one MP)	
	Ripon Division (one MP)	
	Spen Valley Division (one MP)	
Northern Division of the West Riding (two MPs)	Elland Division (one MP)	Divided into five single-member divisions.
	Keighley Division (one MP)	
	Shipley Division (one MP)	
	Skipton Division (one MP)	
	Sowerby Division (one MP)	
Southern Division of the West Riding (two MPs)	Barnsley Division (one MP)	Divided into eight single-member divisions.
	Colne Valley Division (one MP)	
	Doncaster Division (one MP)	
	Hallamshire Division (one MP)	
	Holmfirth Division (one MP)	
	Morley Division (one MP)	
	Normanton Division (one MP)	
	Rotherham Division (one MP)	

Universities

University representation was not altered by the act.

Before 1885	After 1885	
Cambridge University (two MPs)	Cambridge University (two MPs)	No change.
London University (one MP)	London University (one MP)	No change.
Oxford University (two MPs)	Oxford University (two MPs)	No change.

WALES

Anglesey (Representation decreased from 2 to 1 MPs)

BOROUGHS		
Before 1885	After 1885	
Beaumaris district of Boroughs (Amlwch, Beaumaris, Holyhead and Llangefni)		Abolished.
COUNTY DIVISIONS		
Before 1885	After 1885	
Anglesey (undivided) (one MP)	Anglesey (undivided) (one MP)	Absorbed Beaumaris District of Boroughs.

Breconshire (Representation decreased from 2 to 1 MPs)

BOROUGHS		
Before 1885	After 1885	
Brecon (one MP)		Abolished.
COUNTY DIVISIONS		
Before 1885	After 1885	
Breconshire (undivided) (one MP)	Breconshire (undivided) (one MP)	Absorbed abolished parliamentary borough of Brecon.

Cardiganshire (Representation decreased from 2 to 1 MPs)

BOROUGHS		
Before 1885	After 1885	
Cardigan District of Boroughs (one MP) (Cardigan, Aberystwyth, Lampeter and Adpar)		Abolished.
Cardiganshire (undivided) (one MP)	Cardiganshire (undivided) (one MP)	Absorbed abolished Cardigan District of Boroughs.

Carmarthenshire (Representation unchanged (3 MPs))

BOROUGHS		
Before 1885	After 1885	
Carmarthen Boroughs (one MP) (Carmarthen and Llanelly)	Carmarthen Boroughs (one MP) (Carmarthen and Llanelly)	No change.

COUNTY DIVISIONS		
Before 1885	**After 1885**	
Carmarthenshire (undivided) (two MPs)	Eastern Division (one MP)	Divided into two single-member divisions.
	Western Division (one MP)	

Carnarvonshire (Representation increased from 2 to 3 MPs)

BOROUGHS		
Before 1885	**After 1885**	
Carnarvon District (one MP) (Carnarvon, Bangor, Conway, Criccieth, Nevin and Pwllheli)	Carnarvon District of Boroughs (one MP) (Carnarvon, Bangor, Conway, Criccieth, Nevin and Pwllheli)	No change.
COUNTY DIVISIONS		
Before 1885	**After 1885**	
Carnarvonshire (undivided) (one MP)	The Northern or Arfon Division (one MP)	Divided into two single-member divisions.
	The Southern or Eifion Division (one MP)	

Denbighshire (Representation unchanged (3 MPs))

BOROUGHS		
Before 1885	**After 1885**	
Denbigh Boroughs (one MP) (Denbigh, Holt, Ruthin and Wrexham)	Denbigh Boroughs (one MP) (Denbigh, Holt, Ruthin and Wrexham)	No change.
COUNTY DIVISIONS		
Before 1885	**After 1885**	
Denbighshire (undivided) (two MPs)	Eastern Division (one MP)	Divided into two single-member divisions.
	Western Division (one MP)	

Flintshire (Representation unchanged (2 MPs))

BOROUGHS		
Before 1885	**After 1885**	
Flint Boroughs (one MP) (Caergwrle, Caerwys, Flint, Holywell, Mold, Overton, Rhuddlan and St Asaph)	Flint Boroughs (one MP) (Caergwrle, Caerwys, Flint, Holywell, Mold, Overton, Rhuddlan and St Asaph)	No change.
COUNTY DIVISIONS		
Before 1885	**After 1885**	
Flintshire (undivided) (one MP)	Flintshire (undivided) (one MP)	No change.

Glamorganshire (Representation increased from 6 to 10 MPs)

BOROUGHS		
Before 1885	**After 1885**	
Cardiff District of Boroughs (one MP) (Cardiff, Cowbridge and Llantrisant)	Cardiff District of Boroughs (one MP) (Cardiff, Cowbridge and Llantrisant)	Parliamentary Borough of Cardiff extended to include entire municipal borough.
Merthyr Tydfil (two MPs)	Merthyr Tydfil (two MPs)	No change.
Swansea District of Boroughs (one MP) (Aberavon, Kenfig, Loughor, Neath and Swansea)	Swansea, District (one MP) (Aberavon, Kenfig, Loughor, Neath and suburban areas of Swansea) Swansea Town (one MP)	Reconstituted as Parliamentary Borough of Swansea without alteration of boundaries. Representation increased to two MPs. Divided into two single-member divisions.
COUNTY DIVISIONS		
Before 1885	**After 1885**	
Glamorganshire (undivided (two MPs)	Eastern Division (one MP)	Divided into five single-member divisions.
	Mid Division (one MP)	
	Rhondda Division (one MP)	
	Southern Division (one MP)	
	Western or Gower District (one MP)	

Merionethshire (Representation unchanged (1 MP))

COUNTY DIVISIONS		
Before 1885	**After 1885**	
Merionethshire (undivided) (one MP)	Merionethshire (undivided) (one MP)	No change.

Monmouthshire (Representation increased from 3 to 4 MPs)

BOROUGHS		
Before 1885		
Monmouth Boroughs (one MP) Monmouth, Newport and Usk	Monmouth Boroughs (one MP) Monmouth, Newport and Usk	Parliamentary Borough of Newort extended to include entire municipal borough.
COUNTY DIVISIONS		
Before 1885	**After 1885**	
Monmouthshire (undivided) (two MPs)	Northern Division (one MP)	Divided into three single-member divisions.
	Southern Division (one MP)	
	Western Division (one MP)	

Montgomeryshire (Representation unchanged (2 MPs))

BOROUGHS		
Before 1885	**After 1885**	
Montgomery District of Boroughs (one MP) (Llanfyllin, Llanidloes, Machynlleth, Montgomery, Newtown and Welshpool)	Montgomery District of Boroughs (one MP) (Llanfyllin, Llanidloes, Machynlleth, Montgomery, Newtown and Welshpool)	No change.
COUNTY DIVISIONS		
Before 1885	**After 1885**	
Montgomeryshire (undivided) (one MP)	Montgomeryshire (undivided) (one MP)	No change.

Pembrokeshire (Representation decreased from 3 to 2 MPs)

BOROUGHS		
Before 1885	**After 1885**	
Pembroke District of Boroughs (one MP) (Pembroke, Milford, Tenby and Wiston)	Pembroke and Haverfordwest District of Boroughs (one MP) (Fishguard, Haverfordwest, Pembroke, Milford, Narberth, St David's, Tenby and Wiston)	Districts of parliamentary boroughs of Pembroke and Haverfordwest merged.
Haverfordwest District of Boroughs (one MP) (Fishguard, Haverfordwest, Narberth and St David's)		
COUNTY DIVISIONS		
Before 1885	**After 1885**	
Pembrokeshire	Pembrokeshire	No change.

Radnorshire (Representation decreased from 2 to 1 MPs)

BOROUGHS		
Before 1885	**After 1885**	
Radnor District of Boroughs (one MP) (Cefnllys, Knighton, Knucklas, New Radnor, Presteigne and Rhayader)		Abolished.
COUNTY DIVISIONS		
Before 1885	**After 1885**	
Radnorshire (undivided) (one MP)	Radnorshire (undivided) (one MP)	Absorbed abolished parliamentary boroughs.

SCOTLAND

Burghs and Districts of Burghs

BURGHS AND DISTRICTS		
Before 1885	**After 1885**	
Aberdeen (one MP)	Aberdeen, North Division (one MP) Aberdeen, South Division (one MP)	Representation of parliamentary burgh increased to two seats. Divided into two single-member divisions.
Ayr District of Burghs (one MP)	Ayr District of Burghs (one MP)	No change. Comprised five parliamentary burghs: Ayr and Irvine in Ayrshire, Campbeltown and Inverary in Argyllshire and Rothesay in Buteshire.
Dundee (two MPs)	Dundee (two MPs)	No change.
Dumfries District of Burghs (one MP)	Dumfries District of Burghs (one MP)	No change. Comprised five parliamentary burghs: Annan Lochmaben and Sanquhar in Dumfriesshire, Dumfries in Dumfriesshire and Kirkcudbrightshire, Kirkcudbright in Kirkcudbrightshire.
Edinburgh (two MPs)	Edinburgh, Central Division (one MP) Edinburgh East Division (one MP) Edinburgh South Division (one MP) Edinburgh, West Division (one MP)	Boundaries widened to include entire municipal burgh. Representation of parliamentary burgh increased to four seats. Divided into four single-member divisions.
Elgin District of Burghs (one MP)	Elgin District of Burghs (one MP)	No change. Comprised five parliamentary burghs: Inverurie, Kintore and Peterhead in Aberdeenshire, Banff and Cullen in Banffshire, and Elgin in Elginshire.
Falkirk District of Burghs (one MP)	Falkirk District of Burghs (one MP)	Comprised five parliamentary burghs: Airdrie, Hamilton and Lanark in Lanarkshire, Linlithgow in Linlithgowshire and Falkirk in Stirlingshire. Boundaries widened to include entire municipal burgh of Hamilton.
Glasgow (two MPs)	Glasgow, Blackfriars and Hutchesontown Division (one MP) Glasgow, Bridgeton Division (one MP) Glasgow, Camlachie Division (one MP) Glasgow, Central Division (one MP) Glasgow, College Division (one MP) Glasgow, St Rollox Division (one MP) Glasgow, Tradeston Division (one MP)	Boundaries widened to include entire municipal burgh. Representation of parliamentary burgh increased to seven seats. Divided into seven single-member divisions.

Greenock (one MP)	Greenock (one MP)	Boundaries extended to include entire municipal borough.
Haddington District of Burghs (one MP)		Abolished. The five parliamentary burghs that comprised the district were each merged into their respective parliamentary counties: Lauder into Berwickshire; Dunbar, Haddington and North Berwick into Haddingtonshire; and Jedburgh into Roxburghshire.
Hawick District of Burghs (one MP)	Hawick District of Burghs (one MP)	Comprised three parliamentary burghs: Hawick in Roxburghshire and Galashiels and Selkirk in Selkirkshire. Boundaries extended to include entire municipal burgh of Hawick.
Inverness District of Burghs (one MP)	Inverness District of Burghs (one MP)	No change. Comprised four parliamentary burghs: Forres in Elginshire, Inverness in Inverness-shire, Nairn in Nairnshire and Fortrose in Ross and Cromarty.
Kilmarnock District of Burghs (one MP)	Kilmarnock District of Burghs (one MP)	Comprised five burghs: Kilmarnock in Ayrshire; Dumbarton in Dumbartonshire; Rutherglen in Lanarkshire and Renfrew and Port Glasgow in Renfrewshire. Boundaries of parliamentary burghs of Kilmarnock, Port Glasgow and Renfrew extended to include entire municipal burghs.
Kirkcaldy District of Burghs (one MP)	Kirkcaldy District of Burghs (one MP)	Comprised four burghs in Fife: Kirkcaldy, Burntisland, Dysart, Kinghorn. Extended to include entire municipal burgh of Kirkcaldy.
Leith District of Burghs (one MP)	Leith District of Burghs (one MP)	No change. Comprised three burghs in the County of Edinburgh: Leith, Musselburgh and Portobello.
Montrose District of Burghs (one MP)	Montrose District of Burghs (one MP)	No change. Comprised five burghs: Arbroath, Brechin, Forfar and Inverbervie in Forfarshire and Montrose in Kincardineshire.
Paisley (one MP)	Paisley (one MP)	Boundaries widened to include entire municipal burgh.
Perth City (one MP)	Perth City (one MP)	Boundaries widened to include entire municipal burgh.
St Andrews District of Burghs (one MP)	St Andrews District of Burghs (one MP)	No change. Comprised seven burghs in Fife: Anstruther Easter, Anstruther Wester, Crail, Cupar, Kilrenny, Pittenweem and St Andrews.

Stirling District of Burghs (one MP)	Stirling District of Burghs (one MP)	No change. Comprised five burghs: Dunfermline and Inverkeithing in Fife; Queensferry in Linlithgowshire; Culross in Perthshire and Stirling in Stirlingshire.
Wick District of Burghs (one MP)	Wick District of Burghs (one MP)	No change. Comprised six burghs: Wick in Caithness; Kirkwall in Orkney; Cromarty, Dingwall and Tain in Ross and Cromarty; Dornoch in Sutherland.
Wigtown District of Burghs (one MP)		Abolished. The four constituent burghs were merged into the parliamentary counties of Kirkcudbrightshire (New Galloway) and Wigtownshire (Stranraer, Whithorn and Wigtown).

Aberdeenshire (Representation unchanged (2 MPs))

COUNTY DIVISIONS		
Before 1885	After 1885	
Eastern Division (one MP)	Eastern Division (one MP)	No change.
Western Division (one MP)	Western Division (one MP)	No change.

Argyllshire (Representation unchanged (1 MP))

COUNTY DIVISIONS		
Before 1885	After 1885	
Argyllshire (undivided) (one MP)	Argyllshire (undivided) (one MP)	No change.

Ayrshire (Representation unchanged (2 MPs))

COUNTY DIVISIONS		
Before 1885	After 1885	
Northern Division (one MP)	Northern Division (one MP)	No change.
Southern Division (one MP)	Southern Division (one MP)	No change.

Banffshire (Representation unchanged (1 MP))

COUNTY DIVISIONS		
Before 1885	After 1885	
Banffshire (undivided) (one MP)	Banffshire (undivided) (one MP)	No change.

Berwickshire (Representation unchanged (1 MP))

COUNTY DIVISIONS		
Before 1885	**After 1885**	
Berwickshire (undivided) (one MP)	Berwickshire (undivided) (one MP)	Absorbed the abolished parliamentary burgh of Lauder, previously part of the Haddington District of Burghs.

Buteshire (Representation unchanged (1 MP))

COUNTY DIVISIONS		
Before 1885	**After 1885**	
Buteshire (undivided) (one MP)	Buteshire (undivided) (one MP)	No change.

Caithness (Representation unchanged (1 MP))

COUNTY DIVISIONS		
Before 1885	**After 1885**	
Caithness (undivided) (one MP)	Caithness (undivided) (one MP)	No change.

Clackmannanshire and Kinross-shire (Representation unchanged (1 MP))

COUNTY DIVISIONS		
Before 1885	**After 1885**	
Clackmannanshire and Kinross-shire (undivided) (one MP)	Clackmannanshire and Kinross-shire (undivided) (one MP)	The constituency consisted of the combined parliamentary counties of Clackmannanshire and Kinross-shire, and also included the parishes of Tulliallan, Culross and Muckhart in Perthshire, the Perthshire portions of the parishes of Logie and Fossaway, and the Stirlingshire part of the parish of Alva.

Dumfriesshire (Representation unchanged (1 MP))

COUNTY DIVISIONS		
Before 1885	**After 1885**	
Dumfriesshire (undivided) (one MP)	Dumfriesshire (undivided) (one MP)	No change.

Dumbartonshire (Representation unchanged (1 MP))

COUNTY DIVISIONS		
Before 1885	After 1885	
Dumbartonshire (undivided) (one MP)	Dumbartonshire (undivided) (one MP)	No change.

County of Edinburgh (Representation unchanged (1 MP))

COUNTY DIVISIONS		
Before 1885	After 1885	
County of Edinburgh (undivided) (one MP)	County of Edinburgh (undivided) (one MP)	No change.

Elginshire and Nairnshire (Representation unchanged (1 MP))

COUNTY DIVISIONS		
Before 1885	After 1885	
Elginshire and Nairnshire (undivided) (one MP)	Elginshire and Nairnshire (undivided) (one MP)	No change The constituency consisted of the combined parliamentary counties of Elginshire and Nairnshire.

Fife (Representation increased from 1 to 2 MPs)

COUNTY DIVISIONS		
Before 1885	After 1885	
Fife (undivided) (one MP)	Fife, Eastern Division (one MP)	Divided into two single-member divisions.
	Fife, Western Division (one MP)	

Forfarshire (Representation unchanged (1 MP))

COUNTY DIVISIONS		
Before 1885	After 1885	
Forfarshire (one MP)	Forfarshire (one MP)	No change.

Haddingtonshire (Representation unchanged (1 MP))

COUNTY DIVISIONS		
Before 1885	After 1885	
Haddingtonshire (undivided) (one MP)	Haddingtonshire (undivided) (one MP)	Absorbed the abolished parliamentary burghs of Haddington, Dunbar, and North Berwick formerly part of the Haddington District of Burghs.

Inverness-shire (Representation unchanged (1 MP))

COUNTY DIVISIONS		
Before 1885	After 1885	
Inverness-shire (undivided) (one MP)	Inverness-shire (undivided) (one MP)	No change.

Kincardineshire (Representation unchanged (1 MP))

COUNTY DIVISIONS		
Before 1885	After 1885	
Kincardineshire (undivided) (one MP)	Kincardineshire (undivided) (one MP)	No change.

Kirkcudbrightshire (Representation unchanged (1 MP))

COUNTY DIVISIONS		
Before 1885	After 1885	
Kirkcudbrightshire (undivided) (one MP)	Kirkcudbrightshire (undivided) (one MP)	No change.

Lanarkshire (Representation increased from 2 to 6 MPs)

COUNTY DIVISIONS		
Before 1885	After 1885	
Northern Division (one MP)	Govan District (one MP)	Reorganised as six single-member divisions.
	Mid Division (one MP)	
	North Eastern Division (one MP)	
	North Western Division (one MP)	
Southern Division (one MP)	Partick Division (one MP)	
	Southern Division (one MP)	

Linlithgowshire (Representation unchanged (1 MP))

COUNTY DIVISIONS		
Before 1885	After 1885	
Linlithgowshire (undivided) (one MP)	Linlithgowshire (undivided) (one MP)	No change.

Orkney and Shetland (Representation unchanged (1 MP))

COUNTY DIVISIONS		
Before 1885	**After 1885**	
Orkney and Shetland (undivided) (one MP)	Orkney and Shetland (undivided) (one MP)	No change.

Peeblesshire and Selkirkshire (Representation unchanged (1 MP))

COUNTY DIVISIONS		
Before 1885	**After 1885**	
Peeblesshire and Selkirkshire (undivided) (one MP)	Peeblesshire and Selkirkshire (undivided) (one MP)	No change. The constituency consisted of the combined parliamentary counties of Peeblesshire and Selkirkshire.

Perthshire (Representation increased from 1 to 2 MPs)

COUNTY DIVISIONS		
Before 1885	**After 1885**	
Perthshire (undivided) (one MP)	Perthshire, Eastern Division (one MP)	Divided into two single-member divisions.
	Perthshire, Western Division (one MP)	

Renfrewshire (Representation increased from 1 to 2 MPs)

COUNTY DIVISIONS		
Before 1885	**After 1885**	
Renfrewshire (undivided) (one MP)	Renfrewshire, Eastern Division (one MP)	Divided into two single-member divisions.
	Renfrewshire, Western Division (one MP)	

Ross and Cromarty (Representation unchanged (1 MP))

COUNTY DIVISIONS		
Before 1885	**After 1885**	
Ross and Cromarty (undivided) (one MP)	Ross and Cromarty (undivided) (one MP)	Comprised the combined counties of Ross-shire and Cromarty.

Roxburghshire (Representation unchanged (1 MP))

COUNTY DIVISIONS		
Before 1885	After 1885	
Roxburghshire (undivided) (one MP)	Roxburghshire (undivided) (one MP)	Absorbed the abolished parliamentary burgh of Jedburgh, previously part of the Haddington District of Burghs.

Stirlingshire (Representation unchanged (1 MP))

COUNTY DIVISIONS		
Before 1885	After 1885	
Stirlingshire (undivided) (one MP)	Stirlingshire (undivided (one MP)	No change.

Sutherland (Representation unchanged (1 MP))

COUNTY DIVISIONS		
Before 1885	After 1885	
Sutherland (undivided) (one MP)	Sutherland (undivided) (one MP)	No change.

Wigtownshire (Representation unchanged (1 MP))

COUNTY DIVISIONS		
Before 1885	After 1885	
Wigtownshire (undivided) (one MP)	Wigtownshire (undivided) (one MP)	Absorbed abolished parliamentary burghs of Stranraer, Whithorn and Wigtown, previously part of Wigtown District of Burghs.

Universities

Before 1885	After 1885	
Edinburgh and St Andrews Universities (one MP)	Edinburgh and St Andrews Universities (one MP)	No change.
Glasgow and Aberdeen Universities (one MP)	Glasgow and Aberdeen Universities (one MP)	No change.

IRELAND

Antrim (Representation increased from 6 to 8 MPs)

BOROUGHS		
Before 1885	**After 1885**	
Carrickfergus (one MP)	Belfast, East Division (one MP)	Abolished.
	Belfast, North Division (one MP)	
	Belfast, South Division (one MP)	
	Belfast, West Division (one MP)	
COUNTY DIVISIONS		
Before 1885	**After 1885**	
Antrim (undivided) (two MPs)	East Antrim (one MP)	Divided into four single-member divisions, absorbing abolished parliamentary borough of Lisburn.
	Mid Antrim (one MP)	
	North Antrim (one MP)	
	South Antrim (one MP)	

Armagh (Representation unchanged (3 MPs))

BOROUGHS		
Before 1885	**After 1885**	
Armagh (one MP)		Abolished.
COUNTY DIVISIONS		
Before 1885	**After 1885**	
Armagh County (undivided) (two MPs)	Mid Armagh (one MP)	Divided into three single-member divisions, absorbing abolished parliamentary borough of Armagh.
	North Armagh (one MP)	
	South Armagh (one MP)	

Carlow (Representation decreased from 3 MPs to 1)

BOROUGHS		
Before 1885	**After 1885**	
Carlow (one MP)		Abolished.
PARLIAMENTARY COUNTY		
Before 1885	**After 1885**	
Carlow County (undivided) (two MPs)	Carlow County (one MP)	Representation reduced to one member, absorbed abolished parliamentary borough of Carlow.

Cavan (Representation unchanged (2 MPs))

COUNTY DIVISIONS		
Before 1885	After 1885	
Cavan (undivided) (two MPs)	East Cavan (one MP)	Divided into two single-member divisions.
	West Cavan (one MP)	

Clare (Representation decreased from 3 to 2 MPs)

BOROUGHS		
Before 1885	After 1885	
Ennis (one MP)		Abolished.
COUNTY DIVISIONS		
Before 1885	After 1885	
Clare (undivided) (two MPs)	East Clare (one MP)	Absorbed abolished parliamentary borough of Ennis. Divided into two single-member divisions.
	West Clare (one MP)	

Cork (Representation increased from 8 to 9 MPs)

BOROUGHS		
Before 1885	After 1885	
Bandon (one MP)		Abolished.
Cork (two MPs)	Cork (two MPs)	No change.
Kinsale (one MP)		Abolished.
Mallow (one MP)		Abolished.
Youghal (one MP)		Abolished.
COUNTY DIVISIONS		
Before 1885	After 1885	
County Cork (undivided) (two MPs)	East Cork (one MP)	Absorbed abolished parliamentary boroughs of Bandon, Kinsale, Mallow and Youghal. Divided into seven single-member divisions.
	Mid Cork (one MP)	
	North Cork (one MP)	
	North East Cork (one MP)	
	South Cork (one MP)	
	South East Cork (one MP)	
	West Cork (one MP)	

Donegal (Representation increased from 2 to 4 MPs)

COUNTY DIVISIONS		
Before 1885	**After 1885**	
Donegal (undivided) (two MPs)	East Donegal (one MP)	Divided into four single-member divisions.
	North Donegal (one MP)	
	South Donegal (one MP)	
	West Donegal (one MP)	

Down (Representation increased from 4 to 5 MPs)

BOROUGHS		
Before 1885	**After 1885**	
Downpatrick (one MP)		Abolished.
Newry (one MP)	Newry (one MP)	No change.
COUNTY DIVISIONS		
Before 1885	**After 1885**	
Down (undivided) (two MPs)	East Down (one MP)	Absorbed parliamentary borough of Downpatrick. Divided into four single-member divisions.
	North Down (one MP)	
	South Down (one MP)	
	West Down (one MP)	

Dublin (Representation increased from 4 to 6 MPs)

BOROUGHS		
Before 1885	**After 1885**	
Dublin (two MPs)	Dublin, College Green Division (one MP)	Representation increased to four members. Divided into four single-member divisions.
	Dublin, Harbour Division (one MP)	
	Dublin, St Patrick's Division (one MP)	
	Dublin, St Stephen's Division (one MP)	
COUNTY DIVISIONS		
Before 1885	**After 1885**	
Dublin County (undivided) (two MPs)	North Dublin (one MP)	Divided into two single-member divisions.
	South Dublin (one MP)	

Fermanagh (Representation reduced from 3 to 2 MPs)

BOROUGHS		
Before 1885	**After 1885**	
Enniskillen (one MP)		Abolished.
COUNTY DIVISIONS		
Before 1885	**After 1885**	
Fermanagh (undivided) (two MPs)	North Fermanagh (one MP)	Divided into two single-member divisions.
	South Fermanagh (one MP)	

Galway (Representation increased from 4 to 5 MPs)

BOROUGHS		
Before 1885	**After 1885**	
Galway Borough (two MPs)	Galway Borough (one MP)	Representation reduced to one MP.
Galway County (undivided) (two MPs)	County of Galway, Connemara (one MP)	Divided into four single-member divisions.
	East Galway (one MP)	
	North Galway (one MP)	
	South Galway (one MP)	

Kerry (Representation increased from 3 to 4 MPs)

BOROUGHS		
Before 1885	**After 1885**	
Tralee (one MP)		Abolished.
COUNTY DIVISIONS		
Before 1885	**After 1885**	
Kerry (undivided) (two MPs)	East Kerry (one MP)	Absorbed abolished parliamentary borough of Tralee. Divided into four single-member divisions.
	North Kerry (one MP)	
	South Kerry (one MP)	
	West Kerry (one MP)	

Kildare (Representation unchanged (2 MPs))

COUNTY DIVISIONS		
Before 1885	**After 1885**	
Kildare (undivided) (two MPs)	North Kildare (one MP)	Divided into two single-member divisions.
	South Kildare (one MP)	

Kilkenny (Representation unchanged (3 MPs))

BOROUGHS		
Before 1885	**After 1885**	
Kilkenny City (one MP)	Kilkenny City (one MP)	No change.
COUNTY DIVISIONS		
Before 1885	**After 1885**	
County Kilkenny (undivided) (two MPs)	North Kilkenny (one MP)	Divided into two single-member divisions.
	South Kilkenny (one MP)	

King's County (Representation unchanged (2 MPs))

COUNTY DIVISIONS		
Before 1885	**After 1885**	
King's County (undivided) (two MPs)	King's County, Tullamore (one MP)	Divided into two single-member divisions.
	King's County, Birr (one MP)	

Leitrim (Representation unchanged (2 MPs))

COUNTY DIVISIONS		
Before 1885	After 1885	
Leitrim (undivided) (two MPs)	North Leitrim (one MP)	Divided into two single-member divisions.
	South Leitrim (one MP)	

Limerick (Representation reduced from 4 to 3 MPs)

BOROUGHS		
Before 1885	**After 1885**	
Limerick City (two MPs)	Limerick City (one MP)	Representation reduced to one MP.
COUNTY DIVISIONS		
Before 1885	**After 1885**	
Limerick County (undivided) (two MPs)	East Limerick (one MP)	Divided into two single-member divisions.
	West Limerick (one MP)	

Londonderry (Representation reduced from 4 to 3 MPs)

BOROUGHS		
Before 1885	**After 1885**	
Coleraine (one MP)		Abolished.
Londonderry City (one MP)	Londonderry City (one MP)	No change.

COUNTY DIVISIONS		
Before 1885	**After 1885**	
Londonderry County (two MPs)	North Londonderry (one MP)	Absorbed abolished parliamentary borough of Coleraine. Divided into two single-member divisions.
	South Londonderry (one MP)	

Longford (Representation unchanged (2 MPs))

COUNTY DIVISIONS		
Before 1885	**After 1885**	
Longford (two MPs)	North Longford (one MP)	Divided into two single-member divisions.
	South Longford (one MP)	

Louth (Representation reduced from 4 to 2 MPs)

BOROUGHS		
Before 1885	**After 1885**	
Drogheda (one MP)		Abolished.
Dundalk (one MP)		Abolished.
COUNTY DIVISIONS		
Before 1885	**After 1885**	
Louth County (undivided) (two MPs)	North Louth (one MP)	Absorbed abolished parliamentary boroughs of Drogheda and Dundalk. Divided into two single-member divisions.
	South Louth (one MP)	

Mayo (Representation increased from 2 to 4 MPs)

COUNTY DIVISIONS		
Before 1885	**After 1885**	
Mayo (undivided) (two MPs)	East Mayo (one MP)	Divided into four single-member divisions.
	North Mayo (one MP)	
	South Mayo (one MP)	
	West Mayo (one MP)	

Meath (Representation unchanged (2 MPs))

COUNTY DIVISIONS		
Before 1885	**After 1885**	
Meath (undivided) (two MPs)	North Meath (one MP)	Divided into two single-member divisions.
	South Meath (one MP)	

Monaghan (Representation unchanged (2 MPs))

COUNTY DIVISIONS		
Before 1885	**After 1885**	
Monaghan (undivided) (two MPs)	North Monaghan (one MP)	Divided into two single-member divisions.
	South Monaghan (one MP)	

Queen's County (Representation reduced from 3 MPs to 2)

BOROUGHS		
Before 1885	**After 1885**	
Portarlington (one MP)		Abolished.
COUNTY DIVISIONS		
Before 1885	**After 1885**	
Queen's County (undivided) (two MPs)	Queen's County, Leix (one MP)	Absorbed abolished parliamentary borough of Portarlington. Divided into two single-member divisions.
	Queen's County, Ossory (one MP)	

Roscommon (Representation unchanged (2 MPs))

COUNTY DIVISIONS		
Before 1885	**After 1885**	
Roscommon (undivided) (two MPs)	North Roscommon (one MP)	Divided into two single-member divisions.
	South Roscommon (one MP)	

Sligo (Representation unchanged (2 MPs))

COUNTY DIVISIONS		
Before 1885	**After 1885**	
Sligo County (undivided) (two MPs)	North Sligo (one MP)	Divided into two single-member divisions.
	South Sligo (one MP)	

Tipperary (Representation increased from 3 MPs to 4)

BOROUGHS		
Before 1885	**After 1885**	
Clonmel (one MP)		Abolished.

COUNTY DIVISIONS		
Before 1885	**After 1885**	
Tipperary (undivided) (two MPs)	East Tipperary (one MP)	Divided into four single-member divisions.
	Mid Tipperary (one MP)	
	North Tipperary (one MP)	
	South Tipperary (one MP)	

Tyrone (Representation increased from 3 MPs to 4)

BOROUGHS		
Before 1885	**After 1885**	
Dungannon (one MP)		Abolished.
COUNTY DIVISIONS		
Before 1885	**After 1885**	
Tyrone (undivided) (two MPs)	East Tyrone (one MP)	Absorbed abolished parliamentary borough of Dungannon. Divided into four single-member divisions.
	Mid Tyrone (one MP)	
	North Tyrone (one MP)	
	South Tyrone (one MP)	

Waterford (Representation reduced from 5 to 3 MPs)

BOROUGHS		
Before 1885	**After 1885**	
Dungarvan (one MP)		Abolished.
Waterford City (two MPs)	Waterford City (one MP)	Representation reduced to one member.
COUNTY DIVISIONS		
Before 1885	**After 1885**	
Waterford County (undivided) (two MPs)	East Waterford (one MP)	Absorbed abolished parliamentary borough of Dungarvan. Divided into two single-member divisions.
	West Waterford (one MP)	

Westmeath (Representation reduced from 3 to 2 MPs)

BOROUGHS		
Before 1885	**After 1885**	
Athlone (one MP)		Abolished.
COUNTY DIVISIONS		
Before 1885	**After 1885**	
Westmeath (undivided) (two MPs)	North Westmeath (one MP)	Absorbed abolished parliamentary borough of Athlone. Divided into two single-member divisions.
	South Westmeath (one MP)	

Wexford (Representation reduced from 4 to 2 MPs)

BOROUGHS		
Before 1885	**After 1885**	
New Ross (one MP)		Abolished.
Wexford Borough (one MP)		Abolished.
COUNTY DIVISIONS		
Before 1885	**After 1885**	
Wexford County (undivided) (two MPs)	North Wexford (one MP)	Absorbed abolished parliamentary boroughs of New Ross and Wexford. Divided into two single-member divisions.
	South Wexford (one MP)	

Wicklow (Representation unchanged (2 MPs))

COUNTY DIVISIONS		
Before 1885	**After 1885**	
Wicklow (undivided) (two MPs)	East Wicklow (one MP)	Divided into two single-member divisions.
	West Wicklow (one MP)	

University of Dublin (Representation increased from one to 2 MPs)

Before 1885	**After 1885**	
Dublin University (one MP)	Dublin University (two MPs)	Representation increased to two members.

Appendix E

Dates and Events in the Journey to Parliamentary Reform

1694	The Triennial Act fixed the maximum life of a parliament at three years.
1716	The Septennial Act fixed the maximum life of a parliament at seven years.
1782	Pitt the Younger (then aged 22) proposed that a committee be set up to enquire into the state of representation. The proposal was defeated.
1783	Pitt tried a second time and was again defeated.
1785	Pitt (then prime minister) proposed removing the franchise from thrity-six rotten boroughs and redistributing their seventy-two seats. The proposal was defeated.
1789	The French Revolution commenced.
1791	The Sheffield Society for Constitutional Reform was founded.
1792	The London Corresponding Society was founded.
1793	Wars against France commenced. The Catholic Relief Act advanced the Catholic cause in Ireland.
1795	Acts of Parliament targeted Seditious Meetings and Treasonable Practices.
1801	Great Britain and Ireland united to form the United Kingdom of Great Britain and Ireland. Ireland was given 100 seats (out of a total of 658) in the House of Commons.
1816–17	Three protest meetings were held in Spa Fields, London.
1819	The 'Peterloo Massacre' took place in Manchester.
1823	Daniel O'Connell set up the Catholic Association.
1828	Daniel O'Connell was victorious at the County Clare by-election. As a Catholic he was not able to take his seat.
1829	The Roman Catholic Relief Act removed many of the remaining restrictions on Roman Catholics throughout the United Kingdom. They could vote and be MPs. The county voting qualification was increased from £2 to £10. This was intended to stop Irish Catholics returning too many MPs.
1830	George IV died on June 26. He was replaced by William IV.
	Several Bills promoting reform were defeated.
	The Tories did badly in a general election. The Duke of Wellington continued for a while as prime minister, but then resigned.
	Lord Grey became prime minister as head of a Whig government.
1831	A committee set up to make proposals on reform reported to the prime minister on 14 January.
	Lord John Russell introduced the Reform Bill to the House of Commons on 1 March.

On 23 March the Bill was carried on its second reading in the House of Commons by 302 votes to 301.

On April 20 the government was defeated on a major amendment to the Bill. Shortly afterwards the king dissolved Parliament. The consequent general election returned the Whig government (led by Lord Grey) with a large majority.

A second Reform Bill was introduced and it passed through the House of Commons on 8 October. It was subsequently rejected by the House of Lords. Rejection of the Bill resulted in widespread violence and disorder.

On 12 December Lord John Russell introduced another Reform Bill.

1832   The Parliamentary Reform Act 1832 received Royal Assent. Its provisions included:

– A register of voters was established.

– There was an expansion in the number of county seats and a reduction in the number of borough seats.

– Fifty-six boroughs lost both their two members and thirty boroughs lost one of their two members. Larger centres of population gained extra members.

– In the boroughs adult males owning or occupying property worth £10 a year were given the vote. Adult males who already had the vote kept it, but the right died with them.

– In the counties there were three voting qualifications:
  ◆ adult males owning freehold property worth 40s.
  ◆ adult males with copyhold land worth £10 a year.
  ◆ adult males renting land worth £50 a year.

The Parliamentary Reform Act (Scotland) 1832 received Royal Assent. Its provisions included:

– Scotland was given fifty-three seats, an increase of seven.

– In the boroughs the main voting qualification was occupation of property worth £10 a year. Electors voted directly, rather than indirectly as before.

– In the counties the voting qualifications were:
  ◆ owners of property worth £10 a year.
  ◆ leaseholders with leases over fifty-seven years of property worth £10.
  ◆ leaseholders for nineteen years whose property was worth £10.
  ◆ leaseholders who had paid £500 for their lease.

The Parliamentary Reform Act (Ireland) 1832 received Royal Assent. Its provisions included:

– Ireland was given 105 seats, an increase of five.

– In the boroughs and in the places designated 'counties of cities' owners and occupiers of property worth £10 a year were able to vote. All adult males previously entitled to vote continued to be able to do so, but the right died with them.

– In the counties owners of property worth £10 a year could vote, and so could leaseholders to the value of £10, provided that the leases were for twenty years or more.

1838   The People's Charter containing six demands was published.

1839	The first Chartist Petition, containing just under 1,300,000 signatures, was presented to the Commons. It was rejected by 235 votes to 46.
1842	The second Chartist Petition, said to contain 3,315,752 signatures, was presented to the Commons. It was rejected by 187 votes to 49. This was followed by strikes, and in some cases violence and arson.
1848	A Chartist Convention was called and a demonstration was held on Kennington Common. The third Chartist Petition was then delivered to Parliament. The Chartists claimed that it contained 5,700,000 signatures, but a Commons Committee said that the true number was 1,975,496 and that some of them were obviously false. The Commons overwhelmingly voted to reject the petition.
1850	The Irish Franchise Act 1850 ended the 'certification' system and replaced it with a system based on the occupation of property. As a consequence the size of the electorate in Ireland roughly tripled from about 50,000 to about 150,000.
1852	Lord John Russell introduced a Reform Bill, the main feature of which was to give the vote to householders owning property of lower value. The Bill was withdrawn before it got to a vote in the Commons.
1854	Lord John Russell introduced another Reform Bill. This was very similar to the 1852 Bill, but with a slightly more cautious property valuation requirement. Due to the onset of the Crimean War this Bill was withdrawn before it got to a vote in the Commons.
1858	Chartism had declined since Parliament's rejection of the Third Petition in 1848. The last Chartist National Convention was held in 1858.
	The Property Qualification for Members of Parliament Act became law. This abolished the property qualification for MPs; it was the first of the Chartist's demands to be achieved.
1859	A Conservative Bill that proposed many changes was defeated in the Commons by 330 votes to 291. The Conservative government then resigned and the Liberals, led by Lord Palmerston, returned to office.
1860	Lord John Russell prepared yet another Bill, but it was withdrawn due to lack of support from Lord Palmerston and backbench Liberal MPs.
1866	Gladstone, with Prime Minister Russell in the Lords, introduced another Reform Bill. It was defeated on an amendment that was taken as a vote of confidence and the government resigned.
1867	The Reform Act (England and Wales) 1867 (The Second Reform Act) received Royal Assent. Its provisions included:

- In the boroughs the vote was given to all householders who had been resident for a year, and to all lodgers who paid rent of at least £10 a year and who had been resident for at least a year.
- In seats in the boroughs that returned three MPs, each elector only had two votes. In seats that returned four MPs each elector only had three votes. Electors with more than one vote had to cast them for different candidates.
- In the counties the franchise was given to owners (or lessees on sixty year leases or longer) of property worth £5 a year, and occupiers of lands with

a rateable value of £12 a year, who had paid poor rates on the property.
- There was a modest redistribution of seats.
- It was no longer necessary to hold a general election following a change of monarch.

1868   The Reform Act (Scotland) 1868 received Royal Assent. There was a redistribution of seats and the number in Scotland increased from fifty-three to sixty. The franchise principles were similar to those in England and Wales, but because of Scottish law no lodger franchise was necessary.

The Reform Act (Ireland) 1868 gave the vote in the boroughs to occupiers of property worth more than £4 a year, and also to lodgers.

1869   The Municipal Franchise Act gave women the right to vote in local elections. However, three years later a legal judgment restricted this to unmarried women and widows.

1872   The Ballot Act brought in the secret ballot.

1883   The Corrupt and illegal Practices Act was passed. Its provisions included the following:
- The amount that could be spent on election expenses was limited.
- Legitimate expenses were closely defined.
- Each candidate was required to name a single agent. This person alone had the right to settle expenses.
- A certified statement of expenses with receipts had to be submitted.
- Treating was identified as corrupt practice.

1884   Gladstone's government introduced a Bill that would eventually become the Third Reform Act. John Stuart Mill's amendment to give votes to women was rejected by 271 votes to 135, but the Bill passed the Commons. It was rejected in the House of Lords by 205 votes to 146. Gladstone planned to recall Parliament and represent the Bill.

After a hullabaloo a compromise was agreed. The Conservatives agreed to accept the Bill so long as a Redistribution Bill followed shortly. The parties agreed the outline and procedure for this.

The Third Reform Act was entitled The Parliamentary Reform Act 1884. Its main provisions were the following:
- In the counties the 1867 franchise relating to freeholders, copyholders and leaseholders was unchanged, but the borough qualifications were added to them. These were the £10 occupation, the lodger and the household franchises.
- The £50 rental qualification was abolished.
- In the boroughs the so-called 'ancient right' franchise was retained.
- The main effect of the Act was to align the franchise in the counties with the franchise in the boroughs.
- The total electorate was raised from around three million to around five million, or perhaps slightly more. About 60 per cent of men, or slightly more, had the vote.

1885   The Redistribution Act 1885 was a very comprehensive attempt to rationalise parliamentary boundaries in England, Wales, Scotland and Ireland. An extensive analysis is given in Appendix D.

1886	Gladstone's first home Rule Bill failed to pass the Commons. A section of his party (MPs and peers) broke away to form the Liberal Unionists.
1888	The Oaths Act put beyond doubt the right of MPs and peers to affirm instead of taking a Christian oath.
	County Councils were created. Women were able to vote on the same terms as men.
1893	Gladstone's second Home Rule Bill was defeated in the Lords by the crushing margin of 419 votes to 41.
1903	The Women's Social and Political Union (WSPU) was founded by Emmeline Pankhurst. Its members were later dubbed 'suffragettes'.
1905	The suffragettes began to use illegal methods. They later used violent methods and attacked property.
	A minority Liberal government was formed, with Campbell-Bannerman as prime minister.
1906	The Liberal Party won a landslide victory in the general election held in January/February.
	The Education Bill was withdrawn after being wrecked by the Lords. The Plural Voting Bill was rejected by the Lords.
1908	Asquith became prime minister.
1909	Lloyd George's budget (the so-called People's Budget) was rejected by the Lords.
1910	The January general election returned the Liberal government with a greatly reduced majority. It was dependent on Irish and Labour support.
	Resolutions on the subject of curbing the powers of the Lords were tabled in the Commons in March.
	The Lords passed the 1909 budget in April.
	Edward VII died suddenly on 6 May.
	At the request of George V, a two-party constitutional conference was set up. It broke down in November.
	The king very reluctantly gave Asquith 'guarantees' that he would create 400 to 500 new peers if absolutely necessary.
	The December general election produced almost exactly the same result as the January one.
1911	The Lords passed the Parliament Act and it received Royal Assent on 18 August. Its main provisions were:

- The preamble stated that it was a temporary measure and that in the future the Second Chamber would be constituted on a popular instead of hereditary basis.
- The Lords could only delay money bills for a month.
- The Lords could only delay other bills for up to two years. An exception was made for a bill that extended the life of a parliament beyond five years.
- The maximum life of a parliament was reduced from seven years to five years.
- MPs would receive a salary.

The suffragettes stepped up their campaign and increasingly used arson, violence and intimidation.

1913	The suffragette, Emily Wilding Davison, was killed whilst disrupting the Epsom Derby.
	The Prisoners' Temporary Discharge for Ill-Health Act (dubbed the Cat and Mouse Act) became law. It enabled suffragettes engaged in a hunger strike to be released then re-arrested when their health had recovered.
1914	The First World War commenced.
	The WSPU (the suffragettes) and most other suffrage groups suspended their campaign for the duration of the war. Women (including suffragettes) enthusiastically engaged in valuable war work.
1916	A Speaker's Conference was set up and tasked with making recommendations on franchise reform and other matters.
	On 7 December Lloyd George replaced Asquith as prime minister.
1917	On 26 January the Speaker's Conference presented its report.
1918	On 6 February 1918 the Representation of the People Act received Royal Assent. Its main provisions were:

- The vote was given to all men aged 21 or over. There was a residence qualification of six months.
- The vote was given to all men who had served in the armed forces during the First World War from the age of 19.
- Plural voting was limited to a maximum of two votes per person. This was residence plus either on the basis of business premises or as a graduate.
- Women aged 30 years or over were given the vote if they were entitled to be entered on the Local Government Register or married to a man entitled to be entered on the Local Government Register in respect of property worth £5 per year rental value, or they occupied a dwelling house on the same basis as men who had been entitled to enfranchisement under the 1884 Reform Act. They also had the vote if they were a graduate voting in a university constituency.
- There was a redistribution of seats.
- There was to be an annual electoral register.
- Candidates were no longer required to pay the expenses of the returning officer.
- Voting in general elections was to be on a fixed day.

A general election governed by the terms of the new act was held on 14 December.

1921	The devolved legislature for Northern Ireland (the Parliament of Northern Ireland) came into being.
1922	The twenty-six counties of Southern Ireland left the United Kingdom and became the Irish Free State. The six counties of Ulster became Northern Ireland and stayed within the United Kingdom. Parliament became the Parliament of Great Britain and Northern Ireland.
1925	The Honours (Prevention of Abuses) Act was passed.
1928	The Representation of the People (Equal Franchise) Act was passed. This gave women the vote on the same terms as men.
1948	The university seats and all forms of plural voting were abolished.
	Postal voting was made available to servicemen and, in strictly defined circumstances, to all civilians.

1949   The delaying power of the House of Lords was reduced from two years to one year.

1958   The Life Peerages Act enabled peers to be appointed for their lifetime only. Almost all creations are made on this basis.

1963   The Peerage Act allowed hereditary peerages to be disclaimed.

1969   The minimum voting age for parliamentary elections was reduced from 21 to 18.

1973   The Parliament of Northern Ireland was abolished and replaced by the Northern Ireland Assembly.

1974   The Northern Ireland Assembly was abolished.

1979   A referendum on the proposal to set up a Scottish Assembly failed to get the necessary majority.
        A referendum on the proposal to set up a Welsh Assembly was decisively rejected.

1982   Another Northern Ireland Assembly was set up.

1986   The Northern Ireland Assembly was abolished.

1997   Following a referendum the Scottish Parliament was set up.
        Following a referendum the Welsh Assembly was set up.

1998   The present Northern Ireland Assembly was set up.

1999   The House of Lords Act left ninety hereditary peers (plus the Earl Marshall and the Lord Great Chamberlain) sitting with the life peers. These are elected by all the hereditary peers, using a form of proportional representation.

2006   The minimum age at which it is possible to be a candidate in a parliamentary election was lowered from 21 to 18.

2011   A UK-wide referendum was held on the proposal that the 'alternative vote' system should replace first past the post for parliamentary elections. The proposal was decisively rejected.
        The Fixed-Term Parliament Act provided that Parliament has a fixed term of five years. Subject to exceptions in specified circumstances, polling day must be the first Thursday in May on the fifth year following the previous general election.

2014   A referendum on the proposal to make Scotland fully independent resulted in a 'no' vote. Shortly before the voting all the three main parties in the UK Parliament committed themselves, if there was a 'no' vote, to give considerable extra powers to the Scottish Parliament.
        The prime minister, David Cameron, said that 'the question of English votes for English laws – the so-called West Lothian Question – requires a decisive answer'. A commission to develop proposals was set up and he promised that a Bill would be published in January 2015.

Index

Visit our website and discover thousands of other History Press books.
www.thehistorypress.co.uk